ecpr PRESS

Varieties of Political Experience

Power Phenomena in Modern Society

Gianfranco Poggi

ecpr_{PRESS}

Published by the ECPR Press in 2014

The ECPR Press is the publishing imprint of the European Consortium for Political Research (ECPR), a scholarly association, which supports and encourages the training, research and cross-national co-operation of political scientists in institutions throughout Europe and beyond.

ECPR Press
University of Essex
Wivenhoe Park
Colchester
CO4 3SQ
UK

Typeset by ECPR Press

Printed and bound by Lightning Source

British Library Cataloguing in Publication Data

A catalogue record for this book is available from the British Library

Paperback ISBN: 978-1-907-301-75-9
PDF ISBN: 978-1-910-259-19-1

www.ecpr.eu/ecprpress

Endorsements

'Poggi's essays on central topics in political sociology reflect the formidable depth and breadth of his scholarship. Learned, lively, and with a critical edge, they cast historical as well as contemporary light on many corners of politics, the state, civil society and the economy.'

Charles Raab,
Professor of Government, University of Edinburgh

'Poggi reflects on one of the two central subjects of his life of writing – power, particularly political, and its institutional embodiments. These reflections are deeply enriched by his mastery of another subject – the writings of virtually everyone who has thought well about such matters. The book distils, clarifies and theorises vast and complex historical processes, paying equal attention to the constants of human affairs and to their numerous transformations. These are sorted, and their movements plotted, with magisterial command. He illuminates the nouns of power and politics – state, society, economy, politics, law; the many adjectives by which they come to be qualified, amended and transformed over millennia; and the interactions among all of the above. His ability to bear heavy weight lightly, to combine erudition of remarkable depth with deftness and lightness of touch, also makes this work that rare thing in social science: a truly engaging, spirited, and splendid read.'

Martin Krygier,
Gordon Samuels Professor of Law and Social Theory, Co-Director,
Network for Interdisciplinary Studies of Law
Faculty of Law, University of New South Wales

'Over the decades, Gianfranco Poggi's work has acquired classic status within scholarship on political power, the nature of the state and its historical development. The texts assembled in this volume are testament to the author's unique skills in bridging political theory, political sociology and public law, and link his empirical investigation to the great sociological tradition of the nineteenth and twentieth century from Tocqueville and Marx, to Weber, Parsons and Lipset, including neglected scholars such as Heinrich Popitz. This volume includes new additions to Poggi's invaluable contribution to the understanding of the state in our present time and of the challenges that its national, liberal and social features face in the age of globalisation.'

Daniele Caramani,
University of Zurich

'This collection is simply full of treats. It has all the generosity of spirit and intellect of its author, whose contribution to our understanding of the state and power over the years has been significant. Gianfranco Poggi is not afraid to tackle big issues and survey large conceptual landscapes with refreshingly scant regard to distinctions between sociology, political theory, political science and public law, and with a profound understanding of the classical tradition. These essays – some published, others not, or not yet in English – cover themes he takes to be 'upstream' from the state: power and the political. He writes here with his customary energy, panache and infectious enthusiasm. This alone would make this a very welcome contribution, but he has a further gift for the Anglophone reader: a translation of a section of Heinrich Popitz's Phänomene der Macht.'

Alan Scott, Professor of Sociology,
University of Innsbruck

ECPR Press Series Editors:
Dario Castiglione (University of Exeter)
Peter Kennealy (European University Institute)
Alexandra Segerberg (Stockholm University)
Peter Triantafillou (Roskilde University)

ECPR Essays:

Croce, Gramsci, Bobbio and the Italian Political Tradition (ISBN: 9781907301995) Richard Bellamy

Choice, Rules and Collective Action: The Ostroms on the Study of Institutions and Governance (ISBN: 9781910259139) Elinor Ostrom (Author), Vincent Ostrom (Author), Paul Dragos Aligica (Editor) and Filippo Sabetti (Editor)

From Deliberation to Demonstration: Political Rallies in France, 1868–1939 (ISBN: 9781907301469) Paula Cossart

Hans Kelsen and the Case for Democracy (ISBN: 9781907301247) Sandrine Baume

Is Democracy a Lost Cause? Paradoxes of an Imperfect Invention (ISBN: 9781907301247) Alfio Mastropaolo

Just Democracy (ISBN: 9781907301148) Philippe Van Parijs

Learning About Politics in Time and Space (ISBN: 9781907301476) Richard Rose

Maestri of Political Science (ISBN: 9781907301193) Donatella Campus, Gianfranco Pasquino, and Martin Bull

Masters of Political Science (ISBN: 9780955820335) Donatella Campus, and Gianfranco Pasquino

On Parties, Party Systems and Democracy: Selected Writings of Peter Mair (ISBN: 9781907301780) Peter Mair (Author) Ingrid Van Biezen (Editor)

The Modern State Subverted (ISBN: 9781907301636) Giuseppe Di Palma

ECPR Classics:

Beyond the Nation State (ISBN: 9780955248870) Ernst Haas

Citizens, Elections, Parties: Approaches to the Comparative Study of the Processes of Development (ISBN: 9780955248887) Stein Rokkan

Comparative Politics The Problem of Equivalence (ISBN: 9781907301414) Jan Van Deth

Democracy Political Finance and state Funding for Parties (ISBN: 9780955248801) Jack Lively

Electoral Change: Responses to Evolving Social and Attitudinal Structures in Western Countries (ISBN: 9780955820311) Mark Franklin,Thomas Mackie, and Henry Valen

Elite and Specialized Interviewing (ISBN: 9780954796679) Lewis Anthony Dexter

Identity, Competition and Electoral Availability: The Stabilisation of European Electorates 1885–1985 (ISBN: 9780955248832) Peter Mair and Stefano Bartolini

Individualism (ISBN: 9780954796662) Steven Lukes

Modern Social Policies in Britain and Sweden: From Relief to Income Maintenance (ISBN: 9781907301001) Hugh Heclo

Parties and Party Systems: A Framework for Analysis (ISBN: 9780954796617) Giovanni Sartori

Party Identification and Beyond: Representations of Voting and Party Competition (ISBN: 9780955820342) Ian Budge, Ivor Crewe, and Dennis Farlie

People, States and Fear: An Agenda for International Security Studies in the Post-Cold War Era (ISBN: 9780955248818) Barry Buzan

Political Elites (ISBN: 9780954796600) Geraint Parry

Seats, Votes and the Spatial Organization of Elections (ISBN: 9781907301353) Graham Gudgin

State Formation, Parties and Democracy (ISBN: 9781907301179) Hans Daalder

System and Process in Iternational Politics (ISBN: 9780954796624) Mortan Kaplan

Territory and Power in the UK (ISBN: 9780955248863) James Bulpitt

The State Tradition in Western Europe: A Study of an Idea and Institution (ISBN: 9780955820359) Kenneth Dyson

Please visit www.ecpr.eu/ecprpress for up-to-date information about new publications.

Contents

Acknowledgements

I am most grateful to Marcella, my wife, for the assistance she has variously lent me once more during the preparation of this book. I acknowledge the contributions to the writing of it made by my friends and colleagues Giuseppe Di Palma and Joerg Friedrichs. I am indebted to Laura Pugh of the ECPR Press for her high-grade professional input into the process of finalizing the text that follows.

Some of the essays here included were previously published in either English or other languages. The original place of publication is cited at the start of the relevant piece. They are here reproduced in a revised form with the kind authorization of the publishers, which I gratefully acknowledge. In particular, I am grateful to J.C.B. Mohr Publishers, for allowing me to print my own translation of the first chapter of Heinrich Popitz, *Phänomene der Macht*, from their second edition of 1992.

Gianfranco Poggi
June 2014

Preface

One source of my interest in the empirical study of political phenomena (which incidentally has not respected the conventional distinction between political sociology and political science) lies probably in one distant circumstance. When, way back in the fifties, I signed on as a graduate student in Berkeley, its Sociology department hosted a number of significant scholars who pursued creatively that same interest, though along diverse lines: Lipset, Bendix, Selznick, Kornhauser, Linz. At Padua, where I had just graduated, my favourite subjects had been in the field of public law, and this coincidence motivated me to take advantage of that circumstance.

Of course the Berkeley doctoral program required attention to a number of other sociology fields; among these, the study of classical social theory particularly attracted my attention. As a result, from that point on, for many decades my teaching and my research activities were focused mainly on two areas of social science scholarship: politics, and the legacy of the 'sociology greats'. Those themes overlapped to an extent, particularly in the case of Tocqueville, Marx, and Weber; but among my publications one can easily distinguish between these two lines of work.

The collection that follows assembles only writings of mine dealing with political phenomena. Most are characterized by a sustained concern with political institutions (over against, say, political behaviour or the history of political thought), the most significant of which in the modern political environment is *the state*. However, the collection of essays that follow (some previously published, others not; some originally written in English, others in Italian, presented here in my own translation) is focused on two other themes, however closely related with one another, and with that of the state itself: the concept of power (especially but not only political) and the nature of the 'political'. One could say that conceptually both themes lie *upstream* of that of the state, and to that extent their treatment complements two books and several other writings of mine (including some entries in reference works) expressly concerned with the state itself.

As an exception, however, I have included in this collection a previously unpublished piece of mine on the Treaty of Westphalia (1648), which established normatively various aspects of the institutional physiognomy of the state, in particular the notion of sovereignty.

The circumstances under which I wrote the various texts assembled here, and where (if anywhere) they were previously published, are briefly indicated in a note to each of the contributions. All of them have undergone some editing on my part, but do not indicate expressly where and how the version presented here differs from previous ones (if any).

Most of the assembled writings, while they originated in different circumstances and different formats, deal with a relatively specific set of themes – essentially, the dealings between political power and other major institutions and processes. As a consequence, there is some overlap between the different texts, for which I apologize to the reader.

One final point. Time and again, in thinking and writing on the concept of power and on related topics, I have drawn on the contributions to this theme made by a contemporary German social theorist – Heinrich Popitz (1925–2002). A book of his dealing expressly with power which I personally consider a masterpiece (*Phänomene der Macht*, 1992 [1986]) has so far not received anything like the attention it deserves, for the simple reason that it, like other significant writings of Popitz's, is still available only in German.

The ECPR Press has given me a welcome opportunity to remedy this situation by appending to this collection of my writings my own unpublished translation of the introductory chapter of *Phänomene*. On this account, it may well be the case that the most significant text in a collection of essays which bears my name happens NOT to be of my own making (except as a translator). But that's a consequence I am happy to live with.

Gianfranco Poggi
June 2014

To my grandchildren
Catherine, Bodo, Adam and Laura Johnson

Chapter One

Varieties of Political Experience*

What follows is an elementary discussion of the nature of political experience (alternative labels for this theme could be 'the political phenomenon' or 'the political'). To begin with, it refers to the insights into this topic attained by a few generations of ancient Greek writers. The unprecedented originality, intellectual sophistication and literary quality of their writings (dialogues, treatises, speeches, histories, passages from poems, tragedies, comedies) had a powerful impact on subsequent Western reflections on political experience, many of these produced in Latin during the Roman republic and the later Roman empire. The impact continued to make itself felt after the end of the 'Dark Ages' and in the Renaissance, in the course of which many Greek contributions to the theme appeared in the original Greek or were translated into Arabic and/ or various 'vulgar' European languages.

The Greek legacy

The reference to the Greek heritage had very significant effects, and constituted for many subsequent generations of thinkers and writers a shared body of discourses on political experience, spelling out its nature, identifying its main aspects, debating its most significant theoretical, moral and practical issues. However, the intellectual stature of that heritage laid significant boundaries on the Western political imagination, for to a large extent it articulated and commented upon a unique historical experience: the formation and development (and subsequently the decay) of the Greek *polis*. This was (as the Greeks were proudly aware) a highly peculiar development, a self-consciously unprecedented way of constituting and managing collective activities. Those activities were arranged and governed very differently elsewhere, in contexts which the Greeks conceived as non-political – small village communities, the possessions of a lord, or vast imperial domains.

To the Greeks, the *polis* represented political experience tout court; it gave full expression to two closely related powers of human nature which the Greeks felt they had first embodied in ongoing arrangements for collective existence – *language*, and *reason*. They viewed as *non*-political all forms of

---

*   This essay is published here for the first time. The first presentation of its content was occasioned, in 1997, by an invitation from the Faculty of Political Sciences of the University of Florence. It consisted in three talks which I delivered from notes, in Italian, and subsequently wrote out in English as below.

collective existence repressing and denying such powers, or reserving them exclusively to very few privileged, exalted individuals.

Each *polis* had the prerogative of constituting and governing itself by means of one distinctive activity – people talking to one another as members of a collectivity of free and equal individuals, sharing the opportunity of (and bearing the responsibility for) first constituting the *polis*, then – over the generations – producing and modifying its standing arrangements and its policies. People did this, in principle, by voicing their own views and preferences about such matters; debated those advanced by others; sought to persuade one another; finally, ascertained and validated the opinion prevailing among them, often by means of voting. Furthermore, each participant could in principle be empowered to lead (and serve) the others in performing one of more of their jointly deliberated collective activities; but such title was attributed temporarily, for express purposes, and according to agreed procedures such as election, demonstrated qualifications, or the drawing of lots. The upshot of such processes was the orderly production and execution of decisions considered as willed by and for the collectivity as a whole, and as such sanctioned and made binding on everyone.

Such an understanding of political experience (formulated above in rather idealized terms) was possible only within a *polis* encompassing a relatively small population, sharing a number of significant commonalities. On this account, larger human aggregates (such as the whole settled population of the Greek islands and territories) took the form of a number of discrete, reciprocally autonomous *poleis*. Each of these constructed and operated collective arrangements of its own, dealt with other ones on the basis of agreed rules (including those concerning the recourse to war), and competed with them in order to maximize its own access to scarce possessions and invidious advantages.

Such competition often led to wars between the *poleis*, and sometimes to the establishment of relatively durable hegemonies of some of them over others. But for many centuries these phenomena remained compatible with a keen sense among the Greeks that all the *poleis* shared some significant values – a commonality periodically reasserted and celebrated on various occasions, in particular the Olympic games.

Some of those values (for instance *isonomia*, that is the equality of citizens before the law) continue to orient to some extent the political experience within contemporary states – the constituent units typical of the modern political universe. On this account contemporary reflections upon political experience – especially philosophical ones – are still to some extent inspired by the way the Greeks conceived it, although they mostly argue (regretfully or otherwise) that the Greek views are not closely applicable to current circumstances.

For instance, authors comparing and contrasting the *polis* with the modern constitutional state often argue that in both political institutions are to some extent bounden to the value of *freedom*. (Incidentally, the Greek term itself for freedom – *eleutheria* – probably did not have a close equivalent in the other languages known to them.) But the content of freedom itself has long been recognized as being significantly different for 'the ancients and the moderns'.

Beyond the Greek legacy: The constitutive role of coercion

To those asserting the continuing significance of the Greek legacy, however, one can object: why should political experience as such have anything to do with freedom anyway? In fact the Greek understanding of that experience, intellectually powerful and morally compelling as it may be, is not the only plausible understanding. Put otherwise, the Greeks privileged excessively a historically peculiar political phenomenon – the *polis* itself – where an ensemble of free and equal individuals consider themselves as belonging together, and express that feeling by periodically gathering in public to argue how they should live together, what values and interests they share, and how they should jointly attain them and secure them.

The modern understanding of political experience, as for example Machiavelli and Hobbes construe it, differs from the Greek one by self-consciously opening a much wider prospect than that offered by the *polis* itself. The Greeks had focussed on the *horizontal* dimension of the latter – on 'politics' let us say, and on the role played within it by the free and equal individuals making up a collectivity. The modern understanding is focussed on something broader and more general, which one might call 'the political', and emphasizes its *vertical* dimension – the sharp difference between the roles played in political experience respectively by leaders and by their subjects.

That difference should not be seen simply as another aspect of the social division of labor and on that account as serving common interests, although it is often presented as such. (A sociological joke denounces such ideological use of the comparison: *Let's have some division of labor around here. I divide, YOU labor.*) To each end, top and bottom, is normally associated a set of interests in more or less marked contrast with that of the other end. Basically, it is in the interest of leaders to maintain their subjects in a position of subordination, thus as far as possible to deny them the opportunity of defining and pursuing interests of their own, compelling them to serve instead, in some manner or other, those of the leaders themselves. Viewed this way, political experience is essentially one expression of a broader phenomenon – *social power*.

This understanding of political experience is the point of arrival of an intellectual itinerary often undertaken, more or less self-consciously, by modern social theory, and which finds exemplary expression in the thought of Max Weber. First, Weber presents a very broad concept of (social) power, as consisting in an asymmetry, between two parties (individual or collective) to a social relationship, in the probability that each can 'realize its own will even in spite of the other's opposition, on whatever grounds such probability rests' (Weber 1978: 53).

In general terms, such grounds are constituted by one party's superior control over a significant resource; thus, different forms of social power can be conceived as resulting from the specific nature of the resources under a given party's privileged control. Political power, in particular, exists insofar parties differ substantially in the respective ability to make the interests of one of them prevail by threatening or exercising organized coercion on the other. It is one member of a trio of power forms which Bobbio has defined as follows:

> One may distinguish three great classes within the concept of power – respectively, economic power, ideological power, and political power. The first avails itself of the possession of certain goods […], in a situation of scarcity, in order to induce those deprived of them to adopt a certain conduct. Ideological power rests on the influence which ideas formulated in a certain manner, originating in certain circumstances, by persons enjoying a certain degree of authority, put abroad through certain processes, exercise over the conduct of members of a collectivity. […] Finally, political power rests on the possession by a party of instruments for the exercise of physical force (weapons of any kind and degree): it is coercive power in the strictest sense of the expression (Bobbio 1983: 828).

To restate this conceptual distinction in terms echoing a characteristic Marxian expression, three fundamentally distinct forms of social power depend on a part of society's privileged access respectively to the 'means of production, means of persuasion, and means of coercion' of critical significance within that society. Once more, the political form rests on the latter. Political power exists insofar within a society or social group there is a significant, durable asymmetry between its parts as concerns the access of each to means of coercion and the ability to control their employment.

One can construe political experience in other ways than either recalling the Greek understanding of it or evoking expressly (and, one might say, crudely) the phenomenon of coercion. But such ways in fact presuppose, without articulating it, the ultimate significance of that phenomenon. One can for example conceive of the political process as involving primarily the settlement of 'non negotiable' social conflicts. But it can reach such a result only to the extent that one part of society can override the presence or absence of a shared commitment by both parties to make mutual adjustments between their respective interests by imposing and enforcing coercively a settlement favoring its own interests.

One can also characterize political experience by focussing on the phenomenon of 'command'. *Commands* whoever is in a position, by expressing its own will, to commit the activities of others to the pursuit of its own interest, or at least to induce others to 'cease and desist' from hindering that pursuit. But although often the command 'do this/do not do that' does not expressly contemplate the possibility of being contradicted and the consequences of such contradiction, it can only constitute a true command only insofar as it presupposes, overtly or covertly, the threat to punish those contradicting it.

One may also view as central to political experience the particular intensity with which one human collectivity perceives the *otherness* of another that comes across its path. But there are ways of dealing with this situation which are not expressly political. One collectivity may be content neutrally to take into account the existence of the other, can assess the ways it differs from itself, can imitate selectively some of those ways, can enter with the other into mutual exchanges focussed on each party's distinctive resources. The *political* way of dealing with the situation comes in when one subject perceives the other as the source of a threat, as a challenge to its own existence. Here, the possibility of coercion is in the first instance imputed to the Other-than-oneself, but it induces Oneself to 'go on a war footing', to threaten in turn the other's existence or integrity.

Carl Schmitt's famous text, *The Concept of the Political*, emphasizes this aspect, focussing on the contrast between friend and enemy, and making the potential or actual experience of war central to the whole political realm. It is true that peace is also comprised within that realm; but, one observes, peace is made – or not – with the enemy not the friend (Schmitt 1996).

Finally, one can place at the center of political experience of *collective decision* the conscious choice between alternatives on behalf of a plurality of associates. But what renders one decision *political* is its being binding for that plurality, which in turn rests on the possibility of enforcing it (coercively if necessarily) also upon those who have not taken or shared such decision. At bottom, what allows one part of society to conduct itself as the whole of it is its ability to commit the resources of other parts which, if left to themselves, would put those resources at the service of interests of their own.

In sum, even theoretical itineraries with points of departure different from the concept of social power, end up at the same point of arrival. However one understands it, political experience is a wheel revolving around one hub – coercion – no matter how distant its rim may be from that hub. Or, to borrow a metaphor from Foscolo's eulogy of Machiavelli in *I sepolcri*, if you whittle away the laurels adorning the sceptre of rulers you inevitably discover that it drips tears and blood. (In fact, at the beginning of *Iliad* Ulysses uses the 'golden sceptre' symbolizing his royal status as a hard stick in order to teach a lesson to a pesky plebeian, Tersites.)

Institutional modalities of coercion: **Quis? Quis quem?**

Placing coercion at the center of political experience does not mean treating the latter as a night in which all cows are black. One can consistently focus on coercion but acknowledge that coercion itself manifests itself in that experience differently from time to time, from place to place. To do this, one need only ask a few elementary questions, expressed below in Latin, about the position held by the threat or exercise of coercion in any given society:

QUIS? that is: *who*, within that society, is in a position to threaten or exercise coercion in that context? One may object that this phrasing unduly presupposes that in all societies (to return to Weber's definition of social power) *someone* can threaten or employ coercion to suppress or neutralize the others' resistance to the realization of its own interests. However, some anthropologists call 'a-cephalous' (literally: head-less) societies, said to have existed in the past and perhaps to still exist, where either no one disposes of coercive resources or all dispose of them approximately to the same extent. Activities of social control which elsewhere presuppose a marked internal inequality in coercion-capacity would be carried out in such societies on the basis of the consensus of all members, or (more often) of the chiefs of all groups composing the society.

One may register the exception represented by a-cephalous societies but still acknowledge that answering the *quis?* query points to a most important feature of all other societies. In principle, the coercion-capacity may EITHER be dispersed among relatively many subjects, rendering each a more or less autonomous source of political activity, OR be the prerogative of a single component of society – typically, the (modern) state, defined by Max Weber as a social entity which monopolizes legitimate coercion within a territory.

QUIS QUEM? (literally: *who whom?*) Answering this query requires comparing the social identities of those in a position to threaten or exercise coercion with the social identities of those upon whom coercion is threatened or exercised. The significance of such a comparison is suggested by a theory chiefly developed by German and Austrian scholars, in the first part of the twentieth century. Its basic contention was that all significant inequality, including political inequality, was the outcome of a previous, momentous event where two very differently constituted populations, which previously had ignored each other, had more-or-less suddenly encountered and confronted one another. The primordial manifestation of political experience (as of other forms of inequality) was essentially a product of that encounter and confrontation.

Typically, each of the populations, as conceived in the theory, possessed a high degree of ethnic and linguistic homogeneity and of social, economic, and cultural equality. However, one population was nomadic; its mode of subsistence rested chiefly on hunting by mounted men, and the crafts associated with this practice led to the emergence of a minority within it capable of aggressive warfare. The other population was settled on a territory and relied for its subsistence chiefly on agriculture; it was typically peaceable and unfamiliar with military resources and practices.

The more historically significant instances of the encounter between such different populations involved a clash of arms between the two types of society, and typically led to the forcible 'superimposition' (*Überlagerung*) of the former on the latter. One population vanquished militarily the other, invaded its territory, and undertook first to rob it of its produce then to arrange the long-term exploitation of further production by the local population. Mostly the fighting and invading was done by only a minority of the first population, but their outcome, if successful, benefitted all of it. Typically, over time that minority would settle on the invaded territory, and avail itself of its persistent military superiority to establish and manage its own rule over the other population.

In the theory (rendered here in the most simplified form possible) the inequality in coercive capacity between the two populations was the original manifestation of political experience; in due course this may have been complemented by other forms of inequality, all of them presupposing the original difference between the social identities of two distinct populations. But if that relationship between the two populations endures, it may come to comprise various forms of mutual accommodation and merger, and in the long run lead to the development of a single, larger, integrated, relatively homogenous population with a collective identity of its own. (The complexity and unpredictability in such events is magisterially expressed by Horace's reflection on the evolving relationship between Rome and Greece: *Graecia capta ferum captorem cepit, et artes intulit agresti Latio* – conquered Greece conquered the brutish conqueror and brought her arts into rustic Latium.)

The characteristic contention of the *Überlagerungstheorie* – there has *always* been, at the root of the relationship between those in command and those under command, a high degree of ethnic, cultural, linguistic difference between two populations, leading to the forcible subjection of one by the other – is not tenable on those terms. But it fits a number of significant historical circumstances. It also constitutes a somewhat intemperate way of representing as the root of political experience in general, the confrontation with 'otherdom' which as we have seen is sometimes considered critical.

Together, the queries *quis?* and *quis, quem?* make us aware of a significant variable in that experience – what portion of a given population possesses some degree of political capacity, is institutionally entitled to take an interest in the structure and the operations of the political center, and seeks to influence its choices, to participate in the making of its choices, or to influence their content.

For instance, 'the politics of aristocratic empires', according to a book with this title, vest all political capacity in the prince on the one hand and on the other the components of the aristocracy (whether individually or corporatively) (Kautsky 1997). There is no place in such politics for the remainder (that is, the overwhelming majority) of the population, deprived (to use a current expression) of a 'political subjectivity' of its own, and left encapsulated within local contexts, each subject to the lordship of single aristocrats, thus kept in a position of inferiority, dependency, and (mostly) docility.

In the modern state, instead, a minimum of political subjectivity is an integral component of citizenship, a quality shared by increasingly broader sections of the population. In contemporary democracies that minimum belongs to all adult individuals, whatever their gender, education, and socio-economic condition. On this account the process of democratization involved 'the entry of the masses into politics', thus negated the previous, narrow answer to the *quis?* query and strongly reduced the gradient of the inequality revealed by *quis, quem?*

Institutional modalities of coercion: Quantum?

QUANTUM? This query also views coercion as a constitutive moment of political experience, but suggests that it can play either a relatively major or a relatively minor role with respect to other aspects of that experience. In certain contexts, and particularly within constitutional democracies, the incidence of coercion is markedly reduced. Numerous state activities, though they all presuppose the possibility of coercion, do not explicitly exhibit it or put it into play. 'Politics' in the everyday sense of the term is composed by forms of communication – a party's electoral manifesto, a parliamentary debate, the directives a higher level of administration imparts to lower levels – that do not refer directly to organized coercion, though again they may presuppose its possibility.

For instance, in the modern state, the armed forces and police employ a not insignificant but minor proportion of state employees. Although, as already remarked, the state possesses the monopoly of coercion, which can be legitimately threatened or exercised only by people manning its official organs, the great majority within such people have no military training or access to coercive resources. Their *modus operandi* is appropriate to activities which are mostly managerial in nature and do not require the issuing or enactment of binding commands.

But the modern state, in this as in other respects, is historically exceptional. In other contexts the rule has been for political activities to exhibit much more frequently and expressly the coercive element, to put into play (at least symbolically) the system's own military, punitive, repressive dimension, even in its routine manifestations, including the purely administrative ones. In the Greek *polis*, for instance, the conceptual nucleus of citizenship was an individual's military obligations and qualifications. Successively, for centuries the European aristocracy constructed and projected an image of itself, and a justification of its economic and status privileges, centered on a variously evoked and symbolized vocation and responsibility for military command – for instance, through such practices as horse riding, the carrying of swords, the hunt and the duel.

Even some states undergoing modernization have sometimes presented archaic traits emphasizing military or semi-military modes of selection, training, self-representation, performance of politico-administrative activities. For instance, even functionaries engaged in bureaucratic offices with no military content were often expected to wear a uniform, and to conduct themselves in ways which evoked a military understanding of their mission. (However, according to an anecdote, when the Tuscan notable Bettino Ricasoli was informed that wearing a uniform was expected of him as the prime minister of the newly unified Kingdom of Italy, he objected that 'the house of Ricasoli has never worn a livery'.)

Institutional modalities of coercion: De quo?

DE QUO? [literally: à *propos* of what?] That is: what are the issues, the objectives, the tasks of political activity? Such activity (and thus, directly or indirectly, also coercion) is engaged in doing what? The answer varies greatly from context to context, from situation to situation for a given context. In fact, Weber argued, the very nature of politics made it impossible to bind it to any given set of tasks.

> A state cannot be defined sociologically in terms of the content of what it does. There is almost no end which some political organization has not at some point taken upon itself, on the other hand no task of which it can be said that at all times has been made their own exclusively by those organizations today designated as political – by states or by those which historically were the precursor of the states (Weber 1994: 311).

Note that Weber does not in the least deem irrelevant the question of the ends of political action; indeed, a concern to limit those ends is a distinctively liberal feature of his political thinking. It is not in normative, but in empirical terms, that that question, according to him, does not admit of a definitive answer.

In fact, different socio-historical contexts display a whole range of answers to the *de quo?* query. At one extreme, political action is charged at most with two fundamental interests – the maintenance of the internal order and the defense of the territory. At the other, the resources accumulated and managed by the political order are made to serve an open-ended ensemble of diverse (and often conflicting) social interests, some of which concern not directly the society as a whole but single sectors of it. But exactly because the responses to that query are intrinsically contingent, the answers given to it in a context become a central issue of its entire political process.

The main answer represented by the modern state went through two main phases. Early on the state laid significant boundaries upon its own activity through two major, historically unique operations (each undertaken in the various countries with a different timing, and in diverse forms). First – through a process often labelled *secularization* – it reduced or even set aside the state's own previous concern with matters of religious faith and its own entanglement with ecclesiastical authorities. Second, it entrusted the production and distribution of wealth chiefly to the self-interested market activities of profit-seeking private firms. (The latter development is epitomized in the dictum 'to the prince all and only the *imperium*, to private individuals all and only the *dominium*', where *dominium* designates – as in Roman law – the exclusive faculties of acquisition, possession and disposition over material property vested in private individuals.)

To these self-limitations the modern state imposes on its own activities (not always willingly and consistently) corresponded the emergence of 'civil society' – a sphere of legitimate interests and relations which the state acknowledges as lying outside its own normal operations. With respect to this sphere its coercive activities have chiefly one role: to authorize and sanction the pursuit of private interests, but leave its outcomes to its autonomous dynamics.

In the successive phase, which in many Western countries begins in the second half of the nineteenth century, states progressively widen the perimeter of their own activities, committing more and more of their own resources to regulating, controlling, and promoting a number of varied socio-economic interests. Over several decades (during which this phenomenon is massively fostered by two world wars) the list of tasks undertaken by the state, all funded essentially through coercive levies on stocks and flows of private wealth or through public debt, and carried out by a vastly increased and more and more complex body of public employees, becomes very extensive and diverse.

This does not always mean that the state so to speak usurps such tasks from the civil society, whose on-going modernization develops in turn ever new subjects, resources, facilities, and social needs. Some of latter, indeed, are *ab initio* recognized as proper targets of state activity. Even a conservative thinker such as Luhmann (1975) attributes to the welfare state the legitimate function of integrating the individual into an ever-changing, more and more differentiated society, where s/he runs various new risks, including that of feeling lost and insecure of her/his own identity.

To some extent, however, the massive enlargement of the state's role in the management of the social process in the course of the first three quarters of the last century, has displaced the civil society and especially the market. In the last few decades, such development has been problematized by neo-liberal thinking, which has had considerable success in halting the trend prevailing during the previous decades in a society's answer to the *de quo?* query. Needless to say, that success has generated massive problems of its own, not to be discussed here.

Institutional modalities of coercion: Quomodo?

A final query is – QUOMODO? Immediately after excluding that the nature of a political organization can be determined conceptually by considering its *ends*, Weber suggests:

> One can instead define sociologically the state only with reference to one specific *means* which belongs to it as well as to every political organization – physical coercion [...] Physical coercion, naturally, is not the normal or the sole – there is no question of that – means of the state, but one which is specific to it (Weber 1994: 312).

Thus, the answer to the last query consists in the different ways in which coercion is organized and managed in various socio-historical contexts. In Weber's thinking that answer must lay particular weight on one phenomenon – the legitimation (if any) of political power. Western political thought had long recognized its significance, for instance in Rousseau's statement: 'The strongest [man] is never strong enough to be always master, unless he transforms his force into right, and obedience into duty' (Rousseau 1993: 184).

But there are two aspects to that phenomenon. To begin with, a quantitative aspect: *to what extent* can a given political system rely on a compliance with its commands motivated by its subjects' own conviction that – to put it this way – the commander has a *right* to command and the commanded a *duty* to obey?

The answer of course varies from context to context. It is a frequent but serious error to assume that for Weber such a conviction – and thus legitimacy – was always present in the relation between a system of rule and its subjects. Legitimacy stabilizes the system by reducing the necessity for it to constrain the subjects' obedience by threatening or exercising coercion. But even systems which for whatever reasons find themselves having to *do without* legitimacy may nonetheless become established and operate reliably for long periods of time. For instance, in the second half of the last century, in the countries of the Soviet system (though perhaps not the Soviet Union itself) political rule was maintained for decades in spite of its lack of legitimacy in the eyes of the great majority of individuals.

But Weber emphasizes a second, qualitative aspect of the legitimacy phenomenon. Assuming that, as suggested above, political authority can to some extent expect its subjects be motivated to compliance by a sense of dutiful obligation, what is in turn the *content* of that motivation? On what grounds do respectively rulers and ruled construe subjectively their relationship, justify the asymmetry constitutive of it? In one of his most original contributions to modern social theory, Weber responds by formulating three contrasting ideal-types of legitimation, which he labels traditional, charismatic and legal-rational. An important aspect of his argument is that each of the types indicates not only how political authority construes its claim to obedience, but also how it is constituted and functions. Systems differing in the nature of their legitimacy generally differ also, for instance, in how those exercising authority provide themselves with economic resources, or how punishment is imposed on criminals. But Weber's own attention goes chiefly to administration – the day-to-day exercise of political power – and produces another of his most significant theoretical legacies, the concept of bureaucracy.

The legitimacy phenomenon been further elaborated in Heinrich Popitz's theory of the institutionalization of political power. It comprises three basic processes:

> To begin with, relations of power become depersonalized. Power is no longer undistinguishable from a given individual who at a given moment enjoys a significant advantage over others, but increasingly appears connected with functions and positions which transcend the individual. Furthermore, power undergoes formalization: that is, its exercise is increasingly oriented to rules, procedures, and ritualized practices. (This does not exclude that power may be exercised arbitrarily. But one can speak of *arbitrium* – or of favor – only when one can contrast arbitrary decisions – or acts of favor – with what takes place as a rule). A third aspect of power institutionalization is the growing integration of power relations within a more comprehensive order. Power gears itself into a social edifice of which it is a part: supports it and is in turn supported by it (Popitz 1992: 38–39).

Again, the institutionalization of power has both a quantitative aspect – in any given context, to what extent has power become institutionalized? – and a qualitative aspect – in what ways has it done so? A valid answer to the second question would probably show considerable differences even between political systems that have achieved the same level of institutionalization. For example, in the 'classical' Chinese empire the main mode of institutionalization consisted in the meticulous and exacting performance of *traditional rituals* centered on the Emperor who currently enjoyed the 'mandate from heaven'. In the typical modern state, instead, the main mode is the systematic reference to constitutions and other components of the state's own *juridical system*, which can be enacted according to stated procedures. Their content, for that reason, is intrinsically contingent and can more easily deal with changing threats and opportunities confronting the political system.

As Weber points out, in the task of depersonalizing and standardizing the state's political and administrative practices, the knowledge of relevant legal documents by specialized personnel is complemented by other bodies of expert knowledge and the relative experts: economic, financial, managerial, sociological, statistical knowledge. (The term 'statistics' itself suggests the original intent of such knowledge: to monitor empirical reality on behalf of public authority, orienting and if necessary modifying its practices of rule.)

Further instruments of the institutionalization of modern, Western political power, are an increasingly diversified and complex administrative system; the conception of 'the nation' as a unified political subject; the notion of popular sovereignty; finally the participation in the political process of broader and broader sections of the population.

This last development affects particularly deeply the nature itself of modern political experience. On the one hand the society at large projects itself as the constituency of political power, and purports to govern itself via popular participation in the political process. But political participation has a further import, often inadequately attended to. Although one envisages the whole society as an active participant, the etymology itself of *participation* suggests that within that process the various components of a divided society take sides, and typically entrust the political promotion of their own socio-economic and other interests to different parties. This second meaning of 'participation' lends itself to negative valuation, as shown by expressions such as 'factionalism', 'partisanship' and 'sectionalism'.

On this account, the contemporary political process is to a large extent adversarial, bent upon mutual contestation and adversary confrontation. The extent to which it is publicly and legitimately conflictual echoes, however weakly, the original Greek meaning of 'politics' as the open, peaceable confrontation between diverse bodies of opinion and policy preferences. State activities respond to a considerable (though variable) extent to inputs vehicled by popular participation; they are preceded, oriented, accompanied by a discursive process in which in principle each citizen can have her/his say; s/he is allowed and encouraged to exercise her/his own judgment and decide with which other citizens to associate her/himself in the political context.

Thus, the electoral mechanism induces the parties periodically to challenge each other. The peculiar institution of *legitimate opposition* allows a persistent confrontation between the policies put forward by the majority and undertaken by the government and alternative policies pushed by minorities. The resulting tensions are to an extent constrained by the parts' consensus over constitutionally guaranteed political principles and values and particularly by the 'rules of the game'. But sometimes that consensus is revealed to be weak and precarious, and needs to be re-negotiated.

All this renders the political process intrinsically dynamic. From a certain point on, when the entire adult population is entitled to a vote, the increasing complexity of society and the multiple cleavages traversing it, engender ever new demands for public policy, often pushing it into new areas. This tendency, however, may diminish the effectiveness of the parties themselves, their capacity to articulate claims and propose coherent and fiscally plausible demands for political action. At some point, such demands may be conveyed to the states by other conduits – interest groups, social movements, consultants, professional lobbies, corruptive practices.

Furthermore, the state's growing involvement in the management of the social process at large is pushed not only by various sections of society demanding policies favoring them but also by the growing size and internal differentiation of the state's own administrative apparatus, whose diverse components seek each to assert its autonomy and increase its funding. From a certain point on, such endogenous impulses to a greater societal involvement by the state may even become more significant than the exogenous impulses originating from the citizenry. To the extent that this happens, it reduces the significance, of the political inputs conveyed by popular participation. The latter becomes increasingly mediated and controlled (and manipulated) by a large organization; its fundamental mode of expression (the electoral contest) becomes just an occasional event, where a small number of more and more constant and generic issues are raised, while the actual concerns of public action change, increase in number, become more diverse.

On these accounts the citizenry, while remaining formally endowed with certain capacities and opportunities for political impact, becomes in fact increasingly depoliticized, among other reasons because its attention and involvement are increasingly captured by media which distract and manipulate opinion.

Chapter Two

Power: An Outline of the Concept and of its Manifestations[*]

Why is power so hard to define?

In a discipline such as sociology, notorious for the difficulty it experiences in establishing widely and durably agreed definitions of its concepts, that of *power* (at any rate *social power*, which is our only concern here) stands out as one whose definition is particularly contentious and unstable. This in spite (or perhaps on account) of the fact that, however understood, that concept signals a particularly significant social phenomenon, arguably entitled to a central position in the discipline's vocabulary and in its discourse.

Before reviewing some controversies over the content to be attributed to the power concept, one may reflect briefly on *why* it should indeed be so controversial. One reason may be that, at any rate in the Western cultures, those in a position of social power often find it awkward to acknowledge expressly that they indeed occupy such a position, and enjoy the advantages it brings them.

Again, *why*? The phenomenon of social power necessarily entails an asymmetry between parties which to some extent posit each other as equal, as standing on the same plane. This was pointed out by Simmel (1971) in his essay on the relationship he called 'superordination and subordination'. We should not think of it as vesting in the superordinate party a *total* control over the conduct of the subordinate, for that would deprive the latter of all autonomy, all subjectivity. This, in turn, would render her/him unable to 'act back' on the former, to place at the superordinate's disposal, energies the superordinate does not directly possess, and on that very account seeks to deploy to its own advantage from the subordinate. At the same time, in order to do this the superior must bind and constrain, thus to an extent deny (typically, through commands) that very autonomy and subjectivity.

On this and other accounts (perhaps in view of a connection between power and *responsibility* which, under certain circumstances, they find threatening to themselves) very frequently (though by no means always) those possessing

---

[*]   This text reproduces (with some minor emendations) the entry 'Power', which I wrote for the *Cambridge Dictionary of Sociology* (Cambridge: Cambridge University Press, 2006), pp.464–469.

power *over* others do not publicly aver that they do, no matter how aware they are of the advantages this brings them, and how keen they are on continuing to enjoy them. Typically, it is those *under* power who declare themselves so to be. They impute the possession of power to others, and more or less bitterly point to the attendant advantages denied to them. In the *Magnificat*, a passage in the Gospels where the Virgin Mary's comments on the announcement to herself that she will bear God's son, she celebrates Him among other things for His capacity to 'depose the powerful from their seat'.

Sometimes, the powerless seem to take pride in their powerlessness, as in other disadvantageous aspects of their social position – witness the semantic shift undergone by expressions such as *sans-culottes* or *descamisados*, which the higher strata respectively of Ancien Regime France and of modern Argentina originally used to denigrate and make fun of the lower ranks, until these turned such expressions into proud symbolic self-identifications.

In sum, there is something invidious about social power, in two closely related meanings of 'invidious': that which evokes envy, and that which one is not keen to acknowledge having oneself, but is willing to attribute to others. Possibly such ambivalences attached to the expression – and indeed to the experience – of social power, contribute to making it 'essentially contested'; they also account for the fact that the concept itself has been so controversial even in the context of scientific discourse.

The dispute on Weber's definition

Some significant controversies taking place among sociologists and political scientists in the twentieth century, concern, expressly or otherwise, the definition of power (*Macht*) phenomenon offered at the beginning of the century by Max Weber. In one version, that definition characterizes power as 'the chance of a man or a group of men to realize their own will in a social action even against the resistance of others who are participating in the action' (Weber 1978: 926).

Some expressed or implied elements of this definition were *not* considered controversial. In particular, it was widely agreed that one should think of (social) power not as a substance but as a relationship – a point implied in Weber's reference to both parties' participation in 'social action'. In other terms, power is not something to be held, so to speak, in one's hand, but as something obtaining *between* two parties, such that A may hold it *vis-à-vis* B, but not *vis-à-vis* C.

Weber's expression 'chance' was seen as entailing two further plausible, closely related characteristics of power. First, power refers to a *probability*, not (so to speak) to a 'dead cert', to the complete assurance of a given party's success. Second, power is always *potential*, refers not so much to the doing of something (to the actual 'production of effects', proposed by others as an alternative definition of power) but to the *capacity* to do something, to produce effects if and when one chooses.

In other terms, power does not need to be exercised (by overcoming opposition or otherwise) in order to exist. Paradoxically, it was suggested, the exercise of power may so to speak consume it and/or subject it, when actually brought to bear, to the risk of being found wanting, incapable in fact of doing its number. Rather, power is at its most powerful, as it were, when those subject to it demonstrate their subjection without power being actually exercised; when it operates through the subjects' memory of past exercises of it or their imagination of future ones; when it needs to be at most symbolically represented rather that actually put into action. (One may connect to this intuition a number of enlightening discourses by political scientists, historians, sociologists, on the *symbolic* aspects of the power phenomenon.)

However, some aspects of Weber's definition became controversial in the post-World War Two discussion on the power concept. For instance, Weber's reference to the 'will' of the party in power became an issue. It was questioned whether that reference implied intentionality. Does the existence of a power relationship depend on the powerful party's awareness of its own preference for a given, existent or future state of things and on its conscious commitment to obtain it? Does it depend on its ability to superimpose its own over the other party's will? Is the overcoming or the potential overcoming of actual or virtual resistance an essential component of the relationship? What of situations where the asymmetry between the parties is so great that the inferior party is not even aware of having interests contrary to those of the superior party, but routinely cooperates in the attainment of them, or at any rate does not seek to hinder that attainment? Is not the superior party's ability to keep certain present or future states of things from becoming an issue between itself and the other party – its ability to *control the agenda*, it was said – a particularly privileged condition (Lukes 1994)?

Some contributors to the debate, while assuming that Weber's conceptual construct was essentially acceptable – whatever the qualifications and modifications to it suggested by the answers to some questions we have mentioned – labored to establish its boundaries by comparing-and-contrasting it with cognate concepts, such as authority (or domination), influence, force, or manipulation (Wrong 1980).

Methodological concerns

In the second half of the twentieth century the concept of power, with reference to the Weberian definition of it or otherwise, was the object also of methodological arguments concerning the possibility of grounding it empirically. The discussion involved both sociologists and political scientists, especially those associated with the 'behaviorist' approach, itself much inspired by sociology. It often concerned, besides the power concept itself – or an elaboration of it, 'power structure' – that of elite. Attempts to put such concepts to use in empirical research, through varying methodological approaches, were conducted in the US both at the local level (for instance by Floyd Hunter and Robert Dahl) and at the national level (for instance by C. Wright Mills). They led to interesting developments, for instance the study of 'interlocking directorates', carried out with reference to numerous corporations or other economic units, such as banks, or the study of 'decision making' within political bodies.

Some scholars went further in the attempt to 'operationalize' the power concept and indeed to measure various parameters of a power relationship. Some aspects of these are in principle amenable to quantitative assessment. For instance, over how many subjects can the holder of power exercise it? Over how many aspects of their existence? How significant are those aspects?

Also, assuming that power entails the ability to inflict negative sanctions on those subject to it, one can put those sanctions in some kind of ordinal sequence. The 'power over life and death' which Roman law attributed to the *paterfamilias* can plausibly be assumed to stand at the high end of that sequence – although in the *Iliad* Achilles seeks to top that by denying burial to the corpse of Hector, whom he has just killed. (In the Victorian era, an Ottoman ruler expressed his dismay and surprise to a British envoy, on learning that the Queen could *not*, as he did, have anybody's head chopped off on her own say-so.) But there are variations in the manner in which a subject can be put to death. (As a Roman citizen, Paul had over Peter the advantage of claiming the right to die by the sword rather than on the cross.) Below killing lies, say, banishment from the polity, often accompanied by the confiscation of the patrimony of the banished.

The sequence goes down to a rich variety of less and less blatantly damaging sanctions, such as the dismissal from employment of a worker, the blackballing of someone seeking admission to a club, or the exposure to gossip of a member of a social circle. But it is a demanding task to subsume this ordinal arrangement of sanctions into a more sophisticated metric, comprising other aspects of the power relations, and allowing their comparison (the comparison, say, between the threat of a lockout and the threat of a strike) or for that matter to operationalize Michael Mann's useful distinction between extensive and intensive power. In fact, some scholars adopting high standards of methodological rigor, were led by the difficulty of *measuring* power to the conclusion that one might as well dispense with the concept itself!

Fortunately, few scholars took that suggestion seriously. The others continued, more or less explicitly and consistently, to abide by their sense that power was an indispensable concept, pointing to a most significant social experience or indeed a critical dimension, overt or covert, of all social structures. From the late fifties through the mid seventies, in the protracted sociological argument between a theoretical perspective focused on 'order' and one focused on 'conflict', the power concept was often invoked by students associated with the latter perspective. However, it could be employed also to challenge that alternative, arguing that order need not be grounded on normative consensus among all involved in systematic interaction, but rather on the pressure which one part of society, the power*ful* part, imposed upon the other, power*less* part. Even those situations where significant structures were in fact underwritten by some kind of normative consensus valid across society, could be interpreted as outcomes of particularly protracted, routinized, long unchallenged power inequalities.

Another advantage of the emphasis on these was that it gave some conceptual purchase even on social change, on situations where existent arrangements were put into question and order broke down. In its Weberian understanding, the concept itself of power implied the possibility of resistance. It thus suggested that sometimes the power-less but resistant part of society could gain the upper hand and succeed in restructuring society to suit its own interests. Or, a group not favored by the existent power structure could challenge it by developing alternative power sources. Finally, even within a stable power structure, its very existence gave rise to contentions over the occupancy of the favored positions with it, and thus to further occasions for change.

A challenge to Weber's definition

Arguments of this kind, as we have seen, often appealed to Weber's authority. The debate became more intense, and more significant, when the central imagery of the Weberian construction was called into question. To simplify matters, an intrinsically tough-minded view of power was challenged by a tender-minded one.

The Weberian imagery, we have suggested, emphasized the asymmetry between individuals or between groups acting in the presence of one another, and the advantages enjoyed by those located at the upper end of the asymmetry. It implied that, at any rate in a stable and consistent power relationship, whatever its sources and its scope, all the power there laid at that end – in other terms, the relationship was a *zero-sum* one.

Yet Weber himself had connected that relation with the involvement of both parties in 'social action'. Whether he intended this or not, this consideration (together with others) suggested to some authors that one could view the power relation, in spite of its intrinsic asymmetry, as a functional feature of that social action, a fixture, as it were, of a shared social space, not only as something appropriated by one party and by the same token denied the other and used to keep it at bay. A given part's *power over* the other could be viewed also as something both parties benefited from, as a component of their *power to* attain some shared end, as a *collective facility*.

This bold reconceptualization of power was put forward in the late fifties by Talcott Parsons, in a belated but impressive rebuttal of a criticism often made of his theories, to the effect that these ignored the power phenomenon and the related reasons for conflict and change. It was taken further by Niklas Luhmann, who expressly reproached Parsons's critics, and his own, for their bloody-minded insistence on the power asymmetry, on the distribution of power within a group. The time had come to consider the extent to which the institutionalization of power relations empowered the group as a whole, making it more capable of pursuing collective goals.

In this perspective, power could be considered a *medium* through which selections made in one part of society could be conveyed to others, and thus as analogous to money. In the same way that, in a society where it has been invented or adopted, money allows and fosters the rationalization of economic activities, the development within a society of power relations could strongly assist a society's pursuit of non-economic goals.

The gain a group or society derives from being the locus of power relationship deserves consideration – and perhaps primary consideration, irrespective of the way in which or the extent to which such relationship favors in the first instance one part of society over against the others. It allows the society as a whole to respond more promptly and energetically to new opportunities and dangers in its environment, to promote and manage new modes of cooperation. It can be likened to a cybernetic device, which monitors the environment, collects, stores, elaborates information, forms decisions which can be the more promptly, coherently and predictably implemented, to everybody's advantage, the more they are backed by sanctions at the disposal exclusively of one part of society – the superior part. (Incidentally, this cybernetic imagery had already been developed, *avant lettre*, in Durkheim's lectures on political power and the state.) Put otherwise, power does not empower *only* those who hold it.

The fact that power can be, and (according to this argument) typically *is* generated and accumulated on behalf of the whole society, although managed by one part of it, is suggested by one significant aspect of political power in particular, emphasized by Weber – its tendency to seek *legitimacy*, that is to generate in those subject to power a disposition to obey commands grounded on a sense of moral obligation. Yet, Parsons's own strong emphasis on legitimacy (and the attendant processes of legitimation, and its variety) while in keeping with his own strongly normative (and Durkheim-inspired) conception of the social process at large, is only to a limited extent supported by Weber's own discourse on power. Here, the ideal-typical discussion of the subjective processes presiding over the subjects' obedience points to two alternative dispositions to obey: a subject's totally unreflected, automatic habit of submission to another's will; a subject's calculation of the advantages and disadvantages of obedience *vs* non-obedience and of the probability and significance of the attendant application or non-application of sanctions. Obedience grounded on a sense of moral obligation comes in only as a third answer – though one on which Weber himself lays emphasis, by offering a particularly creative treatment of it.

Weber in fact treats legitimacy itself as a significant but contingent qualification of a power relation previously established on strictly factual grounds, and which can if necessary reassert itself and maintain itself, at any rate in the short/medium period, even in presence of a 'legitimation crisis'. Furthermore, in the context of 'big-time politics' – the context, that is, of international relations, where the competitive interactions between sovereign polities take place – there is not much place for legitimacy, which is instead a feature, if of anything, of domestic political relations. In the international realm, instead, military might is necessarily the ultimate stake and medium of political action. And legitimacy is irrelevant to such might, only its effectiveness counts.

Varieties of power

Furthermore, Weber was keenly aware that political power itself, that to which the notion of legitimacy could apply, at any rate (as we have seen) in the domestic context, was only one form of social power. A programmatic sentence from an unfinished essay of his makes this clear: 'Now: "classes", "status groups" and "parties" are phenomena of the distribution of power within a community' (Weber 1978: 927).

In Weber's view, power exists between a community's component groups if and to the extent that one of these secures exclusive or highly privileged access to and control over a critical social resource. This allows that group to lay enforceable boundaries on the activities of the others groups. It can induce them to desist from opposing or hindering the pursuit of its own interests, or indeed direct them to commit some of their own activities, willy-nilly, to that very pursuit.

The power phenomenon, then, can be differentiated conceptually by considering the social resources a group must have at its disposal if it is to have this degree of control over others. In Marxian language, those resources are of three kinds: means of production (on which economic power is based, and which is the main object of the relations between classes); means of violence (these ground political power, and the possession and employment of them is contended over by parties – in a very broad meaning of this expression); means of interpretation.

This last concept needs some further elaboration, for it points to the elusive domain of 'the imaginary'. Michael Mann (1993), without using the expression 'means of interpretation', convincingly argues their significance on the basis of three 'anthropological' considerations. Human beings need cognitive frameworks by means of which to experience and to handle reality; need normative frameworks to sustain and routinize their cooperative activities and to moderate and settle their contentions; need ritual and aesthetic practices by means of which to express particularly meaningful emotions and symbolize and sustain their identities. 'Ideological' power emerges to the extent that a distinctive group establishes privileged control over the social activities and the cultural artifacts relating to the satisfaction of *these* needs, and to that extent can direct those social activities and allow access to those cultural artifacts.

Mann however dissents from the above tri-partition of the power phenomenon by giving separate conceptual status also to *military* power. Other students dissent from the tri-partition by explicitly or implicitly asserting that the notion of power should be applied only to what has been previously named *political* power.

Popitz on the institutionalization of political power

A sustained argument to the effect that social power can manifest itself in different ways was developed, toward the end of the twentieth century, by the German sociologist Heinrich Popitz. The title itself of his book on this topic, *Phänomene der Macht*, conveys this, for 'Phänomene' is a plural noun. In particular, Popitz argues, power can be acquired and managed also to the extent that, through 'technical action', some people can shape and modify to their own advantage the objective circumstances under which other people live, the factual constraints under which they operate.

> Technical action has three essential moments, all relating individuals with things: 'making use of', 'modifying', 'producing' objects. 'But such subject-to-object relations always affect also those between subject and subject. This does not simply mean that technical action has social conditions and consequences. Rather, that action itself plays a role in establishing the social conditions of human beings. Behind the 'making use' of objects necessarily lies the question of property claims; behind the 'modifying' of objects a particular form of the exercise of power, and not just power over the objects themselves; the 'producing' of objects entails the differentiation of activities and thus a form of division of labor (Popitz 1992: 160–61).

Another of Popitz's significant contributions, however, is chiefly concerned with political power, which he, with Weber, grounds on violence, and particularly with its institutionalization. He conceptualizes three main *aspects* of this process: the 'depersonalization' of power, the 'formalization' of its exercise, and its 'integration' (the latter meaning the increasing extent to which power gears itself into other social activities, is supported by them and contributes to them).

Popitz also outlines an ideal-typical sequence of *phases* in the institutionalization of political power. The recourse to violence (or the threat of it) as a way of inducing others' compliant behavior may go beyond its *sporadic* phase insofar as means of violence are made ready for repeated uses, and brought to bear on recurrent situations, from which those threatened with violence cannot easily escape. Power can then move on to a *norm-making* phase, where it does not just induce the subjects to momentary compliance but seeks to program and routinize their compliant activities and dispositions. Further, it can be *positionalized*, that is connected with the occupancy of distinctive social roles (the earliest of which have been those of the patriarch, the judge, and the war leader). In the next phase, those and other such positions come to be supported by a *staff*, an *apparatus* – a set of individuals who steadily and reliably collaborate with each position's holder. The final phase sees the emergence of a *state*. Here the ensemble of the holders of power positions and of the related apparatuses effectively claims the monopoly of three essential functions: norm-making – jurisdiction – enforcement.

The modern state shares with a few other polities, such as the Greek *poleis*, the Roman republic, some medieval city-states, a particularity of great cultural significance: the polity's norms address and seek to regulate the activities not just of those subject to its power but also of the polity itself. In all cases, this is done by means of a few recurrent practices, such as establishing a public sphere, recognizing some entitlements the subjects may hold *vis-à-vis* the power center itself, making the occupancy of power positions depend on certain procedural arrangements.

The recognition that social power has different sources and takes different forms, including *at least* political and economic power, brings to bear a specifically sociological perspective on a phenomenon – power itself – which for centuries had been attributed primarily or indeed exclusively to the political sphere. Indeed, as Luhmann has written, until the advent of modernity Western philosophers and other students of social and cultural affairs 'thematized' society itself chiefly in its aspect as a polity, a 'realm', as bounded territory whose inhabitants are perceived in the first place as suitable objects for rule (Luhmann 1975: 89–127).

Economic *vs* political power

Only in the course of modernization, in fact, the sphere of the economy has strongly asserted its autonomy from that of politics, and economic power has separated itself institutionally from political power. However, according to Franz Neumann (1986), this historically unique development has by the same token posed the problem of how those two power forms would relate to one another, whether and how they would assist or oppose one another, establish alliances with one another, or seek to maximize their own autonomy of one another, their own superiority over one another.

This problem cannot be settled by conceptual fiat, for it has different aspects, and finds different solutions, in varying empirical circumstances. For instance, the Marxian characterization of the state as 'the executive committee' of the bourgeoisie was not terribly off the mark when it was proposed, but needs at the very least strong qualifications and modifications if one wants to apply it in later circumstances. Here it became more enlightening to think of 'politics' and 'the market' as the institutional loci of intrinsically different, and potentially competing, power processes. T. H. Marshall's duality of 'citizenship and social class' points in this direction. The relation between the capitalist, democratic West and the collectivist Soviet system, which constituted the key story of the 'short' twentieth century (1917 to 1991), can be roughly conceptualized as representing a contrast between two very different ways of settling the relationship between political and economic power.

The contrast in question finds a (however remote) echo also in contemporary theoretical debates in the social sciences. The superiority of the economy is implicitly asserted in the extension of the rational choice approach to spheres of social existence, including the polity, where previously other approaches prevailed.

Peter Blau (1964) gave equal time to 'exchange' and 'power' (where power stands for political power) in the title of a book, where however the derivation of the latter from the former was the *pièce de résistance*. The economist Oliver Williamson construed the emergency of 'hierarchies' as the outcome of particular circumstances under which the individuals' purely market behavior, viewed as the paradigm of all social conduct, failed to deliver all its goods.

Whatever the insights yielded by these econo-centric perspectives, one must remark their persistent tendency to identify power with political power, and thus to treat the power phenomenon itself as something in principle extraneous to the economic realm. Power so conceived can be at best complementary to that realm, service its need for political support and regulation. At worst, it tends to prey upon it, and thus to damage the economy's disposition to produce 'efficiency.' (Here once more an intrinsically economistic criterion is unproblematically put forward as the single criterion by which to judge all social arrangements.)

As long as such perspectives prevail, they do little to prepare the sociological imagination to deal with the continuing story of the relationship between economic and political power. The main content of that story is, in the early twenty-first century, the globalization process. This can be roughly conceived as a (partly) novel way in which economic processes seek to proceed with a maximum of support, and a minimum of interference, on the part of political power centers. The novelty lies in the ever-growing availability to economic forces of largely de-territorialized spaces and resources. This deeply challenges the still prevalent loci of political power – states which exercise jurisdiction over distinctive territories, and extract resources from economic units stably located within those.

The challenge is increased by the fact that economic forces control not only expressly economic processes, but also those concerned with the production and application of scientific knowledge, as well as with the production and distribution of objects addressing the ever-growing demand for a 'collective imaginary'. In other terms, economic power has largely subsumed ideological power under itself.

An appreciation of the extent to which these ongoing phenomena find in social power both their target and their medium, requires among other things the continuing awareness of the significance and complexity of the power concept itself. Once more it is not a *conceptual* question, whether the relationship between political power and economic power, in particular, is primarily one of collusion or of collision. But one can assume that the answer to that question – or indeed the answers, since these will continue to vary from time to time and from place to place – will throw light on historical and contemporary phenomena of great human significance.

Chapter Three

Political Power Un-Manned:
A Defence of the Holy Trinity from
Michael Mann's Military Attack[*]

This brief contribution addresses only one of the problems raised by Michael Mann's imaginative and substantial discussion of the military phenomenon in his *magnum opus* (Mann 1986–2012). The problem concerns the conceptual status Mann confers upon that phenomenon by considering it as the locus of a distinctive, relatively self-standing source of social power, on which it falls occasionally to play an autonomous role in the making and unmaking of societies, and which in any case interacts with the other sources as the custodian of a resource – organized coercion – which *they* don't control while *it* does.

Put otherwise, I question, below, Mann's decision to stage his show by

---

[*] Most contemporary social scientists are aware of, and indebted to, the highly original, full-scale treatment of the relations between different forms of social power which Michael Mann has offered in a monumental work (4 vols!), *The Sources of Social Power*. This unique, most impressive work is characterized by two main features: Mann's masterful survey of an enormous range of events and arrangements, ranging from pre-history to our own times; and his reasoned, consistent reference to a conceptual scheme embracing four main power forms – ideological, economic, military, political.

In proposing and elaborating this scheme of his own making, Mann differs from one more-or-less expressly proposed by many authors, Max Weber among others, by adding military power to the conventional trio of power forms: political, economic, and ideological (the expression for this last form varies within the literature). As it happens, in pursuing my own interest of long standing in the relations between various forms of social power – *see* some essays in this collection, as well as my *Forms of Power* (Poggi 2001) – I have always abided by that trio.

A few years ago the editors of a collection of essays evaluating the massive scholarly significance of Michael Mann's masterpiece for contemporary social science (Mann 1986–2012) asked me to contribute to that collection. At that point, I boldly decided to present at some length my own reasons for (as it were) begging to differ from Mann on one single, merely conceptual point – the contrast between his own four-fold classification of power forms and the more conventional three-fold one. I even had the nerve to give a cheeky title to my contribution.

Though my own contribution to the volume did affirm my debt to and admiration for most other aspects of Mann's work, my contribution's single-minded insistence on that contrast rendered it something of a dissenting voice. On this account, readers wanting to evaluate my own argument (reproduced here with minor variants) will do well to consider those passages which, in Mann's own 'Response' to the contents of the volume, vigorously restate his views. Both my own essay and Mann's response appeared in J. Hall, and R. Schroeder, *An Anatomy of Power*, (NY: Cambridge University Press, 2006).

adding to the trio of political, economic, and ideological power a fourth: protagonist military power – a decision he represents in the acronym IEMP. In doing so, he expressly and, one might say, gleefully, sets himself against the trinitarian orthodoxy. I contend that, on purely conceptual grounds, this is a doubtful decision, though I concede that occasionally it finds some justification in specific empirical circumstances.

Mann's dissent from the conventional trio of power sources

In making that decision, I believe, Mann was carried away by the intensity of his dissent from much of the social theorizing prevalent at the time he conceived and planned *The Sources of Social Power*, where the military phenomenon was sometimes ignored, more frequently treated diffidently and without an adequate sense of its nature and significance. By adding military power to the orthodox trinity, Mann placed it on the high ground, and made it axiomatic that a valid, theoretically inspired account of the story of human civilisation required, among other things, a sensitivity to the nature and dynamics of organized violence – not *just* those of the material metabolism between human beings and nature, of the construction and maintenance of collectivities via relations of command and obedience, or of the elaboration of authoritative understandings of what is true, proper, or beautiful.

While recognising the significance of this theoretical concern, and the relevance of the insights it has produced in the writings of Mann himself and of other scholars, I suggest that at the conceptual level none of this justifies abandoning the conventional trinity of political, economic, and ideological power.

One must admire Mann's courage in refusing to abide by that trinity, for a multitude of diverse sources affirm it, imply it, or assume it. I, for one, find it all over the place. Recently, Runciman has forcefully restated it in his treatise (Runciman, 1983–88). Weber's opening sentence in 'Class, status group, and party' asserts it almost explicitly (Weber 1978: 926). Etzioni's typology of compliance structures in complex organisations uses it (Etzioni 1975). One of Gellner's best book titles, *Plough, Sword and Book*, echoes it (Gellner 1969); so does his view that the fusion between political, ideological and economic powers in the Soviet system made of it a unique example of 'Caesaro-Papist-Mammonism' (Gellner 1994). Statements about the nature of economics suggest that the discipline deals with only the first of three modes of allocation – contract, custom, command. Books and essays I come across often pattern on the Marxian notion of 'means of production' those of 'means of coercion' and 'means of interpretation'. Kant has a parallel trinity of three evil dispositions, 'hankering after lordship', 'hankering after possessions', and 'envy', where the last one with a little massaging can be rephrased as 'hankering after recognition'.

I am sure Mann himself could easily add other entries to this haphazard list of trinitarian views on power; but no matter – to him, they are all out of step. Military power deserves equal time with the members of the established trio, as his own Grand Narrative intends to prove, at any rate to his own satisfaction. Not entirely to mine, though, for two main reasons.

First – apart from my own stubborn preference for conceptual trinities, at any rate over against quartets if not always over against pairs: for, let us face it, *omne trinum est perfectum* – I sense that, if he read Mann, Ockham would reach for his razor. Although for Mann the phenomenon of organized, technically assisted capacity for sustained coercion, performs a significant amount of analytical and empirical labor, such labor does not justify promoting that phenomenon to the rank of a fourth source of social power.

Weaknesses in Mann's understanding of political power

One significant reason for opposing that promotion is the fate it would inflict on a particular member of the established trio – political power. The latter is, as it were, un-manned by being denied its conventional grounding in organized violence, and rendered sterile. Mann's operation of placing the discourse on power no longer on a tripod but on a four-legged table is deceptive, since one of the other three legs is rendered lame by the operation itself, which deprives political power of the conceptual identity bestowed upon it by centuries of theoretical reflection.

This is no place to review the intellectual itinerary which grounded that conceptual identity in coercion. I will just mention that it began, of course, in Greece; but on the face of it the Greeks, by inventing and naming politics, did not subscribe to my own bloody-minded identification of politics with coercion. Indeed the Greeks had a fancy notion that politics was based on the humans' capacity for talk, which allowed them, under appropriate conditions – those characteristic of the *polis*, which they proudly considered an exclusive, privileged product of their own making – to collectively envision conceptions of virtue characteristic of each *polis*, and to design institutions oriented to those.

Where is the coercion in all this? Well, ask the (relatively) old man who in *Crito* rattles on to his horrified friends and disciples (who have arranged to save Socrates' life by spiriting him out of Athens) about the only way he can show his own true devotion to the city's Laws – drinking the hemlock. The point is that even discursively generated laws, produced by politics understood in that fancy Greek manner, have to be sanctioned by collective coercion.

Coming straight to our own times, we do find notions of politics which on the face of it do not ground it in violence. Bertrand de Jouvenel (Jouvenel 1962) and Jean-Yves Calvez (Calvez 1995), for instance, claim that politics arises, instead, from a collectivity's confrontation with Other-dom – *l'autruité*.

But there are ways of dealing with The Other which are not political – we can be curious about The Other, we can traffic with It, we can ignore It. The ways that are political turn out to revolve on the decision to fight It, submit to It, or incorporate It, that is subsume It under a community bounded, again, by the enforceability of is norms.

Field and Higley (1980) understand politics as the settling of conflicts which the parties do not allow themselves to negotiate – but for this very reason the settlement must be coercively *imposable* if not always coercively *imposed*, otherwise it would not settle matters. The frequent reference in other American literature to the 'binding' nature of political decisions coyly points in the same direction. Witness Mann's own, 4-point definition of the state, 'much influenced by Weber', where the last feature is: '4. some degree of authoritative, binding rule making, backed up by some organized physical force' (Mann 1993: 55).

When it comes to the state, the central political institution of modernity, Weber's definition, with its 'monopoly of the legitimate use of force', seems absolutely *de rigueur* these days, and we know from Anter's work (Anter 1996) that it was widely shared in Weber's own time. Parts of Weber's own 'Politik als Beruf' become mystifying without that definition – particularly its discussion of the Machiavellian problem, the moral dangerousness of political leadership. Many successive theorists, from Elias to Tilly, have discussed it at length. But that monopoly is an elaboration (quantitatively and qualitatively *variable*) of a conceptually (and historically) prior relationship, once more, between political power in a generic sense, and not-yet-monopolised physical force. In sum, politics is a recurrent, constitutive aspect of social life among humans *because,* as Popitz states, 'there is no social order based on the premise that violence does not exist' (Popitz 1992: 67).

While 'loosening', as he says, the ties between military and political power, Mann repeatedly and emphatically stressed instead the relationship between political power on the one hand and territoriality, centrality and administration on the other. About none of these three features, however, one could say, as Popitz suggests about violence, that no social order is thinkable without it. To me, this suggests that political power as Mann construes it is without anthropological grounding.

As against this, the construction of the 'classical trinity' offered by Popitz (I often refer to this author, who died recently, because in my judgment he has received within anglophone sociological circles nothing like the recognition he deserved), anchors each of its components in a distinctive kind of inescapable human vulnerability – respectively, vulnerability to death and suffering (political power), to hunger and deprivation (economic power), to a sense of personal insignificance and cosmic meaninglessness (ideological power.) I wonder what human vulnerability is addressed, presupposed, managed by a power characterized by centrality, territoriality, and administration.

Or, seeing that Mann himself derives ideological power from a distinctive set of human needs, and economic power from another set, I wonder from what human needs he would derive political power as *he* understands it. In fact, in the text I have in mind he does not mention human needs, but derives political power from 'the usefulness of territorial and centralized administration'. Usefulness to whom, one wonders, given that in the course of both prehistory and history hundreds of populations lived cheerfully enough without the benefits of administration, let alone its centralised and territorial forms. And as concerns many of the populations which did experience administration, its benefits, one suspects, had to be imposed upon them, at any rate early on. *Guess how?* By the threat or exercise of coercion, that is by expressly and compellingly addressing the first of Popitz's vulnerabilities.

Another standard way of conceptualizing different power sources grounds each not (at the passive end) on distinctive needs or vulnerabilities, but (at the active end) on distinctive resources. For instance, my former colleague at the University of Virginia, Murray Milner, Jr. has developed in his *Status and Sacredness* a sophisticated 'resource-based' theory of status which juxtaposes it to power and privilege (Milner 1994). Again, Mann's understanding of political power must part company with this approach, for administration, centralised and territorial or otherwise, is not a resource, but a task.

Mann *vs* Weber

In dealing with these matters, Mann knows he stands in a (to say the least) uneasy relationship to Weber's theoretical legacy, given the latter's trinitarian conception of power. Mann is not as aware as he should of the extent to which he differs from Weber on a related question: the conceptual relation between political power and the state. To him, 'political power means *state* power' (Mann 1993: 9). To Weber, it doesn't. Underlying this difference is another one: in most texts of Weber's, and probably in all the more significant ones, in the expression '*modern* state' the adjective 'modern' is pleonastic. The state as he characterises it (particularly in other definitions than the one quoted above, which do not limit themselves to the above 'monopoly of the legitimate use of physical force') is another of those distinctive Western historical products Weber writes about in the 'Author's Introduction' to *The Protestant Ethic*, and indeed belongs, among those, in the subset of specifically modern ones. This does hold NOT for the way Mann understands 'the state'; though he does devote special attention to the *modern* state, he is willing to call 'states' all manner of other polities.

This is of course a perfectly legitimate preference, and one which Mann shares with a number of other authors, though my impression is that these are outweighed if not outnumbered by those who stand with Weber on this question. Yet that preference leads to some awkwardness when Mann tries to square it with Weber's own. In the second volume of *SSP2*, for instance, after quoting the standard Weberian definition, focussed again on the monopoly of the legitimate use of physical force, Mann claims to differ from it 'on one point. Many historic states did not 'monopolize' the means of physical violence' (Mann 1993: 55).

Now, I find this confusing, for three reasons. First, the category of 'historic' states, so far as I remember, is not used by Weber, which makes it difficult to see against what background of understandings shared with Weber, Mann posits his one difference from him. Second, Mann shifts from Weber's *use* of physical violence to the *means* of it – not an insignificant shift, since the notion of legitimacy invoked can be applied only to the *uses* of violence, not to its *means*. Finally, given that Weber never imputed *his* monopoly to other than the (modern) state, what's the use of reminding him (so to speak) that it does not hold for other polities?

Mann's last quoted passage goes on to say that 'even in the modern state the means of physical force have been substantially autonomous from (the rest of) the state' (Mann 1993: 55). This clause is again conceptually untidy, for 'means' as such cannot be autonomous or otherwise – the subjects who wield them can. It also surprises one by conceding a lot to the argument Mann is opposing, for it implies that, at any rate in the modern state, those means are a however wayward *part* of the state itself – *quod NON erat demonstrandum*. Against these petty objections to the clause in question must be set the fact that it opens Mann's way to a number of significant, empirically grounded arguments, as I shall soon argue.

A final difficulty with Mann's treatment of both the political and the military components of his quartet lies in his insufficiently elaborate and differentiated discussion of physical force, violence, coercion or what you will. What drives Mann to give 'separate and equal' status to military power is essentially his intent to give full conceptual recognition to the difference which *armies* have repeatedly made at a number of significant points in history, to the contribution which 'men on horseback' have recurrently made to the course of Western history in particular. Here again he both agrees with Weber and differs from him.

The difference lies chiefly in the fact that, although Weber was fully aware of the historical significance of the military factor and of related institutions (especially fiscal ones), when he emphasises the significance of physical force for his concept of politics and the (modern) state, he seems to have primarily in mind its employment by domestic agents of the executive and the judiciary: bailiffs, policemen, tax collectors, customs officers, prison guards, truant officers, executioners – *and* soldiers when they play a direct role in repressing aggressive manifestations of popular discontent and in re-establishing the public order at the behest of the authorities.

This is in keeping with Weber's keen sense that the state, like other polities, is in the first place a set of institutional and material arrangements for the domination of one part of society by another, and it is this domination which the employment or the threat of employment of organized physical violence primarily grounds, expresses, and sanctions.

This emphasis is reflected also in the place held by the notion of legitimacy in Weber's political thinking. There is no place for such a notion within 'politics between nations', at any rate in the Westphalian/Hobbesian/anarchical understanding of such politics which presumably Weber shared. For him legitimacy is a (contingent) quality of the 'vertical' relationship between the dominant and the dominated part of society, a (contingent) aspect of the command/obedience relation – and there is no such thing as command/obedience in the 'horizontal' relationship between sovereign nation states.

A digression on Weber's own understanding of politics

At this point I would like to digress briefly on whether and how, in his understanding and appreciation of politics, Weber squared the emphasis on domestic aspects I just attributed to him with his passionate commitment to the might of the German nation and thus to the 'primacy of foreign policy'. Perhaps it is not unjustified that most commentators distinguish between Weber's *political* writings and his *politological* ones, placing those focussed on the 'primacy of foreign policy' among the former rather than the latter. But in Weber's own mind, of course, that distinction sometimes gets short-circuited.

It is my impression – I voice it hesitantly, for to turn it into something more than just an impression would require a revisitation of the sources I cannot undertake at this point – that this happens in particular in a most significant piece of writing, the published version of his talk *'Politik als Beruf'*.

This talk was given early in 1919, at which time unavoidably (whether Weber wanted and admitted this or not) his thinking about politics was chiefly preoccupied with the question, how to make sure that Germany, a recently and disastrously defeated nation, would soon resume its rank as a most significant European and world power. Weber was a revanchist. Did he not say at Versailles, to some representatives of the allies, 'we shall meet again, gentlemen, on the field of honor', or words to that effect? (Incidentally, I have long felt that this imagery, appropriate to the joust or the medieval battlefield, was almost shockingly inappropriate in the mouth of someone who well knew how men in their thousands had died, say, at Tannenberg or at the Somme.)

That preoccupation, I sense, lays a heavy mortgage, in particular, on the conception of democracy presented in *'Politik als Beruf'*, giving it its peculiar plebiscitarian twist, and possibly informing also Weber's famous conception of an ethic appropriate to the political realm. As late as 1917, in texts foreshadowing changes to be introduced in the German constitution after the war – which he still hoped Germany might win – Weber had carefully discussed institutional arrangements for ensuring the *accountability* of parties and bureaucracies. In *'Politik als Beruf'* this no longer matters as much, and

Weber holds forth about something as rum – let us say it outright – as 'the ethic of *responsibility*' central to The Leader's sense of personal honor.

One reason for this, I suspect, is that *patriai tempore iniquo* Weber's thinking is thrown all in the direction of foreign policy and thus, when all is said and done, of war. Hence its occasionally disturbing overtones, remindful of the later Schmittian definition of 'the political' as an ambit of decision revolving around the question who's friend and who's foe, a question unavoidably 'existential', the answer to which must ultimately rest on the judgment of a single person. Or, put otherwise, in the situation of early 1919 the cry 'Bismarck, Bismarck, where art thou now?' becomes more and more compelling for Weber, and biases many aspects of his understanding of politics.

Mann's emphasis on the military uses of violence

With this, we can return to the contrast between Mann's and Weber's ideas. While, as I argued, when Weber discussed the state, the 'professionals of violence' involved in domestic affairs were chiefly on his mind, the second volume of Mann's *SSP* contains a useful, brief discussion of the relationship between police forces and armies, but the latter markedly predominate in Mann's thinking. This is common among authors who make much of the relationship between politics and violence in interpreting (in particular) European history, and most particularly, of course, among those who emphasize the impact of the changing technology of warfare on political institutions. Among significant contemporary writers perhaps only Foucault has theorized the relationship between coercion and the state by emphasizing instead the domestic, repressive, law-and-order-keeping uses of the former: and in this he agrees with Weber – and disagrees with Mann.

Perhaps one reason for Mann's opposite emphasis is that in a work such as *SSP*, with its focus on momentous changes and a narrative approach, it makes little sense, when dealing with organized violence, to emphasize those forms of it that from the material standpoint have changed *relatively* little in the course of history. For instance, the firepower deployable in operations of law enforcement and repression has certainly undergone remarkable quantitative and qualitative changes in the course of modern history, but nothing as remarkable as those undergone by firepower on the battlefield. Even when the army is called out to repress domestic disturbances, it is typically its most archaic component – mounted troops – that first makes its appearance. (Incidentally, in some countries those troops are not supposed to charge at a crowd before playing the bugle three times!)

Oddly enough, Mann's definition of politics-and-the-state, with its focus on territoriality, centrality and administration, shares the conceptual emphasis I attribute to Weber on the domestic side of the political enterprise. However, he deprives it of its coercive edge, by turning over most of the nasty stuff to a separate fourth power source, where the name of the game is not *just* repressive and punitive violence inflicted on individuals or on groupings of individuals, but, at bottom, mass killing.

The alternative would have been, to stick to the conventional conceptual trinity, confirm the intimate, constitutive relationship between political power and force, and emphasize that the actual recourse to force tends to be exceptional, being routinely replaced by material and symbolic ways of threatening that recourse and keeping it available as a last resort. It would have been possible, then, to thematize the oscillation, in the conduct of political business, between a minimum and a maximum of actual or symbolic use of force – between hegemonic, consensus-building moments and repressive moments, between carrot and stick, between welfare state and warfare state, between one and the other of the typical postures of the contemporary state toward the lower orders in particular theorized by Piven and Cloward (Piven and Cloward 1971).

Such oscillations could have been correlated (the direction of causal influence might of course be difficult to determine) with the ways in which and the extent to which 'even in the modern state the means of physical force have been substantially autonomous from (the rest of) the state'. I have already quoted this passage, and although on that occasion I had typically gone out of my way to find something *conceptually* wrong with it, I had also suggested (untypically, this time) that it has a lot to recommend it at the *empirical* level. I shall develop this point by drawing on a chapter of a book of mine (Poggi 2001).

Why the relation between political authority and a differentiated military is to an extent problematical

First, let me restate the trinitarian view I am 'pushing' here, by quoting the definition of 'politics' in Collins's *Conflict Sociology*;

> What we shall deal with here is the ways in which violence has been organized in society [...] In this fashion we can deal with all questions that might arise about politics [...] Politics, in this approach, involves both outright warfare and coercive threats. Most of what we refer to as politics in the internal (but not external) organization of the modern state is a remote version of the latter [...] Much politics does not involve actual violence but consists of manoeuvring around the organization that controls the violence (Collins 1975: 157).

The expression 'the organization that controls the violence' has some implications worth teasing out. First, 'organization' implies a built-in capacity, a readiness to exercise (or threaten) violence; the violence exercised or threatened is a product, a manifestation of pre-constituted, abiding arrangements. Second, 'organization' implies that these arrangements constitute an expressly contrived, differentiated, relatively self-standing aspect of a broader social reality. Third, the notion of 'control over violence' suggests that from the standpoint of that broader reality, the phenomenon of violence has costs (including the risk of being challenged and overcome by greater violence, or the risk of being overused) which it is the task of organization to evaluate and keep under control.

The institutionalization of political power in general and, more specifically, the development of the state, point up the complex and sometimes paradoxical relationships between these implications. The state tends to restrict the play of diffuse violence in the society and thus to pacify society, in two closely related ways. It declares illegitimate much of the violence people would otherwise indulge in – *much*, not all; as feminist critics have pointed out, the violence exercised and threatened by men in their dealings with women has mostly *not* been considered illegitimate. And it tries, more or less consistently and successfully, to reserve to itself the social and material devices that make violence more formidable – from uniforms to military and police command systems to weapons.

This last one is the critical process in the curbing of domestic violence. The political center vests in a part of itself, specifically organized to deal with it, an overwhelmingly superior capacity for violence. Thus, individuals or groups which might otherwise attempt to engage in violence on their own behalf are persuaded to cease and desist from such attempts. What pacifies society, thus, is not the disappearance or the utter rarity of social and material devices for restraining, killing, maiming, destroying, but the fact that these are vested, in principle, only in the political system, which entrusts them in turn to a specialised part of itself. To the extent that this happens, a paradox presented by Hobbes is confirmed: as the *potential* for violence increases, its *actual* exercise (or the threat of it) diminishes. This requires that the part of the political system entrusted with the potential for violence be – again – an 'organization': a purposefully contrived and coherently controlled set of practices, people, resources, specialised in building up and maintaining that potential. The political system must ensure that the organization in question packs enough of a punch to 'pacify' the social process at large and, when necessary, to keep outside political forces from interfering with it. It must also ensure that the potential for violence it assigns to the organization does not become dispersed into the rest of society by a kind of osmosis or entropy. Finally, the organization itself should not, as a whole or in its parts, exercise or threaten to exercise violence on its own behalf, against the larger society or the political system itself.

Let us restate this argument. The larger society can be secured against internal disorder and external aggression only if, through its political system, it possesses itself of a potential for violence which is *formidable* – in the etymological sense of the expression, meaning 'such as to evoke fear'. Organization serves this aim, for it entails that violence will be primarily (indeed, as far as possible, exclusively) engaged in an effective, workmanlike fashion by trained, competent specialists. It also serves the aim of differentiating institutionally the business of violence from the remainder of the social process.

Here comes the tricky part. Exactly that institutional differentiation creates an awkward possibility: the specialists in question may use their own exclusive guardianship of a critical social resource (organized violence) to affect the definition of public interest entrusted to other parts of the political system, and the related policies. The organization they inhabit may become self-absorbed, relatively unresponsive to the requirements and expectations of the rest of society. It can foster its own autonomy of other parts, increase its claims upon the resources they produce and manage, or seek to impose on the rest of the political system a self-interested understanding of what the larger society, taken as a whole, can and should do.

These possibilities are enhanced by the fact that any organization built around violence tends to have a strongly hierarchical structure. This, on the one hand allows it to confront promptly and effectively the contingencies requiring violence to be threatened or exercised; on the other, it allows the top levels of the structure to deploy the organization's resources in a coherent and unified fashion. Thus the organization can present more of a challenge *also* to other parts of the political system. The guardians and practitioners of organized violence may deal with the rest of the system *as if* from the outside, disregarding or subverting their own subordination to other parts, including those instituted to stand for the whole of the political system. In this fashion, the relationship between organized violence and political power, although it is a part-to-whole relationship, may come to resemble those between ideological or economic power on the one hand, and political power on the other.

There is of course great diversity in the extent to which the top-level military personnel act as a semi-independent elite, in the nature of the claims they advance, and in the content of the arguments by which they support those claims. Some countries have occasionally experienced the outright usurpation of political power by military leaders; in others these have successfully blackmailed the political elites into undertaking policies (sometimes of no direct military significance) different from those they had intended to pursue; in others yet the military have traditionally been, at worst, a pressure group seeking to increase or maintain its share of the state's budget (Finer 1976).

(Incidentally, in the Italian version of the book on which I am drawing here, I argue at some length that analogous phenomena can occur also in the relation between a political system and *its* police force. This may happen to such an extent as to affect deeply the constitutional framework of the exercise of rule, generating a *police state* (Poggi 1998).)

Two major issues in the relation

In spite of the variety in the phenomenon we are dealing with, it is possible to identify, among the recurrent issues, two particularly significant ones: on the one hand, how significant is, in the context of political experience in general, the problem of war and of the preparedness for it; on the other hand, how necessary it is that the institution specifically committed to handling that problem be granted a large amount of autonomy. I will comment briefly on these themes.

In the context of the modern state, and particularly in the West, the first theme – the persistent significance of war – has had a complex career. On the one hand, in the nineteenth century the war phenomenon, from time immemorial the central issue and the central instrumentality in the relations between states, acquired a monumental, ominous dimension, first fully displayed in the mass carnage of the American Civil War; and in the first half of the twentieth century, two world wars enormously amplified and deepened that experience. Through most of the second half of the century, the capitalist West and the collectivist East stood in a relationship which some claimed to be akin to war, and which occasionally seemed to push them toward the brink of an unprecedented kind of warfare of total mutual annihilation. Besides, a distressing number of highly murderous wars took place outside the areas directly occupied by the blocks, and without involving them in direct military confrontation, though many of those wars were related to the blocks' policies.

On the other hand, even in the West/East contest, it was widely felt that the key issue was not the military might of the two blocks, but the productive capacities of the respective socio-economic systems, and their ability to promote industrial growth both in the countries of each block and in the so-called Third World. Only in the USA and the USSR (especially, perhaps, in the latter), were the military elites spared the suspicion that their role in the politics of the respective countries had become a recessive one.

Naturally enough, this was for military elites a threatening feeling. They often reacted to it by arguing that, for all appearances to the contrary, war unavoidably remained the overriding concern of states, and organized, armed might their bottom-line resource. In some cases, military elites acknowledged that all-out war (not just nuclear, but also conventional) had become a highly improbable option. However, they began to prospect alternative uses for their own distinctive competences, and developed a set of neologisms and euphemisms for such uses – for instance, counter-insurgency measures, low-intensity military operations, peace-keeping or humanitarian interventions, aid to civil authority.

The persistent centrality of the military phenomenon to political experience is not, however, the sole theme to which military elites connect their claims. Another is the necessity that, for many intents and purposes, the military institution be run according to criteria exclusive to it, and enjoy a high degree of autonomy with respect to other political and social institutions. In order to understand this requirement, we may consider the utter peculiarity of the core activity of fighting soldiers, which (when all is said and done) consists in their seeking to kill people who in turn seek to kill *them*.

Soldiers are supposed to carry out this activity in a frame of mind well conveyed by the meaning of the expression 'mission' in the military context. This entails that one is *sent* to accomplish a task not of one's own, but in the accomplishment of which one is to invest all one has and is. 'Mission' also suggests that the task in question is a distinct phase or aspect of a broader project, of which one may not be even aware. The responsibility for formulating and assigning the task, and of coordinating it with other phases or aspects of the same project, falls to others. The connection between one's specific activity and those of others assigned the same mission, or between that mission and other missions, can only be ensured by prompt and thorough obedience to commands.

However, the execution of commands by a soldier, while (so to speak) *oriented* by obedience, must also be *motivated* by a sense of personal engagement. It would not be safe for this to be provided exclusively by the soldiers' attachment to their personal survival and bodily integrity, for all-too-often this might induce soldiers to flight rather than to fight. (In French, *sauve-toi*, literally 'save yourself' also means 'run away'.) An additional, and sometimes an overriding, motivational ingredient must instead be solidarity – a keen sense that one has a significant personal stake also in the survival and bodily integrity of others with whom one is closely associated. One might say that obedience provides a vertical tie between the individual soldier's conduct and that of his or her superiors; and solidarity a horizontal linkage between the individual soldier and his or her peers. A further emotional requirement is that, in the combat situation, soldiers should feel called upon to *prove themselves* in the face of an extremely testing and threatening situation.

What soldiers are to prove about themselves, used to be characterized as manliness; if this notion is to be disposed of because of its sexist connotations, one should replace it with another one bearing the same complex semantic freight. This comprises the capacity, in extremely stressful situations, to give and execute commands; to demonstrate solidarity toward one's associates; to perform complex activities; to endure deprivation, suffering, the prospect of painful death. It also encompasses a willingness to engage in violent, armed aggression and to overcome others' resistance to it.

In the context of a more-or-less modernised society, such psychical dispositions tend to be rare, as well as potentially dangerous. Their inculcation, therefore, requires a specialised environment, which insulates those who impart them, as well as those in the process of acquiring them, from the rest of society, and thereby both protects the society itself and maximises the probability of having those dispositions duly learned and experimented with. The insulation is both symbolic (for instance, the wearing of uniforms, the ceremonies of induction of soldiers) and physical. (As an Italian saying goes, the reason army barracks are guarded by sentinels is – to *keep out* common sense.) Above all, it is institutional; that is, a set of publicly acknowledged, sanctioned practices structure military life differently from all other forms of social life, for instance by attaching high value to obedience, solidarity, and various aspects of what, again, one used to call manliness, in comparison with attitudes and dispositions rewarded instead by the larger society.

As Mann has shown in his writings, typically a state's military component is not content with being an object of public controversies over its nature and significance, but actively intervenes in them in order to assert its autonomy of other parts of the state, and maximize its leverage on the state's policies. This is indeed something Weber himself knew a lot about, though he preferred to discuss similar tendencies with reference to the state's bureaucratic apparatus rather than its army. (We know however that he resented the semi-dictatorship Ludendorff imposed upon German public life during the last phase of the Great War.)

I think Mann has rendered us all a service by reminding us of the military's drive toward autonomy. This results from its position as a relatively segregated and highly specialized institution, entrusted with formidable resources which, if it disregards or 'suspends' its constitutional position as a mere executor of political decisions made by other state organs, can be mobilized to affect their policies, or even to take over the state's commanding positions.

Mann knows and relates a great deal about the diverse phenomena generated by that drive, and emphasizes those moments and aspects of it which have made a significant difference at various salient points in modern history, sometimes through complex 'intertwinings' between what he calls military power on the one hand, economic and/or political power on the other.

Conclusion

The question remains, whether any of this authorises Mann's view that military power has the same conceptual status as political, economic, and ideological power. As is clear from all the above, I would answer that question in the negative, though I concede that in certain contexts the relationship between military and civilian elites comes to resemble that between two self-standing powers. But my sense is that even when this happens, it happens *within and about the state*, and thus confirms the higher conceptual status of political power over against 'military power'.

Take the Pinochet episode, for instance. It was a classical military take-over of *state* power, brutally bringing organized violence to bear in order to change the *Chilean state's* constitution, regime, and policies, in alliance with and in the service of domestic (and foreign!) economic power. One *part* of the state sought to increase its sway over *other* parts and thereby over the *whole* of the state. One constitutive component of institutionalised political power prevailed upon and subordinated others – it did not try to 'go it alone'. The point of the exercise was to place the main levers which controlled the state machine in the hands of the military leaders. In this, the episode confirms, rather than negating, the institutional identity of the military as the custodian and the specialised practitioner of that most distinctive and fearsome resource on which *political* power grounds its institutional identity – organized, armed violence. No less – and no more.

Chapter Four

State and Society: Modern Trends of a Problematic Relationship[*]

An unsettled distinction

The conceptual couple 'state/(civil) society' is a product of the protracted effort through which, starting with the Enlightenment, a few generations of European intellectuals sought to gain a purchase on the process of modernization. The juxtaposition of 'state' to '(civil) society' emphasises one major aspect of that process: the growing differentiation between, on the one hand, the structures and events directly connected with public authority, with the constitution and management of the polity, and on the other the structures and events which individuals generate as they pursue their private interests, express their emotions, acquire and exercise their capacity for judgment, establish and manage relationships with one another.

Speaking of a 'juxtaposition' between two concepts, however, somehow prejudges the question of how they relate to one another, suggesting that they lie on the same plane and are, simply complementary to one another. But this is not the only relation in which those concepts have stood to one another. In an earlier relation, which might be called fusion, the two concepts were closely overlapped. In a philosophical and juridical vocabulary that originates with Aristotle and, transmitted through scholastic philosophy, lasts until Kant, the expression 'civil society' designates a condition in which humans have exited from the state of nature by establishing, and subjecting themselves to, political authority; one wrote of *societas civilis SIVE res publica*. Here, what made a society civil was the very fact of its being policed and governed.

Hegel breaks with this fusion of the two concepts in the *Philosophy of Right* of 1821. He sets alongside the civil society – a realm where individuals engage in the competitive pursuit of their private interests (chiefly economic) – the state, understood instead as an institutional site where are identified, and pursued through the actions of public authorities, interests collective in nature. These may be, in the dealings of states with one another on the international

---

[*]   What follows is the revised text of an entry written for the *International Encyclopedia of the Behavioral and Social Sciences* edited by Neil Smelser and Paul Bates, and published by Elsevier in 2001.

scene, the increase of each state's might and security. Or – on the domestic scene – the maintenance of public order or a degree of regulation of private traffics.

But this juxtaposition is loaded with tensions which induce Hegel to introduce conceptual entities – embodied in such institutions as the family, the corporation, or the 'police' (which here means: public administration) – intended to moderate those tensions. In fact, the juxtaposition comes to be perceived as an immanent contrast between state and society, leading thinkers to take sides with the one OR the other. Hegel himself opts for the state, but already Lorenz von Stein (1921), who places the paired concepts state/society at the center of a great work on the changes taking place in the France of his time, resolutely opts for society.

In a sense, so does Karl Marx. He derives from Hegel the view of civil society as the locus of the formation and confrontation of private interests of an economic nature. However, he endows it with a powerful, self-sustaining dynamic, grounded on means and relations of production, with respect to which the state itself loses the creative, autonomous power to drive historical development attributed to it by Hegel.

In contemporary theory, and sometimes in intellectual quarters very distant from the Marxian tradition, there are still instances of this tendency to prioritise one of two concepts and subsume under it the other. Oliver Williamson's theory of markets and hierarchies, for instance, posits the exchange phenomenon as the primordial form of social relation, and derives from 'market failures' the emergence of hierarchical, command-based relations, and thus of organizations (Williamson 1975). However implicitly, also in this view society, conceived in the first instance as the locus of market relations, precedes and in a sense justifies the state (seen as a particularly commandeering hierarchy). This priority of society, naturally, imposes tight limitations on what the state can and should do.

Arguments of this kind suggest that envisaging a true dichotomy between state and society is not appropriate, because one concept can be made to posit and encompass the other instead of accepting it as sharing its own standing. But there are also arguments to the effect *not* that two concepts are too many, but that they are too few, and three are needed.

To begin with, one may object to the Hegelian/Marxian reduction of the civil society to the political economy or the market, and suggests a different referent for it. A model of a social realm focussed on intellectual pursuits, and constituted and regulated without recourse to political mediation and to power relations, can be found in the eighteenth century *imperium litterarum*, the international cosmopolis of *savants* and literati. Or one may seek to comprise within civil society the phenomena of culture and religion, or the institutions concerned with play, emotions, aesthetic expression, and other inter-individual relations *not* reducible to exchange. The market itself may either be made to adjust itself to the presence, under the conceptual umbrella of 'civil society', of these new and rather different referents, or be viewed instead as a third realm all of its own acknowledging its peculiarly powerful and demanding dynamic.

For instance, Jean Cohen and Andrew Arato, whose work has played a particularly significant role in re-launching, as it were, the conceptual career of 'civil society', expressly exclude from its ambit the forces and relations relating chiefly to the economy: in advanced societies there are *three* fundamental institutional complexes – the state, the market, civil society (Cohen and Arato 1992). The latter, rather than revolving around the pursuit of individual interest, is conceived instead as the locus (among other things) of the development of collective identities, of solidarity, of the formation and transformation of institutions by social movements.

In this perspective, *tertium datur*, and Lindblom's 'Politics and markets' (Lindblom 1977) do not exhaust the social space. In the early 1970's, without express reference to the concept of (civil) society, Richard Titmuss's analysis of the arrangements through which individuals – respectively in Great Britain and in the United States – were induced to transfer some of their blood to strangers, suggested that the supply of even goods and services of the greatest significance could be entrusted to sentiments of solidarity and commonality which transcend the boundaries of the family and the neighbourhood. Titmuss argued for the intrinsic superiority of this way of securing that supply. Leaving it either to the state, by means of the particular resource of coercion, or to the market, which appeals to individual interest, would produce various negative effects (Titmuss 1971).

Historical roots of the distinction

One reason why, at the purely conceptual level, the relations between the two terms are so unsettled, may be that 'state' and '(civil) society' are not, and should not be conceived as, universal categories. Whether we conceive them as juxtaposed or counterposed to one another, both expressions refer to highly distinctive, historically unique ways of establishing and regulating both political and economic processes (and socio-cultural ones, if a tripartition is accepted as more plausible). As suggested at the beginning of this article, the couple 'state/(civil) society' conceptualises an aspect of the peculiar story of Western modernisation.

The state/society distinction presupposes, and profoundly modifies, arrangements which had emerged in various European countries in the course of the late Middle Ages, and are often characterized by the German expression *Ständestaat* (literally, 'state of the estates'). In spite of its historiographic success, this expression is potentially misleading, for it may lead one to think of its referent as a 'state' in the modern sense of the term.

To avoid this misunderstanding the Austrian historian Otto Brunner (1956) has proposed replacing that expression with that of *ständische Gesellschaft*. By this is meant a context where the 'estates', through arrangements partly traditional partly expressly negotiated, take an active part in the government of a territory. They do so, however, chiefly by exercising their own privileges, not on a mandate from the central government; and in those privileges political aspects are tightly fused with both economic ones and with *status* ones, relating to honor and rank. The estates' governmental activities are differentiated not as articulations of an overriding political function, rather on the basis of each estate's distinctive prerogatives and responsibilities. (The crown itself may be considered as one of those estates, even if embodied at a given time in a single person; the English king/queen is seen as a *corporation sole*.)

Furthermore, typically the component units of each estate are not individuals, but collective entities with a pronounced hierarchical structure. Across Western Europe in the late middle ages and in the early modern era the typical unit is the 'house', understood as the seat and patrimony of an aristocratic dynasty. To quote from a dictionary entry by the Italian student of the history of institutions Pierangelo Schiera:

> The lord of the house (*Hausherr*), at the same time that he performed the function – which today we consider private in nature – of head of the family, also exercised an authentic political power (jurisdictional, administrative, representative) over the members of the house subjected to him, which tended to include the bulk of the rural population (Bobbio 1983: 1095).

Furthermore, often each 'house' was also a fortified place, an assemblage of autonomous military resources, which the members of the family (again, including their rural dependants) employed at the behest and under the command of the lord. In that capacity each house normally took part in the king's/queen's military undertakings; but by the same token it could also protect its own rights, arms in hand, from encroachments by other houses, including the king's own. (According to a recent formulation, the aristocracy of early-modern France, had not just a 'right' but a 'duty' of revolt) (Jouanna 1989.)

Finally, the typical house constituted an *oikos*. That is: it was the seat of a complex plurality of activities intended to make it economically self-sufficient, as much as possible without recourse to exchange. The monitoring and organization of those activities (including, critically, the periodic, coercive, delivery to the lord's household of unpaid produce and labor by the rural dependants) engaged the lord's faculties of jurisdiction and coercion.

The crisis of the *ständische Gesellschaft*

Accounts of the 'decline and fall' of these arrangements generally emphasize their incompatibility with the most distinctive aspect of state formation, the gathering at the center of a country of the faculties and facilities of organized violence, culminating, according to Max Weber's well known formula, in the monopoly of legitimate coercion. Exactly because the aristocratic 'houses' were originally the seats of an autonomous military capacity, that same aspect of state formation 'mediatizes' them. That is, when it does not dissolve them outright, it turns them into articulations of an unchallengeable public order, centered on the sovereign, his/her councils, his/her standing army, his/her fiscal, administrative, judicial apparatus. The political autonomy of the houses, and thus of the estates they collectively constitute, is lost. The sovereign's superiority in those terms is such that, while it does not suppress the houses' internal hierarchical arrangements (including, of course, 'patriarchy') it relativises them, flattens them. Seen from the summit of sovereign power, even the most exalted members of a realm begin to appear relatively similar to one another, and relatively powerless.

At the same time that centralized political activities become the prerogative of a sovereign power which seeks to perform them in a more and more unitary and rational manner, economic activities become decentralized. The decisions on what goods and services to produce, through what processes, are taken by an increasing number of subjects acting and interacting each in the pursuit of its own interests and deploying its own resources, no matter how puny these may be in comparison with the great aristocratic fortunes of old. The provision for the needs of the individuals depends more and more on their capacity to enter into traffics with one another on the market.

In the countryside, in particular, the commercialization of resources and of products reduces the part played in a country's economy as a whole both by the aristocratic patrimonies and by the typical rural units of old – villages which shared the aristocrats' preference for self-sufficiency and their hostility to the market. Commercialization also diminishes the significance of city-based productive units whose activities had traditionally taken place under corporate regulation. Those units tended to suppress or constrain market relations; for that very reason, they are progressively marginalized and eliminated. The new arrangements favor economic innovation by giving autonomous market operators the freedom to combine and recombine resources, including the contractually negotiated labor of new subaltern groups.

To sum up: while state building dissolves the *ständische Gesellschaft* by taking over from it tasks, facilities, and legitimacy pertaining to the political sphere, the advance of an economy based on traffics pushes into the market the units let loose by that dissolution. Over against an expressly political organization with a strong vertical gradient, ordering all relations by the ruler's exercise of her/his own *imperium*, stands an open-ended set of more and more numerous social units which, in the pursuit each of its own interest, establish with one another horizontal, or apparently horizontal relations.

The political prerequisites of the civil society

This can only take place, however, insofar as the process of state building has two peculiar aspects: first, the political center takes on *all* expressly political concerns and resources *but only those*; second, it acknowledges the existence of private subjects who, while excluded from the political sphere, act autonomously in others. In both ways, political power expressly limits itself by means of complex and sophisticated institutional arrangements: for instance, the progressive denial of political and juridical significance to the religious concerns of individuals, or the recognition and sanction of private property and of contract.

Heinrich Popitz points up the historical rarity of such arrangements:

Only rarely has it been possible even just to pose the question of how to constrain institutionalized violence, in a systematic and effective manner. This has only taken place with the Greek *polis*, republican Rome, a few city-states, and the constitutional state of the modern era. The answers have been surprisingly similar: the principle of the primacy of the law and of the equality of all before the law (*isonomia*); the idea of setting boundaries to all legislation (basic rights), norms of competence (separation of powers, federalism), procedural norms (decisions to be taken by organs, their publicity, appeal to higher organs), norms concerning the distribution of political responsibilities (turn-taking, elections), public norms (freedom of opinion and of assembly) (Popitz 1992: 65).

Within this set of arrangements that expressly limit political power, not all counterpose two realms we might call 'state' and '(civil) society'. In particular, in the Greek *polis* individuals exist chiefly as soldiers and citizens, and the private dimension of their existence is little valued and expressed. The Roman republic does not exist as a rationally organized ensemble of offices, but only as an ensemble of magistratures sponsored respectively by the senate or the people.

Only *vis-à-vis* the modern constitutional state does (civil) society emerge, through the processes indicated above. In other civilizations the tendency of political power to aggrandize itself, to possess itself of all resources (beginning with labor power) suppresses all autonomy of the society, and locks all individuals in the role of subject or slave.

In the case of the modern West, the acknowledgement of private property in productive resources by the political center plays a critical role, for it allows at least some subjects to stand over against that center as relatively autonomous units. This, according to North and Thomas, has critical effects in the advance of the division of labor and the enlargement of the scope of the traffic economy (North and Thomas 1972); but it has also distinctive political effects, best perceived *a contrario* in the 'decline and fall' of empires which fail to acknowledge and protect property rights and suppress their unique disposition to mobilize and innovate economic resources (Eisenstadt 1993).

The significance of private property has two implications. First, it justifies to an extent the Hegelian/Marxian understanding of civil society primarily as the site of traffics between private individuals. Second, it entails that the civil society should not be envisaged as a 'flat' space, harboring no power relations. In fact property, or at any rate private property in the means of production, engenders a power difference between those who do and those who do not possess it. The state/society difference does not rest on the fact that power is institutionalized only in the former; rather, the latter too is structured (among other things) by power relations of its own, foremost among these those established by property.

Joseph Proudhon well understood this:

A state constituted in the most rational, most liberal manner, inspired by the most just intentions, remains nevertheless an enormous power, capable of crushing everything around itself [...].Where may a power be found that can counterbalance the state's overwhelming might? There is no other than property. Counterbalancing the state, and thus ensuring individual liberty – this is the main function of property in the political system (Proudhon: 1998: 82–83).

State and society in the twentieth century

The power forms that lie on both sides of the state/society divide interact in a complex manner, and their interactions shape to a large extent the dynamics of modern societies. In the twentieth century the prevailing trend called in French *étatisme*, for it saw a considerable enlargement of the scope of state action. In totalitarian systems, this trend freed that action from all institutional limitations, and thus threatened the existence itself of society as a separate realm. In other systems, it pushed back considerably the boundaries of that realm, but this in response *also* to demands originating from that realm itself. Such demands could originate from economically underprivileged strata seeking to maximize the import of citizenship and to reduce that of their market position; or, instead, from economically powerful groups seeking the state's assistance in securing their profits and stabilizing or regulating the market itself, when this for various reasons had lost its self-equilibrating property.

A further component of the trend consisted in the strategies of groups (sections of the 'political class', public employees, members of the so-called 'new professions') whose livelihood and whose opportunities for a greater say in policy formation and implementation depended on an expansive definition of the state's role.

Whatever its protagonists, in non-totalitarian countries the trend in question was to a considerable extent promoted by the existence of a 'public sphere' where social interests of the most diverse kinds could interact, as well as by the institutionalization of adversary politics, which gave voice to broader social strata, and found its most recurrent, legitimate theme in the respective scope of the state and the market. Political parties played the central role in this dynamic, sometimes opposing but more often supporting, the 'étatist' trend. This expressed itself, among other things, in the formation of bodies and agencies which sat astride the traditional divide between the public and the private realm – as with the Italian *para-stato* or the British *quango*'s.

The last two-three decades of the twentieth century saw a problematization of that trend, which social forces expressing themselves politically through conservative and/or right-wing parties sought if not to arrest at least to slow down. Their arguments asserted instead the superior rationality of the market, which re-asserted itself as the chief if not the only institutional site of the civil society.

Apart from constituting a revisitation of the Hegelian/Marxian conception of the civil society, this argument has one considerable merit. It recognizes that in contemporary society also human potentialities and social processes – of a cultural, communicative, symbolic, in any case not on-the-face-of-it economic, nature – which other views consider a tertium with respect to both state and market, are in fact targeted and controlled to a large extent by great concentrations of economic power. These, availing themselves of new material and social technologies, subjected much of the social process to their own logic of accumulation, increasingly focussed on financial resources, and thus particularly 'footloose'. The fact that mostly those technologies are generated and operate transnationally, and thus increasingly escape the reach of the political competences and facilities vested in the states, lends new efficacy to the attempt to reduce, after decades of '*étatism*', the significance of public and political action, and to enhance that of the market.

Also the end of the Cold War operated in that sense, for it reduced the necessity for a strong political/military guardianship of the capitalist order, and loosened the constraints of the keynesian compact which the dominant strata had previously made with the lower orders and implemented largely through state action.

Both dominant trends – the explicit or implicit reduction of civil society to the market, and the slogan prevalent in the advanced countries at the end of the twentieth century: market, *si*, state, *no* – are potentially worrisome. The market itself remains the site of the formation of, and interaction between, large economic forces, endowed with great *power*; and these are increasingly operating in a transnational space, where the state – still wedded to the territory – can no longer perform even its most traditional functions, jurisdiction and police, let alone those functions of guidance of and intervention in the social process at large which it had increasingly exercised during most of the century.

These recent phenomena compromise the institutional tenability of the couple state/society nearly as much as it had been threatened, earlier, by the totalitarian state or by centralised economic planning. A seriously dis-empowered state cannot guarantee, as complementary to itself, an authentically civil society. In this sense, the Aristotelic and medieval vision according to which only a politically organized society can truly call itself 'civil', deserves to be reconsidered.

Chapter Five

Juridical Aspects of European State-Making: A Retrospect[*]

Nearly forty years ago, commenting on the editorial work he was bringing to a close in *The Formation of National States in Western Europe* (Tilly 1975), Charles Tilly regretted that such a significant contribution to scholarship did not consider, among the several aspects of its theme, the role played in state-making by judicial institutions. I remember sharing that regret; perhaps because my first degree was in law, I would indeed have would have liked to see some juridical matters expressly thematized. But I did not then, nor did I subsequently, feel up to the task of remedying that omission in a manner comparable to the treatment that path-breaking book offered on several other aspects of its topic.

Let me say immediately that I do not consider *this* the occasion to try and rise to that challenge. This paper, in fact, disregards the role played in European state-making by judicial institutions in the narrow sense of the term, and merely takes a look at an overlapping theme – some juridical aspects of other components of that process.

An unduly neglected aspect of state-making

In retrospect, I feel a kind of naïve resentment toward works that ignore or slight such aspects. Hirschman's *The Passions and the Interests* – a work of monumental significance – is an example of this (Hirschman 1997). The range of the readings it discusses is impressive, but it ignores the direct and material bearing of its own theme on the European (especially the continental) legal tradition. He suggests that, early on in his main story – the increasing centrality in modern society of the institutionally autonomous market – politically activated coercion and repression were discarded as reliable controls over man's passions because such controls raised an unanswerable *quis custodiet*? objection.

Not a bit, in fact. Over the centuries Hirschman is dealing with, lawyers developed as many as five distinguishable though overlapping legal, coercion-

---

[*]   The text that follows took shape as the written-out presentation of a contribution, offered orally, to various conferences and seminars. Its present form is a slightly edited version of a text prepared for presentation at the American University in Paris in 2010.

based approaches to controlling both the passions (and the interests) of private individuals and the whim and arbitrium of rulers. These were

- the reception of Roman law

- absolutist codifications

- secular natural law

- public law

- constitutionalism.

Though Hirschman crosses many disciplinary boundaries, he seems intent on giving a wide berth to most arguments relating specifically to law. He thus misses, for instance, the extent to which, in eighteenth century Germany, the making or un-making, justifying or critiquing of major political institutions and practices, found their major public vehicle in different lines of discourse about natural law (Tarello 1976). He ignores the interpenetration of juridical with philosophical thinking in Leibniz or of juridical with proto-sociological thinking in Montesquieu.

A more or less self-conscious disregard for (I have suggested) an important aspect of significant political developments, is probably more frequent among American social scientists than among those from other countries (particularly Germany. I'll just mention two names from two generations ago, Franz Neumann and Otto Kirchheimer, and two from a later generation, Jürgen Habermas and Niklas Luhmann). This may be due to the prevalently professional orientation of legal studies in the US, locked into expensive and exclusive law schools and on this account not considered a potential component of a liberal education (which they definitely are or have been in other academic cultures). Or it may reflect the fact that, by virtue of being *about the law* (that is – at bottom – a complex of normative expectations, programs *for* conduct rather than descriptions and accounts *of* conduct) legal thinking expresses and codifies an orientation to what *ought* to be rather than what *is*, whereas modern social science thinking is – or tries to be – oriented the other way.

Law as a medium of institutionalization

At this point, let me characterize conceptually what this paper is about. By 'state' we mean a historically unique way of accumulating, structuring, managing political power – that particular form of social power where a group is in a position to control, activate, block the activities of other groups within the same society by availing itself of its own privileged access to means of coercion. In the routine manifestations of such power, however, coercion needs to be neither exercised nor explicitly threatened, and power operates chiefly through commands which find (more or less) prompt obedience.

Conceptually, one may connect this happy circumstance with the *institutionalization* of political power, that is the extent to which that power has undergone the following three processes, as Heinrich Popitz spells them out in *Phänomene der Macht* (Popitz 1992: 233–260):

- *depersonalization* – that is, commands are issued by individuals in their capacity as occupants of roles, as addressees of sanctioned expectations which indicate more or less explicitly the conditions and consequences of such occupancy;

- *formalization* – that is, in order to be valid, commands need to be expressed in certain ways. (The following is my favorite example. In some European countries, a body of mounted police or of cavalry assigned to make a contentious crowd disperse, *must* give it a warning by sounding the bugle three times before it can go – *Charge!*);

- *integration* – that is, the exercise of power must take into account both its own dependence and its own impact on some non-political resources and practices.

The French social theorist Yves Calvez, without referring to Popitz, and using a less detailed concept of institutionalization, suggested somewhere that we define the state itself as a political organization where power is institutionalized to a particularly large extent (Calvez 1995: 56). When I first encountered this suggestion I thought it plausible; but later it occurred to me that perhaps what characterizes the state as we understand it is not just the *extent* to which, but also the *way* in which its power is institutionalized. Although I know very little about, for example, the Chinese empire, I sense that in it political power was institutionalized to a very considerable extent, but this was done chiefly by means of *ritual*, whereas in the modern state power it was institutionalized largely (by no means exclusively) by means of *law*.

The making of the modern state was, among other things, a highly *discursive* affair. In its course, naturally, the factual resolution of contrasts by means of physical force played a most significant role. Yet it was often accompanied, preceded, and followed, by discursive processes of organization, planning and justification; by appeals to tradition, history, religion, public interest, states of necessity, rationales of various nature, variously grounded entitlements. Now, to repeat my main claim, legal discourse played a distinctive role in those processes.

This consideration, in turn, echoes a point made long ago by Giovanni Tarello, the Italian legal theorist I have already mentioned. All cultures make use of law to two chief ends: punishing and thus preventing anti-social conduct; apportioning between groups or between individuals privileged access to and control over material resources. However, in the West law has long been put to use also in a third pursuit – establishing, activating, controlling polities, and mandating and directing their policies (Tarello 1988). This use of law, and the resulting overlap between legal institutions and discourse on the one hand, and between political institutions and discourse on the other, began in Greece, and was carried forth and intensified in Rome and at other points in the historical career of the West.

To elaborate this point somewhat, let me again quote Popitz:

Only rarely, in the history of society, has one found it possible even just to pose systematically and consequentially the question, how to lay boundaries on institutionalized violence. Essentially, one has managed this only in the Greek *polis*, in republican Rome, in a few other city-states, and in the history of the modern constitutional state. The answers to the question have remained strikingly similar: the postulate of the supremacy of the law and of the equality of all before it (*isonomia*), the idea of delimiting in principle all legislation (basic rights), procedural norms (decisions taken by organs, publicity, appeals to higher authorities), norms on the attribution of offices (turn taking, election), and public norms (freedom of thought and of assembly) (Popitz 1992: 65).

What follows elaborates somewhat Tarello's and Popitz's suggestions by looking at some juridical aspects of the three institutionalization processes spelled out by Popitz.

(1) Depersonalization

Again, the point of this process is to filter the raw will of a person who issues a command, by referring to a role which s/he holds and which authorizes her/him to issue commands. In the modern state this arrangement is taken very far, because each role is in turn a component of a whole complex of roles, or offices. Unlike the Roman republic, which was constituted by a small number of loosely coordinated magistracies, the state is a large set of differentiated organs, with specific facilities and faculties of rule, each further articulated into lower-level units, and so forth.

Typically, the individuals holding various positions have *savoirs* and skills different in scope and content – as different as those of the navy officer, the judge, the diplomat, the politician, the financial auditor, the record-keeper. Yet all this multiplicity and diversity is counteracted by devices for securing unity, which if successful, make the whole system conform to the metaphor of the pyramid. Now, many of these devices are juridical in nature. Consider:

- the superiority of the constitution over normal legislation, first affirmed in the United States;

- the relationship between different layers of the judicial system, empowering the higher to review the verdicts of the lower layers;

- the fact that in many states the yearly budget (in spite of its nature as an accounting document) is formally a kind of statute;

- the phases of the implementation of policy, from the generic statement of a given aim of state action to progressively more specific administrative acts, each authorized, funded, monitored by previous and somewhat broader ones;

- the procedures presiding over the selection of political and administrative personnel, via election or via success in competitive examinations.

(2) Formalization

This process, again, makes the binding-ness of commands depend on their observing some constraints in the way they are formed and expressed. Typically, the Western state not only stylized the external manifestations of political power, establishing where, on what occasions, through what procedures political decisions should be deliberated and announced, by people wearing what garb, pronouncing what formulas, and so forth. It also sought to derive some of those decisions, to a greater or lesser extent, from a certain kind of public discourse – juridical discourse, chiefly derived from and inspired by Roman law.

This was a highly literate, text-based discourse, with a strong conceptual content, and a distinctive penchant for abstraction and systematization. Such discourse lends itself to sustained, sophisticated reasoning; subsumes specific circumstances under general principles; aims to produce conclusions through syllogistic arguments. In this manner, it is meant to select *one* from within *a set* of answers to any given question, all possible in principle, and on that account it is particularly suited for the making of decisions through express deliberation. Also, it validates that one answer largely through the formal qualities of the reasoning leading up to it – its logical rigor, its consistency with the results of related arguments, its reference to generally acknowledged authority, its compatibility with higher-level norms. (The sapiential learning characteristic of the Chinese *literati* typically differed from this discourse in not being oriented to the reasoned formation of decisions. The same can be said of another form of learning considerably employed in Western state-making, the 'new learning' of the Renaissance, drawing upon the rediscovered literary patrimony of antiquity, and of the associated rhetorical practices.)

On this account, in the modern West law constituted for a few centuries the most sophisticated, demanding and rewarding form of public, secular discourse, and as such attracted the attentions and the ambitions of generations of young intellectuals. It also enjoyed (and bestowed on its practitioners) high cultural and social prestige. It was thus among lawyers that, in many parts of the West, states sought (and trained, sometimes through Universities expressly established to that end) much of their leading personnel, which first operated side by side with noblemen and clergymen, and later to a large extent replaced them. The French expression *noblesse de robe* conveys this: those aristocrats not destined by their ancestral heritage for some form or other of military leadership, were chiefly be-robed practitioners of the judicial trade. And the frequency with which, in the potted biographies of many lesser or greater protagonists of French history, one finds the expression *il fit son droit* – meaning 'received his law degree' – reminds us that over several generations a law degree constituted the academic credential *par excellence*, sometimes even for young men seeking employment and recognition not directly associated with law.

Many expressions used historically in talking about significant aspects of political experience show the impact of this way of formalizing power on the public perception of the nature and the tasks of the state. I give a few random examples.

In English, one still uses the expression 'writ' not just to designate a specific legal instrument original vested in the king, but to characterize the ruler's prerogative at large. 'Laying down the law' has long designated the fullness of rule. 'Doing justice' was for centuries a prime obligation laid upon a ruler by folk wisdom, and a standard by which her/his subjects assessed her/ his adequacy or lack of it. In German early-modern political history, the *Herrschaftsverträege* (contracts having as parties a country's ruler at one end, its constituted bodies at the other) were a fundamental institution. Even opponents of monarchical powers, or of some of its practices, would often appeal to folk law, to a country's jural traditions, or to the law of nature. A key institution of private law, contract, was evoked in order to signify a new way of construing and legitimizing the fundamental political relationship, that between ruler and people.

Our own speech about politics bears that imprint. We still use 'jurisdiction' in two (so to speak) politically laden ways. We use it in the singular to characterize a fundamental activity of rule, which the state is expected to perform exclusively. We use it in the plural to point up a fundamental feature of the modern political universe, its being *open at the top*, being made up of several independent centers of rule, each bounded by a distinct territory. 'Constitution' is a juridical expression. Significant political activities routinely find expression in different kinds of juridical instruments, expressing different legal responsibilities and *savoirs*: statutes, decrees, sentences, fines, the proclamation of the winner of an electoral contest, the appointment of a functionary, the declaration of a state of war or of a state of siege.

This interpenetration of law and politics, characteristic of the state, has diverse consequences. It has been stressed by Kelsen, for instance, and taken to imply the essential identity between law and the state itself – a conceptual operation which sort of sublimates away the naked power component of political experience. (Hintze and others took Kelsen to task for this very reason.) More generally, and somewhat less controversially, other authors saw the state's unity as grounded on and expressed by the unity of the legal system – and vice versa.

The purposeful use of legal instruments by the state in order to establish its own organizational components, to fund them and activate them, to dictate policy – in other words, the formation of modern public law – was the driving edge of a broader, redoubtable phenomenon: the positivization of law in general. Previously, Western rulers had sanctioned the law contained in the country's traditions, which often lay judges claimed to 'find'. Subsequently, in a momentous change, the rulers themselves became the sole makers of law – *quod principi placuit legis habet vigorem* – the source of a secular, growing, ever-changing body of law, owing its legitimacy chiefly to the observance of norms about the production of new legal commands. The driving edge of this development was constituted by arrangements establishing and empowering public agencies, forming policy, and regulating from above the relations between the state itself and the subjects.

One may sum up these developments by attributing to them both the politicization of law and the juridicization of politics. The latter phenomenon is the one more frequently theorized, in two rather different versions: the rule of law in England (and subsequently in the United States); the *Rechtsstaat* on the continent.

(3) Integration

The question, here, is whether, how, and to what extent, the state-in-the-making, on the one hand displays a tendency to grow upon itself and to draw upon a growing portion of a society's resources, though on the other acknowledges that it is one component of a larger social reality and, as Popitz says, it 'gears itself' (1992: 38–9)into its operations. The standard formulation of the relationship between these two sets of social processes – on one side those revolving around political power, all the others on the other side – is the distinction itself between 'state' and 'civil society'. (I ignore here the variant it has recently found in the suggestion that we think of a *tri*-partition state, market, and civil society (Cohen and Arato 1992).)

That distinction comes into its own through a long process of institutional differentiation. Rulers progressively reserve to themselves *all and only* the concerns of a political nature, and leave to private individuals two major kinds of social activities, relating respectively to their religious and spiritual concerns and to their economic affairs. This process, too, has a significant juridical dimension, for the individuals in question are seen as the bearers of subjective rights, that is of actionable claims to the autonomous pursuit of interests of their own – and the state itself must acknowledge, protect, and if necessary enforce such laws. Typically, in the pursuit (in particular) of their economic interests, individuals engage in transactions which produce binding agreements between them. Since the binding-ness of such agreements depends on the state, this entails that the state allows a degree of delegation of law-making activity to private individuals.

Those transactions may also produce (and be produced by) asymmetries between the individuals involved in them as concerns their access to and control over certain resources. Such asymmetries may lead in turn to the formation of power relations between those individuals. Again, the state typically acknowledges such relations and secures such powers, as long as they do not involve the direct exercise or threat of violence by any other entity than itself.

A very substantial step forward in the direction of a liberal society takes place when individuals become entitled to exercise their own autonomy and to pursue their own interests not only in their private dealings with one another, but also by entering the public sphere. Here, too, they do so as the bearers of subjective rights, but of a new kind – *public* subjective rights. Schematically put: first individuals are allowed to address one another and to reason jointly on current public affairs, to form and communicate opinions about them in their conversations, through correspondence, via the press. Subsequently, they are allowed to identify interests which they share with a plurality of other individuals, form alignments with those in support of such interests, promote demonstrations, engage in opinion campaigns which support or criticize current state policies, organize themselves into parties and other kinds of collective units.

In this manner, the public sphere comes to represent a hinge between the civil society, as the locus of private pursuits, and the state itself, as the receptor of collective inputs intended to influence and orient the activity which is exclusively its own – the formation and implementation of policy. But since the civil society is itself the locus of significant contrasts between private interests, these tend to map themselves, as it were, on the public sphere itself, where they express themselves through competing alignments. The efforts these make to influence the formation and implementation of public policy necessarily place them at logger-heads with one another.

This phenomenon threatens to introduce an element of *division* in the operations of the state itself, which (by playing up the *topoi* of sovereignty and of the public interest) tends to project itself as the guardian of *unity*. As a result, even within a most sophisticated body of public law doctrine and of administrative science, that was produced in the nineteenth century by generations of German scholars, it took many decades before one such scholar – I believe it was Heinrich Triepel – dared to acknowledge the existence of political parties, and cautiously began to theorize their constitutional role.

The curious catch-phrase, 'Now is the time for all good men to come to the aid of their party' is probably the exception to a rule, whereby for a very long time, in various languages, expressions pointing to the role that contrasting alignments play in the making of policy had negative overtones. (I am thinking, for instance, of *'parti pris'*, *'parteggiare'*, 'sectionalism', 'faction', 'partisanship'.)

The state continued to assert its own unitary mission in various ways, chiefly by trying to tone down the bitterness and combativeness of the contrasts which competing social and economic interests tended to introduce into the political process. The role played by Bismarck in getting the German welfare system started, suggests a *top-down* aspect of the development of citizenship, alternative to the *down-up* processes emphasized in T. H. Marshall's account of that development (Marshall 1950). In any case, again the concept (and the rhetoric) of rights continued to be employed.

Easton's influential book *Systems Analysis of Political Life*, so far as I remember, does not use that concept or any other expressly juridical ones (Easton 1965). Yet, the way he argues for the compatibility of dissent and consent within the political process – roughly: people can agree about the existence of the political community while disagreeing about its regime; can agree about the regime while disagreeing on which team of leaders should be in charge at a given time; can agree about that while disagreeing about policies – once more presupposes, though it fails to stress, juridical arrangements which separate the different levels of the polity.

One final point. The appeal to nationhood, and the multiple, diverse initiatives whereby states pursue 'nation-building', can be seen as ways to attain Popitz's *integration* alternative to the workings of the public sphere, to reduce and moderate the tendency of social and economic conflicts to map themselves on the political realm via that sphere. The state projects itself as being complementary to, and at the service of, 'the nation', construing it sometimes as a social entity which pre-exists to the state itself and attains political expression through it.

Unlike the civil society, the nation is conceived as having political interests of its own which are shared across it, do not tend to become divisive, and indeed (as I suggested) to an extent *bind* the divisions which competing social and economic interests tend to engender in the civil society. The nation can do this, at bottom, because, in Renan's (1997) classic understanding of it, it is a cultural reality through and through. As an 'imagined community' (Anderson 1983), the nation can represent and assert values – especially identity values – which are not intrinsically scarce and thus are not divisive. By the same token, I suggest, the making of a nation is chiefly a matter for poets, historians, and other literati, and does not particularly lend itself to juridical thought and practice.

Let us conclude. What I wrote above about 'the law' has chiefly positive overtones, suggesting that there is much to be said, from the standpoint of significant values, for the part law played in Western state-making. I stand by that judgment, but with two qualifications. First, some very significant aspects of that historical venture had very little to do with law. Second, some legacies of the experiences I have discussed do not deserve much approval in the contemporary context. Legal rationality has some aspects which do not much assist and favor a process which in my opinion our society currently needs – a renewed appreciation of *politics* and its re-activation.

Chapter Six

Citizens and the State: A Retrospective View and an Attempt at Prospecting[*]

This paper is divided into two unequal parts. The first looks back upon the story of the relationship between citizens and the state; the second points at some recent and current developments in that relationship which render it increasingly problematical.

Although it is the longer of the two, the first part is highly schematic. Furthermore, it does not present a narrative, however succinct, of the relations between state and citizens, but merely suggests a number of conceptually distinct aspects of that topic. Finally, it conceives 'the state' itself in a rather conventional manner, as the polity characteristic of the modern West: one with a claim to sovereignty, a bounded territory, and a population which might be more or less reasonably called a 'nation'.

Taking this entity as my point of reference, I have asked myself, below, under what determinations, in what capacities (or in-capacities) citizens typically re-present themselves to the state. One might turn the question around, and consider the state itself as it re-presents itself to the citizens; but to some extent the answers to this second question are implicit in those given to the question I have elected to address. And those which are not so explicit may be left to another essay!

Citizens as subjects

All right, then: what do citizens (as it were) *look like* when viewed from the vantage point of the state? Let us begin with *citizens as subjects*: citizens

---

[*] The text that follows was first presented as a paper at a conference on citizenship held at the European University Institute (Florence) at the initiative of Bo Stråth, who subsequently co-edited with Quentin Skinner the proceedings of the conference, published as Q. Skinner and B. Stråth (eds), *States and Citizens: History, Theory, Prospects* (Cambridge: Cambridge University Press, 2003), in which the paper itself appeared under the title: 'Citizens and the State: retrospect and prospect.' The paper was subsequently presented at other conferences, in the US and in Europe, and in its progress underwent changes registered in the version below.

The theme of citizenship is currently attracting considerable public attention, chiefly on account of neo-liberal policies seeking to reduce drastically the actual significance of the phenomenon. Within the scholarly literature generated by these phenomena, I would like to refer to two recent, impressive contributions: *Genealogies of Citizenship*, by Margaret Somers (2008), and *The Modern State Subverted: Risk and the deconstruction of solidarity*, by Giuseppe di Palma (2013).

appear to the state, in the first place, as its subjects. 'Subject' is a tricky word, and at least some of its politically significant meanings do not coincide with the one I am interested in here, which is best conveyed in the Italian expression *suddito* or the German *Untertan*.

That citizens are in the first place, from the state's standpoint, its 'subjects' is not on the face of it a tenable statement. It is often said, indeed, that one of the most critical aspects of political modernisation is constituted by the fact that the ruler ceases to treat individuals as *subjects* (*sudditi*, *Untertane*) and learns to treat them as *citizens*. This suggests a categorical incompatibility between the two expressions I have emphasised.

However, I would suggest that one gets nowhere by taking too seriously such a categorical transition from the condition of subject to that of citizen, for the (so to put it) subject-ness of individuals persists, and their quality as citizens at best sublimates and qualifies that subject-ness. For the state is essentially a system of rule, a set of arrangements and practices whereby one part of a (politically and otherwise) divided society exercises domination over the other part, whether or not the individual components of the latter are vested with attributes of citizenship.

This applies also to liberal-democratic states. For, as one might put it, 'state' is a noun, 'liberalism' and 'democracy' are adjectives. That is: they are significant but contingent and limited qualifications of a stubbornly asymmetrical relationship, which do not impose upon that relationship a total transformation. Even within liberal-democratic regimes, rule is exercised *over* a population, the key political relationship remains one between those who command and those who obey, and citizens in their great majority, in their routine existence, cannot but experience the state as something different from them, and which lies, so to speak, on top of them.

In fact, according to some interpretations – I am thinking chiefly of Foucault, and in the second place of Giddens – political modernization on the one hand makes rule milder and more humane, on the other hand makes it more penetrating and compelling. In particular, according to this interpretation, even in liberal-democratic systems citizens become more and more exposed to governmental surveillance: *citizens as surveillés* might be a way to phrase this particular determination.

If this formulation usefully points up some ambivalences of the modernization process, I would suggest that there are other ambivalences which, so to speak, run the other way around. Some specific aspects of the original and persistent subject-ness that citizens undergo are considerably modified, in particular, by the advent of liberal democracy. Before considering this development, however, let me suggest a further determination of citizenship.

Citizens as tax-payers

This is a most significant aspect of the political relationship, on both conceptual and historical grounds. The conceptual grounds are suggested by the fact that some authors conceive of the polity, or indeed of the state itself, as essentially a machine for coercively extracting resources from the civil society (envisaged in the first instance as the locus of economic processes). They liken the state to a protection racket, define its key relationship to society, and to the individuals in their capacity as economic actors, as essentially a predatory one. (For a sophisticated and clever contemporary rendering of this view, *see The State*, a redoubtable book by De Jasay, 1998.)

Whatever validity this view may have possessed in the past, especially as regards *pre*-state polities, historically the development of the state, in the West, has witnessed significant modifications in the way in which political 'extraction' took place. Early on, Western rulers had to take into account that many of the resources they intended to extract were directly controlled by a privileged stratum of landlords-and-warriors whose privileges the rulers could not simply do away with. Furthermore, previous to the establishment of an administrative machinery at the ruler's own disposal, in order to gather and deploy economic resources the ruler needed the consent and cooperation of relatively autonomous bodies (the most important often designated in French as *états,* in German as *Stände*). More or less routinely, the ruler had to address numerous assemblies, local and regional, or otherwise constituted corporate entities, whose consent and cooperation could not be simply compelled but had to be negotiated. This necessity is the root of a complex institutional development best summarized by a famous English dictum, *no taxation without representation*, and constitutes the early core of representative government and of constitutional constraints on state action.

Later on, an increasingly expansive state had to find ways of tapping into other forms of wealth, chiefly in the hands of bourgeois and middle-class strata. Typically, such forms are mobile, and if the state is to attain them (without damaging their production and reproduction) its extractive activities must adapt themselves to that mobility, moving towards more and more calculable, predictable, routinised forms of taxation.

As Albert Hirschman argued in *The Passions and the Interests* (Hirschman 1997), this necessity favours – up to a point – the rationalisation of the political enterprise as a whole. Also, Thomas Ertman (1997) has shown what enormous advantage the English state derived from the fact of having become, earlier and more effectively than others, complementary to and compatible with a commercial economy – a development which allowed it, among other things, to finance war through the public debt. In other terms, the modes of extraction are a significant aspect of the general configuration of the political system, including the place (if any) it finds for the notion and the practice of citizenship.

Citizens as soldiers

Again, this determination of citizenship is both conceptually and historically significant. Conceptually, because it addresses directly the question of organized violence, which most authors conceive as the core itself of political experience – and that of statehood, to the extent that such violence is not only organized, but uniquely legitimate.

The historical significance of military obligation is suggested by too many aspects of Western political development for us to review here. It may suffice to mention that already in the Greek *polis* the move away from its institutional design as the exclusive concern of a narrow patrician stratum to one which acknowledges the significance of all individuals – as long as they were male, adult, and free – was closely connected with the advent of *hoplite* warfare. This mobilised as combatants relatively large numbers of individuals supplied with relatively uniform weaponry, and trained to operate in close contact with one another. The resulting military empowerment of the common man assisted and to an extent caused his ascent to relatively protected, active citizenship.

Many centuries later, the link between the military and the political capacities of common men is evidenced, at first in the context of the French revolution – remember *aux armes, citoyens!* – in the parallel between the revolutionary creation of mass armies and the emergence of (at first, relatively) popular suffrage. One might also mention a remarkable connexion between the modernisation and 'totalisation' of warfare on the one hand, and the emergence of (at any rate) particular aspects and moments of the welfare state on the other.

Both the last two aspects of citizenship, tax-paying and military involvement, point chiefly to the burdens involved in the citizenship relation, and to that extent can be seen in the first place as elaborations of their quality as subjects. We may counter this significance with that of a very different determination.

Citizens as rights-holders

This relationship has been masterfully (though not uncontroversially) conceptualised by T. H. Marshall (Marshall 1950). It implies that the citizen/ state relationship is an inter-subjective one. That is: an entity possessing legitimate interests, resources and capacities of its own lies at each end of the relationship and is accepted and recognised as such by the other. It is as if every citizen, puny and insignificant as s/he may appear from the viewpoint of the state, were somehow capable of saying to the state itself, 'do not trifle with me'; or 'I have towards you entitlements you must respect'. (Again, there is a characteristic English phrasing of this phenomenon: *An Englishman's home is his castle.*)

As we shall see below, this capacity not only protects every citizen's private interests, but authorises her/ him to acquire a certain awareness of the state's doings and even to make some input into those doings – and not *just* as they impinge upon her/himself. We owe to George Jellinek one of the most sophisticated statements of this position: under the *Rechtsstaat*, the sphere of an individual's legally protected entitlements may include '*public* subjective rights'. But one may go further, and assert a more advanced (and, one might say, more utopic) position:

Citizens as constituents

This idea is, once more, rooted in the experience of the ancient city, where in some phases, in parts of the Hellenic and the Roman world, the population (or rather, the male, adult, free, militarily competent element of it) was seen as responsible for the city's very existence. The city (*polis*) is perceived as a made-up, historically constructed reality, and it is the population which calls it into being, assumes in it and confirms through it a collective identity (generally, with strong ritual and mythical components). The idea is repeatedly echoed, in the medieval West, by the story or the legend of a *conjuratio* through which formerly discrete and powerless individuals constitute themselves into a new, juridically distinctive, politically autonomous, militarily effective entity – the city itself.

But even the subsequent loss of the city's autonomy, discussed by Weber in the famous essay 'The city' (Weber 1978: 1212–1372) does not entirely dispose of the vision of a plurality of individuals who constitute a political entity of their own. By representing itself as a nation or as a people, a population can project itself as the collective protagonist of a state-building enterprise, and as such attribute to each citizen a portion of the authorship and ownership, so to speak, of the resulting political entity. Not of course *qua* singuli, but *qua universi*, the citizens claim and assert the state as their own, and in this sense can be understood as its constituents.

A stronger formulation of this notion might be '*citizens as sovereigns*' – though in fact sovereignty is more often attributed to 'the people' or 'the nation' rather than to 'the citizenry' or indeed to 'citizens'. In any case, I would insist, the core of the relation of individuals to the state remains their being the state's *subjects*, and on this account all formulations which represent the collectivity as self-ruling, are strongly normative in nature – they point to a regulative idea rather than to a factual relation.

Above, I have referred to the concept of 'nation'. This perhaps deserves to be emphasised by suggesting a further determination:

Citizens as co-nationals

That is: the state often expects citizens to experience their identification with a comprehensive and abiding social and cultural entity – the nation – as distinct from, and in principle more compelling than, the commonalities related to the non-political aspects of their existence (as members of marriages and families, as business partners, as co-religionaries). This expectation (to which the state seeks to give normative force through, among other things, educational activities and public rituals) is markedly at variance with another aspect of modern citizenship, emphasised long ago during the *querelle* over 'the liberty of the moderns as compared with that of the ancients'. This other aspect concerns.

Citizens as private individuals

Note that this is perhaps, in turn, a contradictory concept, for there is an intrinsic tension between the two terms. Citizenship, for 'the moderns', is a qualification or a set of capacities pertaining to individuals who are not *only*, or indeed not *primarily* citizens, but possess resources and interests which do not pertain to the political sphere, and to which they may well attach greater priority than to those which do pertain to that sphere.

The young Marx punningly suggested that modern individuals, in order to become politically aware and involved, must undergo an *ex-stasis*, must as it were jump out of their own skins, overcome the inertia of possibly much more proximate and pressing attachments and sensitivities. Tocqueville emphasised their reluctance to do this: the great majority of individuals, once satisfied that, as far as the public order was concerned, each of them was as good as anybody else – a basic import of the democratic condition – may easily lock themselves into their petty, private cares, and invest in them all their energies and concerns, and neglect instead public affairs. This tendency is favoured by a number of aspects of modern life and culture much 'pushed' by the mass media – particularly consumerism and narcissism.

A troublesome corollary. It is possible *also* for the political involvement and participation of individuals to be motivated and oriented chiefly by a concern of each with his/her private condition. The contemporary debate on state *vs* market is perhaps misleading: it conceals that state and market may be considered as essentially *alternative* ways of securing the *same* result, the maximisation of private welfare across a given society. More generally, one may view contemporary politics as being to an increasing extent 'economicised'. One aspect of this which much worried Max Weber (1994: 328) is the fact that also professional politicians, seeking or exercising leadership, tend more and more to live *off* politics, rather than *for* politics.

This last remark points indirectly to a further component of citizenship of great political significance:

Citizens as political participants/as partisans

The link between these two aspects needs to be emphasised. The conventional understanding of political participation emphasises the 'vertical' flow of influence between the base and the summit of the political system, where policy is made – a flow carried by representative institutions and other ways of generating bodies of opinion and bringing them to bear on the political process. But one should never forget that, in the liberal-democratic state, that process unavoidably takes the form of a legitimate but persistent and often sharp 'horizontal' contrast and competition between different components of a society which is, like all historical societies, internally divided. After all, 'to participate' means 'to take sides', thus to become partisans, to seek to assert some interests of one's own in preference to and against those of others.

The matrix of policy is politics, but the immediate stake of politics is the capacity to take over power positions and to exclude others (however temporarily) from them – *ôte-toi que je m'y mette* – in order to 'reward your friends, punish your enemies'. This reality is masked by the chief ploy of political rhetoric, the presentation of one's partisan interests as general ones – for partisanship is morally dangerous and, one might say, aesthetically unappealing. But the refusal to accept its necessity amounts to a failure of the political nerve; and under contemporary conditions it is encouraged by a pervasive tendency, which we may label:

Citizens as spectators

Rejecting, or trying to reduce as much as possible, the burden of partisanship – including the cost of acquiring information on complex issues – citizens may deem some amount of political involvement justified only if competes successfully with alternative ways of investing their leisure time, and particularly their attention to the media. Hence the well-known trends toward the spectacularisation of politics, its focus on 'personalities', and other ways of packaging and marketing the political game. The danger of this to significant political values is clear: as Rorty suggested somewhere, spectatorship is incompatible with agency.

A final determination of citizenship I would like to mention (though others could easily be suggested) is the following:

Citizens as equals

This is the critical import of the symbolically laden recourse of revolutionary France to the appellation 'citoyen': individuals must address each other, and expect to be addressed, as all possessing equal significance and as sharing certain basic entitlements. One of these, perhaps neglected by Marshall, is the entitlement to a certain degree of respect, to a not inconsiderable quantum of recognition. In Durkheimian/Goffmanian terms, all citizens qua citizens are to an extent sacred objects.

The possibility, the nature and the consequences of modern equality (and thus also of the equality of citizens) are central themes of classical social theory. See for instance

- Tocqueville's warning: The democratic passion for equality can unfortunately be satisfied also by a condition of equal *in*significance and submission *vis-à-vis* the state. There may thus be a tension between two aspects of citizenship: the promise of equality and promise of freedom;

- Marx's concern with the limitations and inadequacies of *mere* political equality. Within modern civil society, the political equality associated with citizenship is often trumped by economic inequalities (themselves, paradoxically, grounded on the juridical guarantee of private rights);

- Mass society theory and its concern with the impact of equality on the possibility for the emergence, the distinctiveness, and the effectiveness of elites (Hayek 1960).

We have thus considered a number of ways in which Western citizenship has been institutionally and conceptually defined. I note in passing that the coupling of the institutional with the conceptual mode of definition is a distinctive and significant feature of the phenomenon itself of citizenship. Perhaps because citizenship was originally an urban phenomenon, and thus presupposed relatively widespread literacy and the possibility of fairly sustained discursive encounters between individuals outside domestic settings, its career has mostly been accompanied and counterpointed by self-conscious, sometimes sophisticated processes of intellectual justification and debate.

Whither citizenship?

I shall now consider briefly some developments which, as I have said at the outset, seriously problematise the whole phenomenon and pose the question, *whither citizenship?* I will assign such developments to three different groupings (though these overlap somewhat).

To begin with, the spheres within which some aspects of citizenship inscribe themselves have long been undergoing material and institutional changes which alter, among other things, the significance of those aspects. Let me take two examples. The relationship between citizenship and the military experience to which I referred before under the heading 'citizens as soldiers' has been affected by at least four distinct (and to an extent contrasting) developments.

First, contemporary modes of warfare have to a significant extent erased the difference between citizens-in-arms and the rest of the citizenry, particularly as concerns that particular 'risk of war' constituted by the likelihood of being killed or injured by the enemy's military action. Second, over the last few decades some armed forces have opened themselves to women. Third, in many circumstances combat can be materially effective only when engaged in by relatively small numbers of highly trained and expensively equipped professional fighters; to that extent the idea itself of a citizens' army (and perhaps that of conscription) has become less and less plausible. However – fourth – the combatants themselves generally need to be supported by larger and larger bodies of civilians: these *are* expected to be citizens, but mostly operate in the capacity of salaried professionals and experts, not of citizens as such.

My second example concerns 'citizens as equals'. As we have seen, modern social theory has controverted over a number of problems relating to this aspect of citizenship. According to the late James Coleman, however, it has not been sufficiently aware of a form of inequality particularly significant in contemporary society, and of its impact on citizenship (Coleman 1974). Advanced societies, Coleman argued, are inhabited by two very different kinds of individuals: physical individuals – corporate individuals. Between the two there is a growing, critical imbalance in power. The state can be considered as the largest and on some counts the most powerful corporate entity, but even in dealing with it, other corporate entities are generally more capable to assert their interests than most physical individuals are. Where does that leave all other supposedly *equal citizens*, one may ask?

The prospects of meta-national citizenship

A second group of developments problematising citizenship relates to the emergence of political entities which encompass (and to an extent 'mediatise') the states themselves, and respect to which the institution of citizenship, originally established at the level of the state, needs to be re-thought and re-constructed. To speak concretely, one may ask oneself what is the actual content, if any, of *European citizenship*, symbolised among other things by the uniform passports currently been issued by the member countries of the EU, and perhaps even by the existence of the Euro (for most if not all the component states of the Union). The point is that many of the determinations of citizenship I have examined in the first part of this essay simply do not make (much) sense at the European level. I'll give four examples.

The European Union is a political entity with extremely limited fiscal powers and faculties, and its revenues consist largely in contributions from member states. This means that 'citizens as tax-payers' does not apply at the Union level. This may be one reason among others for the equally visible weakness of its representative and properly political institutions. Could it be the case that IF *no taxation without representation,* THEN *no representation without taxation?*

Whether for this reason or for others, there is as yet little space also for 'citizens as participants/as partisans' at the Union level. As is often remarked, there are at best only the beginnings, at this level, of a distinct, autonomously institutionalised, party system – one reason (or one consequence?) of the much discussed 'democratic deficit' of the Union.

Thirdly, one barely needs to note that the Union, having no defence policy and no military capacity of its own, has at present no use for 'citizens as soldiers'.

Finally, it is clear that 'citizens as (co)nationals' exist only at the level of the component states (and nations) of the Union; and a similar argument could be made for other determinations of citizenship mentioned above. The big exception is possibly that of 'citizens as private persons'. The Union originally constituted itself as a common market, and to this day its institutional identity is chiefly focussed on the sphere of the economy. To that extent, it accommodates and validates most of the private concerns associated with that sphere. It facilitates the mobility of factors of production, provides uniform regulations for industrial activities, and so on.

On all these counts, we could say that there is a lag between the advances made in Europe toward the establishment of a new political and administrative system, and those realised for the time being in the quantity and quality, so to speak, of European citizenship.

A third set of developments affecting and problematising citizenship relates to so-called globalisation. This complex and controversial phenomenon impinges on citizenship chiefly in two ways. First of all, by weakening the state. As more and more economic (and, especially, financial) resources and processes become to most effects 'extraterritorial', those legislative, fiscal and jurisdictional faculties which states had used, through most of the 20th century, to promote and fund their re-distributive activities, become less and less significant, if not in absolute then in relative terms. In the global economy, as I have already suggested, corporate economic actors, whose presence had always rendered problematical the presumption of equality among citizens, become ever more significant as aggregations of power and as the sources of decisions of overriding importance for which they are not politically accountable. Since they operate on and through the market, they encourage or indeed compel individuals, from one country to another, to behave in turn toward one another as market operators, and to disinvest (so to speak) from their identity as citizens. Directly or indirectly the great corporations also produce, and benefit from, flows of discourse, images, cultural products, opinions, which delegitimise the centres of political power and undermine their cultural and moral standing within the population.

Second, globalisation entails a 'reshuffling of the social matter' – to use Durkheimian imagery – not just within, but between countries. These become more and more permeable to flows from one another of (among other things) people. A presumption that to some extent underlay the Marshallian development of citizenship – the presumption that the individuals affected would be nearly all co-nationals, born in a given country of parents also born in it, and destined to remain stably settled it – is increasingly undermined by massive migration flows. We could say that under these conditions it becomes more difficult to conceptualise a population – a purely demographic aggregate – as a people. It is implausible to think of 'citizens as constituents', and of the individuals currently active in a country as one cohort within a lengthy sequence of generations, each familiar with the country and committed to its culture and involved in its political fortunes by an immemorial compact. As a result, many immigrants are routinely denied some entitlements of citizenship.

This denial, however, looks more and more arbitrary when it affects substantial and ever-increasing numbers of people, who on other counts tend to become undistinguishable from the native population, and in particular become integrated in its economy. Such denial can be expected to appear even more invidious the more the immigrant flows become bilateral and symmetrical – that is, when the probability increases that nationals of a country which denies or restricts the claims of immigrants from another will themselves migrate to the latter.

The most likely response to this situation is likely to be (as is already shown by a number of cases, in particular as concerns social security entitlements) the institutionalization of a principle of reciprocity between the countries in question. The next step is likely to be in the direction of what has been called trans-national citizenship, understood perhaps as a the application to individuals of something like the 'most favoured nation' practice long acknowledged in international law. Or, more ambitiously, an appeal can be made to some understanding of 'human rights' as the ground for a more or less substantial set of portable entitlements, which accompanies individuals wherever they are, and which each state must somehow acknowledge and validate.

On a number of counts, such a development may deserve devoutly to be wished, however difficult its implementation. But we should be aware that it contrasts with the notion of citizenship proper, for that notion (as I see the matter) is intrinsically a particularistic one. It presupposes and substantiates a bond between one set of individuals and one political community, however broad and internally diverse. Also, that particularistic bond is always, conceptually, a compound of rights and duties. Now, it is not clear, in the 'human rights' vision, which expectations would lay upon the individuals as a counterpart to the claims the individuals themselves would hold *vis-à-vis* the states. There is finally a problem – to what extent rights (or duties) held to be constitutive of the human subject as such reflect in fact distinctive cultural preferences masquerading as universals.

Thus, even disregarding the difficulty of establishing institutions which would validate the new understandings of citizenship, the contemporary situation seriously challenges the pre-existent conceptions of citizenship itself, and mandates among other things a much more serious reflection on its historical career than it has been possible to conduct here.

Chapter Seven

Challenge and Response in the Relationship Between the State and the Liberal Public Sphere[*]

The pages that follow seek to interpret in what may be a somewhat unconventional manner some well-known aspects of the political dynamics of the modern state. They focus on a rather complex phenomenon, theorized in an original and penetrating manner, many years ago, in a great book by Jürgen Habermas, *Strukturwandel der Öffentlichkeit* ([1962], English translation 1991).

Historical role of the public sphere

According to Habermas, the development of the key institutions of the Western constitutional state (such as parliamentary representation, the relation between government and opposition, the *adversary* formation of the state's policies) presupposed a previous, relatively less explored phenomenon: the development and the growing autonomy of the liberal public sphere. Modern Western societies had witnessed a unique development: a complex of new structures and processes which enabled an ever-growing number of individuals to form and express opinions concerning social and cultural affairs NOT relating directly and exclusively to their own occupational identities and their interests as property-owners. Such individuals felt entitled to compare their own with other people's opinions concerning matters of shared interest. Drawing on information available to fellow members of the public, each individual could freely communicate to others her/his own views on such a matter by engaging her/his own ability to conduct a reasoned, persuasive argument, whose optimal outcome was a shared, intrinsically tenable view of the merits of the matter. In a proper argument so construed, no participant could appeal to views put forward by pre-constituted authority, and as such not subject to controversy and critique. The principle presiding over the resulting formation and exchange of knowledge, opinions, understandings, was that

---

[*]   The text that follows translates my own contribution to a collection of essays by various authors, intended to celebrate the massive and thematically diverse scholarly oeuvre produced over several decades by the Italian sociologist and political scientist Luciano Pellicani: *Studi in onore di Luciano Pellicani*, edited by S. Maffettone and A. Orsini (Cosenza: Rubbettino, 2012).

'authority is valid insofar as arguments are valid' not 'arguments are valid insofar as authority is valid'.

According to Habermas such a principle had originally asserted itself within narrow circles of socially and economically privileged individuals, all possessing a quantum of *Besitz* and/or *Bildung*, that is possessing some material and/or intellectual capital. Such possession allowed them, among other things, to become members or correspondents of clubs, salons, masonic lodges, artistic or scientific academies, coffee houses, and to purchase books and periodicals, see theatre shows, travel. At first the views they formed, exhibited and confronted with those of others in those contexts, referred exclusively to matters of aesthetic judgment, moral custom, intellectual interest and scientific import. Subsequently, however, the collectivity of those involved in such a process – Habermas characterizes it as *das aufgeklärte, urteilsfähige, räsonnierende Publikum* (a public enlightened, capable of judgment and reasoning) – became larger, due to increasing literacy within the urban populations, the increasing availability to their members of leisure time, basic forms of knowledge, sources of information, elaborate and sophisticated communication codes. Over time, such *Publikum* began to address a further range of themes, comprising some concerning the management of public affairs by constituted authorities, the initiatives taken by governments, the priorities established by official practices between contrasting social interests.

In the long run, such processes – among individuals not only endowed with material and intellectual resources and values, but also capable of forming and expressing controversial opinions and judgments, and often not personally acquainted and directly communicating with one another – led to the formation of social networks which conveyed certain issues and views to a larger and larger public and, in the end, presented them openly to the constituted authorities. What one often refers to as an 'organizational revolution' – the modern practice of self-consciously building and managing permanent social arrangements focussed on specific interests – asserted itself also in this context. There emerged public alignments, networks of associates seeking not only to elaborate shared orientations and judgments, but to promote them to wider and wider circles, involving them in various forms of collective activity.

The most visible and significant such alignment is naturally the political party, especially one that can be designated as a 'mass party', the keystone of a system of political representation which becomes over time more and more wide and comprehensive. In this manner, the public sphere becomes a kind of hinge between the civil society and the state. It confers political *voice* to ever wider strata within the population, and imparts constitutional legitimacy to the most diverse interests, transforming them into claims addressed to the state.

Positive effects for the state of the workings of the public sphere

By doing this, the public sphere enriches and empowers the state itself. It makes it aware of the numerous and changing risks and opportunities produced by social dynamics – in particular the increasingly autonomous workings of the market and of scientific institutions – and by the evolving power relations between states. Furthermore, the public sphere involves greater and greater numbers of individuals into a potentially positive relation with political authority, which for centuries the majority of the population had seen as distant, foreign, incomprehensible and even hostile.

The state and its territorial articulations become the ever more plausible referent of collective identities. As a whole, the state represents itself to *common people* not only as the source of often arbitrary and vexing impositions, but also as the potential addressee of legitimate requests and of dutiful support on the individuals' part. The representative system ascertains opinion shifts within the public, thus allows the state to produce decisions which are intrinsically contingent because controversial and mutable, to acknowledge and weigh contrasting social interests, to deliberate officially about their respective merits. In this manner the state is induced to take into account public views and preferences which it cannot easily ignore or control, to entertain a dialogue with public opinion, to deliberate self-consciously on its policies and articulate expressly the decisions producing them.

Negative effects for the state of the workings of the public sphere

If these phenomena represent for the state the positive effects of an active public sphere, the latter can also have a negative impact on the state. The rest of this paper considers this possibility, and suggest some ways in which the state can avoid or moderate that impact.

We have not stated it so far, but it is a most relevant fact that public sphere theorized by Habermas exists and operates within *divided societies*. All modern societies are divided, on account of their complexity, and harbor conflicting interests. As Rokkan ([1970] 2009) would put it, they are traversed by *cleavages* of various nature – ethnic, linguistic, religious, regional, political, class cleavages. Now, the public sphere necessarily evokes and represents such cleavages in its relations to the state; by doing so, it *maps social cleavages onto the state*; unavoidably it invests them, to a greater or lesser extent, with political relevance, turns them into the legitimate carriers of issues political authority must deal with while forming and implementing its own decisions.

These processes more or less openly and self-consciously put at issue a central aspect of the state's own institutional identity – the fundamental value constituted for it by its *unity*. This aspect is clear for instance in the definition of the state, by Weber and other authors, as a form of political organization possessing a *monopoly* of legitimate violence over a territory. Furthermore, the lack of unity within the society which the public sphere reveals has a very significant implication: the adversarial nature of policy-making. This process not only entails (again) the acknowledgment and thematization of social contrasts of various nature; it also points up the intrinsically contingent nature, thus the unavoidably contestable content, of collective decisions (beginning with legislative ones). In principle this jeopardizes another fundamental value for the state: *continuity*. The root itself of 'state', as a number of Greek expressions suggest, points to something that abides, remains the same across time.

But if the public sphere, by fulfilling its institutional mission and making the state aware of the diverse and mutable opinions of its constituency, poses a challenge to such significant political values, one may ask how the state itself may respond to that challenge *without* blocking the operations of that sphere – an operation incompatible with the state's own constitutional and liberal features.

The state's responses: Emphasis on administration

A first response is embodied in an aspect of the structure itself of the modern state which over time has gained greater and greater significance. Today's state, even when its summit is constituted by representative institutions, cannot but be an *administrative* state. Its bureaucratic apparatus is unavoidably (and increasingly) large and internally differentiated; however, its whole design conveys an aspiration to unity and continuity. It performs ever more numerous, complex, costly tasks of management and regulation of the most diverse social processes. Its operations are entrusted in the first place to professionals qualified as such by specialist knowledge, who operate according to directives originating in principle from a single summit; furthermore, those professionals must observe established routines and as far as possible follow precedent. Thus, at the very center of a contemporary state, whatever its constitutional profile, lies an ensemble of personnel, resources, faculties, operational practices which act as the state's *flywheel*, committed to the unity and continuity of its operations.

Consider some manifestations of this commitment. The dictum *ministers and deputy ministers change, top functionaries carry on* applies to many countries. In France, great leverage on the state's activity is in the hands of the so-called *grands commis*, whose vocation for unity rests on commonalities of social extraction and on the shared educational trajectory through the *grandes* écoles. In many political systems, when a new majority asserts itself in parliament and in the executive, its ability to realize its distinctive program is strongly constrained by the size and the composition of the existing state budget. At most it can introduce incremental (thus, marginal) innovations in the distribution of resources between the branches of the administration.

According to Weber, such constraints make themselves felt even in the face of revolutions; overcoming them would require halting the *business as usual* of the administrative apparatus, and placing at the top of it individuals lacking professional qualifications, thus liable to cause widespread disorder and waste.

Weber saw this judgment confirmed by events in Russia following the October 1917 revolution; in particular, when Trotsky found himself compelled to re-establish within the Red Army command structures and practices of the Tzarist army, and to re-assign important positions to officials previously dismissed. Weber, furthermore, viewed such American practices as the *spoils system* and the popular election of judicial personnel as aspects of the tardy and peculiar process of state formation in the United States, although during his own times those practices were being modified in order to deal with objective necessities.

In sum: a duly established and managed state administration is a vast and complex system operating according to bodies of currently valid juridical or technical knowledge, on which the political leadership can safely draw insofar as it respects the autonomy of the professionally qualified personnel in possession of such knowledge. In particular, states with a liberal-democratic constitution, albeit to a different extent and in diverse fashion, honor in principle the functionaries' expectations of tenure of office and of career progression, which protect them from prejudicial decisions on the part of political leaders.

There are other arrangements which attribute something like a *bipartisan* mission to the administrative system. In Italy as in other countries, for instance, the ministerial structure, at the top of which generally stand political, non-professional officials, is complemented by so-called *authorities* – ensembles of personnel with especially high professional competences, brought to bear on particularly pressing and demanding public problems. Furthermore, while considering measures to be taken, functionaries are often allowed to consult particularly qualified outside experts. Finally, the process whereby administrative decisions on matters of particular public significance are formed often comprises a sequence of *hearings* where interested parties can propose determinate policies, often availing themselves, again, of expert advice.

Such arrangements confirm that the state's administrative system bears the responsibility for safeguarding such values as the unity of the state and the continuity of its political activities, that the public sphere may tend to disregard.

The state's responses: Promotion of citizenship

A keen concern with the value of unity, furthermore, may be said to inspire most contemporary states to construct two very significant – and rather different – sets of policies, (once more: to a different extent and in diverse ways). They counter and moderate the potential challenge to their unity from the liberal public sphere by promoting on the one hand *citizenship*, on the other *nation-hood*.

Let us first consider the promotion of *citizenship* – an expression taken here in T. H. Marshall's (1950) sense with particular reference to socio-economic rights. This line of policy ignores or represses (more or less openly) only the most conflictual and subversive requests advanced in the public sphere; all other requests are in principle allowed to find expression and to seek satisfaction. In this manner, the conflict attendant on such requests becomes institutionalized, and their impact on the unity of the state is reduced. Political claims and proposals to some extent incompatible with one another are moderated and become the legitimate object of compromises between the sections of the public which advance them and the sections which oppose them.

Generally, political initiatives to this effect are associated with progressive parties, but are sometimes taken by conservative forces; for instance, in the nineteenth century some policies characteristic of what was subsequently called 'the welfare state' were undertaken by Bismarck. In any case, socio-economic citizenship entails distributive policies conferring on all citizens, on an equal basis, a quantum of access to, and fruition of, certain *bona* of a material nature. These policies may equip citizens with qualifications allowing them to contribute to the formation of the national product, or compensate for the disadvantages affecting them if rewarded exclusively by the market. In any case, they moderate some of the dis-equalities which otherwise, if emphasized by the public sphere, would have a negative effect for the state's unity.

The state's responses: Promotion of nation-hood

The promotion of *nation-hood* seeks the same result rather differently. It diffuses within the population an emotionally potent sense that all its components share numerous and significant commonalities. It generates a collective identity and a commitment to expressly political interests transcending the divisions generated within the population by the unequal enjoyment of material advantages. The state appears as the unitary embodiment of those interests and the guardian of a shared destiny.

Policies promoting nation-hood, one might say, confer to the *raison d'état* – for generations the exclusive concern of a very narrow, privileged political elite, which cultivated it in the light of judgments and considerations protected by the *arcana imperii* – an increasingly great and deep resonance in the 'hearts and minds' of ever broader strata of the population. Increasingly, within the discourse on basic public issues, the notion of *national interest* becomes the standard and the aim of the political initiatives to be taken. The state projects and justifies itself as the specialized political instrument of the nation – a collectivity grounded on significant pre-political commonalities which seek expression in state policy. National sentiment views the whole population as standing in a close, abiding (primordial, one might say) relation to the state's territory, conceived as the body itself of the state. When the exclusiveness of that relation is challenged from other states, this generates intense indignation and a hankering to restore it, mostly expressed by *nationalistic* claims and aspirations.

There are of course remarkable differences between the contents and the communication practices of these two responses to the potential challenge to the state's unity. Once more, *citizenship* acknowledges the contrasts articulated within the public sphere, and seeks to moderate and to an extent concile them; *nation-hood* seeks to transcend those contrasts. It emphasizes the external relations between states, all exposed to potential or actual threats presented by other states; whereas citizenship addresses in the first instance the relations between its own components.

As one sometimes puts it, the concern with *national* interests represents the 'high' aspects of politics, the focus on the distribution of the national product its 'low', mundane aspect. (Consider the negative charge of such expressions as 'politics of envy' or 'sectional interests'.) The 'discourse of citizenship' places a more or less explicit cognitive focus on the respective contributions and entitlements of various parts of the population. The 'discourse of nation-hood', instead, has a normative and emotional focus; it aims to engender, strengthen and celebrate a sense of belonging. On this account it has a strong symbolic component, supplied to a large extent by 'creative intellectuals' – historians, novelists, musicians, poets, artists – rather than economists or jurists. (A book, which played a most significant role in the cultivation of national sentiment by the Italian educational system between the last part of the nineteenth and the first part of the twentieth, bears the telling title *Heart*.)

The state's responses: The shared privileges of the 'political class'

One can object that this whole argument *hypostasizes* the state, presents it as a self-standing, superior entity, whose practices are (or should be) oriented to interests exclusive to it, such as its unity and continuity. This way of construing the state may have some significance from a philosophical or juridical perspective, but not from that of sociology or of political science, whose prime commitment to register the realities of politics-on-the-ground, necessarily 'deconstructs' the state, views as an arena of constant, unavoidable contrasts between the diverse interests of multiple social components. In particular, the distinctive, 'Machiavellian' focus of the sociological imagination lies on the power differences between the political elite/class at the top of the state and the remainder of the population, even when the latter is politically *enfranchised* as the bearer of more or less significant citizenship rights. As Weber insists, when all is said and done also the state, like all political organizations, is a form of domination of men over men.

However, one may recognize the merits of this Machiavellian vision without denying all significance to what has been said above. Even the political elite/class must somehow defend its own unity from the impact of the public sphere, its tendency to acknowledge and convey significant political and social contrasts. It defends itself largely by increasing and securing the privileges all its components share in spite of what divides them, including the particularly visible contrast, at the top of the political system, between the governing majority and the minority in the opposition.

Contemporary Italy, for example, presents a whole range of such arrangements. All members of representative bodies, at whatever level, enjoy sizeable emoluments and other privileges, such as retirement payments and annuities gained after only few years of service. Even when they fail to be re-elected they often qualify as consultants for various public and private bodies; they can occupy, and be rewarded for, more than one office at the same time. The length of their tenure in office accounts for the markedly gerontocratic composition of the leading personnel in Italian parties, unions and other organizations; the mass media devote much more (and much more respectful) attention to such personnel than happens in other countries. All this constitutes for the political elite/class an insurance policy against the risk of its members not being re-elected or re-appointed – a policy whose premium is ultimately charged to tax-payers.

Similar, though mostly less generous prerogatives attach to office-holders in other countries – in France, for instance, the practice permitting the *cumul* of offices, or, in Britain, those concerning the expense of residing in London for members of Parliament. But such phenomena can also be seen as expressing a legitimate public interest in the continuity of state activities, responding again to a challenge originating from those of the public sphere.

The state's responses: Neutralizing the public sphere

There is a further, broader and more insidious (because largely covert) response. The state, in its various aspects, can seek to 'neuter' the public sphere itself, keep it as far as possible from documenting, articulating, broadcasting public feelings, opinions, policy options which might throw doubt on the legitimacy or effectiveness of current state activities, embarrassing or discrediting those responsible for them. To the extent that the state accomplishes this, the political elite/class protects itself from what it considers excessive or unjustified pressures, by curbing the public's ability to monitor and criticize its own conduct.

Habermas had already characterized this development, in the contemporary context, as amounting to the occupation and colonization of the public sphere by various political, economic, social powers-that-be, each seeking as far as possible to shape public opinion in order to maintain and increase its own autonomy and the leverage it can exercise on state policy. Since the time Habermas wrote, that development has continued to enjoy considerable success. As a result, contemporary societies witness the ever-growing individualization of the concerns and expectations of the members of the public, a reduction of their ability and disposition to act in concert, to engage in collective rather than private pursuit of their interests.

This development – the product of massive and pervasive social trends – is promoted and celebrated by the mass media, whose cultural messages favor the atomization of the public. Their prevalent approach to political affairs is often aptly characterized as *spectacularization*. It plays against one another the individuals taking part in them; it emphasizes, rather than their policy commitments, their personal qualities, and in particular their skills as communicators. In fact those skills are often imparted to politicians by personnel whose professional expertise lies not in the formation of policies, but in the manipulation of information and in the *marketing* of the images of political leaders. The title of a book on the presidential campaign of 1968 in the US, *The Selling of the President*, says it all.

Essentially, even political arguments are addressed to a public constituted by atomized spectators rather than by the holders of legitimate collective interests. Much of the open communication about political affairs becomes a special kind of *infotainment*, carrying a minimum of properly political *signal* in comparison with the massive *noise* addressing other concerns of people. To employ a recent, clever expression: it is in the interest of the holders of political power that the mass media operate as *weapons of mass distraction*.

This behavior of the media has structural roots. At any rate until the recent development of Internet, the possibility itself of emitting messages of this kind (or any other kind) to broad publics required some access to, and control over, media of mass communication. These constitute a business open only to few, large aggregations of financial resources, able to create and manage more and more complex and expensive technological and organizational systems. On the one hand, then, the mass media business can have only few, powerful participants; on the other hand, it thrives on its ability to address communications to large, atomized audiences. On both counts it exercises a very strong attraction not only on the elite/class at the top of the political system, but also on those guiding in possession of great economic resources. Thus, both powerful economic forces and powerful political forces are keenly interested in controlling the media, and using it, as far as possible, as an effective loudspeaker for their messages.

There is a complex relationship between these two sets of forces, and sometimes the one sometimes the other prevails. Roughly, one could say that in the US the control over the media lies in the hands of industrial and financial corporations; in Russia in those of the political oligarchy. But sometimes both contenders share an objective: preventing the formation and operation of a system of communication where information on political issues might be gathered and conveyed by a plurality of reciprocally independent centers; where the significance of those issues is openly controverted and their official interpretation challenged; where alignments can develop between people who share the same views and connect them via open-ended networks; where those alignments are given *voice*, and possibly mobilized in some form of collective action.

One may ask oneself to what extent the 'new media' (the Internet and similar devices whereby individuals not only receive and store information but easily convey it to one another) approximate this vision of a system independent of (and critical of) that of the mass media, capable of preventing the occupation and colonization of the public sphere by established powers criticized by Habermas. Such potential significance of the new media is suggested by Tocqueville's comments on the political role played in nineteenth century America, at the local level, by a great number of competing newspapers, generating and conveying a variety of interests.

Contemporary phenomena such as e-mail, search engines, the social media and the 'blogosphere' may be seen as a similar process, since they expose individuals to multiple, diverse communications, thus contrasting the domestication and neutralization of the public sphere by dominant minorities. Exactly on this count, however, those minorities share an interest in limiting the intrinsic open-endedness of the networks, the highly contingent, thus not easily controlled content of the messages they convey.

Consider the indignant and repressive response of official powers to the *Wikileak* phenomenon, or the attempts by Chinese authorities to censor Internet communications or restrict access to them. For that matter, consider the ways in which various economic power centers seek to extract fees from Internet users. More generally consider a remark made by a correspondent of the American internet site *Salon.com*, under the title 'The Master switch – is the Internet due for a takeover?': 'all information industries cycle from freedom to monopoly' (Miller 2010). If Tocqueville surveyed today the newspaper scene, in the US and in other countries, he might see in it symptoms confirming such a disquieting generalization.

Chapter Eight

Relations Between Political and Economic Power: A Conceptual Narrative[*]

This essay deals with a problem of general and persistent societal significance – the relationship between the political form of social power and the economic form, each of which concerns a distinct dimension of social inequality.

Political power

Political power rests on the asymmetry between two parts of society in the respective degree of control over a peculiar resource – let us call it *means of coercion*. That is: one part is markedly superior to the other as concerns the ability to exercise, or to credibly threaten to exercise, organized physical violence upon the other part, which lacks a comparable measure of control over the same resource. This allows the first part to issue commands and prohibitions which activate or block the other's actions. It can induce it – and if necessary force it – to engage in, or desist from, certain activities, thus fulfilling the first part's own preferences and promoting its interests.

Such ability is of course a very significant social privilege, around which contentions of various kinds are always possible, concerning in particular

- *Who* possesses political power with respect to *whom?*

- On *what* aspects of the existence of the latter can the former exercise power?

- *How*, in what ways can such power manifest itself?

---

[*] In 1998, while teaching at the European University Institute, in Florence, I was asked to contribute a chapter to a book, *Eredità del Novecento* (The Legacy of the Twentieth Century), edited by Giuseppe Bedeschi (Rome: Istituto dell'Enciclopedia Italiana, 2000). I chose as my topic the relations between political and economic power, a theme I subsequently dealt with at greater length in chs 7–9 of *Forms of Power* (Poggi 2001).

Upon revising the earlier Italian text for this volume, I became acutely aware of how inadequate was its treatment of the developments occurring between the last few decades of the 20th and the first decade of the new millennium. Accordingly, the English version (here published for the first time) differs to a considerable extent from that Italian text, chiefly by expounding, however synthetically, the variations undergone by the relationship between political and economic power between the beginnings of modernity and our own times.

Thus understood, *political* power is intrinsically an inter-subjective phenomenon, revolving around the axis of a relation between individuals (*qua* individuals or *qua* components of groups). This is so, even if the execution of commands or of prohibitions is guaranteed, when all is said and done, by the vulnerability of individuals – merely as sentient bodies – to deprivation of bodily liberty, encroachment upon the integrity of their bodies, or the infliction of death.

On this account, political power mobilizes the emotion of fear. But these crude, merely factual makings of it normally undergo a variety of institutional elaborations which communicate its existence and justify it. Commands and prohibitions, after all, operate as such only insofar as those issuing them share symbolic codes with those receiving them, which may generate the phenomenon we call legitimacy.

Economic power

Economic power is constituted rather differently; one can think of it as a social projection of a relation revolving in principle around the human being/nature axis. It exists insofar as one part of society exercises a privileged control over resources which bear upon the production and distribution of goods and services supporting the material existence of the other part. Such control has its most distinctive expression in private property, which in principle confers upon the owner the advantage of living off resources from access to which and use of which s/he can legitimately exclude all others.

Thus the owner's relation to others is in principle a negative one, and applies to the generality. But it also allows him/her to deal with selected specific non-owners not so much by issuing commands and prohibitions to them as by entering with them exchanges advantageous to her/himself.

That is: under variously negotiated agreements, parties acknowledge each other as free and equal; each meets, interacts, and stands back from the other in view of its own perceived interest. In most historical societies, proprietary control is distributed asymmetrically; those to whom it is denied are strongly constrained, in undertaking such agreements, by their lack of resources which they need to survive but are owned by others. They can survive only by committing themselves to relations marked by inferiority and dependence *vis-à-vis* those who control resources.

Consider the final paragraph of Chapter Five of *Capital*. The market sphere in which exchanges take place between money and labor power constitutes – Marx writes – *a true Eden of man's innate rights*, since the two parties who willingly enter it are both equal, free, property-owning individuals. However!

When we leave this sphere […] a certain change takes place, or so it appears, in the physiognomy of our *dramatis personae*. He who was previously the money-owner now strides out in front as capitalist; the possessor of labor-power follows as his worker. The one smirks self-importantly and is intent on business; the other is timid and holds back, like someone who has brought his own skin to market and now has nothing else to expect but – a tanning (Marx 1976: 280).

The distinctively human way to provide for the individuals' needs is mediated by resources (*means of production*, in Marxian terminology) themselves produced by past efforts and successively embodied in objects. Such objects, however, can be put to use not only in directly satisfying needs through consumption, but also in further acts of production, sometimes carried out at the behest of individuals different from those who have previously produced them. Private property allows some subjects to control the further productive employment of pre-existent objects, by mobilizing and controlling the current efforts of subjects deprived of property. These can have access to the means of production, treat them as instruments of their own work, distribute its products, employ them for the satisfaction of their own needs, only if they commit themselves, within more or less markedly unequal exchanges, to the service of property owners.

Marx, of course, is the source of the most elaborate and eloquent statements of this insight. Below, I cite from his *Critique of the Gotha Program* a statement particularly significant because it is formulated in utterly general, anthropological terms. It does not refer to capitalistic exploitation or use the controversial construct *surplus value*, but points up the inequality generated in all historical societies by the relationship between human beings and (the rest of) nature, the disequalizing role played by means of production, division of labor, and property.

From the fact that labor is conditioned by nature follows that a man who possesses no other property than his own labor power, under whatever conditions of society and culture, can only become the slave of other men who have possessed themselves of the objective conditions of labor. He can only work upon their permission, thus only live upon their permission (Marx 2000: 611).

Thus, economic power exists insofar as in a society the ability to dispose of resources essential for the production of material life is distributed in a particularly asymmetrical manner, and most particularly when only a minority can expect political authorities to sanction its own private disposition over means of production of strategic significance in that society. Such power grounds a very marked inequality between a society's property-owning minority and the rest.

To a greater or lesser extent, the other members of the society's component groups see their own existential opportunities (to translate Weber's *Lebenschancen*) restricted by a situation of material scarcity, and are more or less compellingly induced to accept damaging conditions of employment. They may expressly subject themselves to commands and prohibitions issued by their employers; but this is just a contingent aspect of an underlying condition of inferiority. In any case, it seems plausible to speak of the property-owning minority as possessing a distinctive, *economic* form of power.

This form can manifest itself also in asymmetries between collective subjects: firms, different sectors of the national economy, even different national economies. In each case, economic power differentiates subjects as concerns their ability or inability to pursue lines of action of their own, oriented to their own interests, and to lay boundaries on the actions of others. For example, between different firms, even when organizationally independent of one another, some may be *price makers* others *price takers*.

To sum up: political power and economic power represent two different ways in which a part of society establishes and practices its own superiority over other parts. *Political* power manifests itself chiefly through express commands backed if necessary by coercion. Those to whom commands are addressed routinely suspend consideration of their own immediate interests and preferences and treat those commands as valid and binding directives for their own action. In *economic* power, the inferior part has in principle the option of identifying and pursuing interests of its own, but can only do so under circumstances which place them under the superior part's control; on this account the inferior is induced to, so to speak, play the superior's game rather than its own. Given this asymmetry, members of the inferior part are typically compelled to secure their own survival by accepting employment from members of the superior part and by submitting to its express commands. This imparts to their relations a *quasi*-political aspect.

Historical rule: The convergence between the two powers

In spite of this ideal-typical difference between political and economic power, the German legal and social theorist Franz Neumann (1900–1954) convincingly suggests a paradox: in the course of history those distinct and to some extent contrasting power forms are mostly found in close, publicly sanctioned association with one another. *As a rule* whoever possessed one power generally possessed also the other, and by the same token those excluded from one power, or at any rate placed in an inferior position with respect to it, were at a sharp disadvantage also *vis-à-vis* the other (Neumann 1986).

According to Neumann such convergence between the two dimensions of social inequality was not purely a contingent matter of fact. It was dictated by express institutional arrangements that within a given society normally placed both powers in the hands of the same minority. Situations where this did *not* occur were exceptional, and were generally aspects of unsettled, transitional situations.

Typically, within many pre-modern societies whoever controlled the most significant economic resource – landed estates – was also invested with political prerogatives and privileges: defence of the territory; jurisdiction; exaction of levies; recruitment, equipment and deployment of fighting men. Mobile wealth itself, especially when not directly related to commerce, was largely in the hands of a stratum of notables also endowed with political privileges (sometimes, onerous ones). On this account Max Weber qualified as 'political' the type of capitalism prevalent within ancient society, where even relatively modern-looking profit-making activities were generally carried out by putting one's political resources to acquisitive use.

In the West, late- and post-medieval aristocratic regimes generally exhibit the same coincidence between political and economic power. This is conveyed, for instance, by the expression *potens et pauper*, which strikes us as odd because it posits at one end a *politically* privileged stratum and one *economically* underprivileged at the other. The aristocratic lords regularly put their political (military, fiscal, judicial, policing) prerogatives to economic use. Typically, they extracted and expended the surplus produced by a population composed chiefly by rural workers under serfdom, by having recourse, when necessary, to the legitimate threat of coercion.

At a higher level, medieval and early-modern princes themselves treated the territories over which they ruled as their dynastic domains, and routinely derived from them, via the same extractive practices as the aristocratic land-lords (chiefly, feudal dues and unpaid labor), the resources they committed to preserving and increasing those territories. *Below* the level of the princes and of the aristocracy, in turn, some individuals often *bought* offices and lived from the related revenues and perquisites. On this account, the predominant arrangement for administration, that is the day-to-day management of authority relations, is appropriately labelled *patrimonialism*.

Naturally, in pre-modern or early-modern Europe there existed also some accumulations of wealth purely mobile in nature, commercial and financial, which the owners accumulated and managed on the market without recourse to distinctively political privileges, and availed themselves of such wealth also in their dealings with princes and aristocrats. But they existed, to use an expression of Marx's, only 'in the pores' of the prevailing social and political arrangements.

The modern exception: The two powers diverge [...]

Western modernization, in fact, can be considered *also* as a process whereby such forms of wealth attain a more and more visible and autonomous position within the larger society – a process involving novel institutional arrangements. The most innovative of these – those constitutive of modern capitalism – manifested a historically unprecedented dynamic, expressly and exclusively economic in nature, and markedly different from that of political institutions. As to these, a parallel development was signaled by the notion of *raison d'état*, which enjoined rulers unceasingly to maximize each his own realm's security and *puissance*. The advance of modernization, thus, produced two institutionally separate forms of social inequality, within each of which a distinctive elite established its own position of advantage. (Ogden Nash said it all long ago in the title of one of his poems: 'bankers are just like anybody else, except richer'.)

The same process of institutional differentiation (central to the sociological understanding of modernization) affects also other spheres of society and culture, such as the family, scientific knowledge, religion, or the arts. But here our attention goes exclusively to the differentiation between politics and the economy, thus between the respective power forms.

Again according to Franz Neumann, Western modernization violates the historical rule – the institutional fusion between political and economic power. In the absolutist phase of state building, for instance, princes increasingly claim for themselves all and only the *imperium*, the practice of command and the control over organized coercion. They leave to *particuliers* (at first, the aristocratic landowners) all and only the *dominium*, meaning, as in Roman law, a private individual's exclusive possession and management of economic resources, thus control over the production and distribution of wealth.

The same institutional differentiation between the two powers is increasingly found also at lower levels in the political system. Typically, as Tocqueville (1985) relates in *L'Ancien Régime*, early political modernization allows lords to preserve their rents and their prestigious social status, but progressively abridges their previous entitlements as the protectors and military chiefs of the *manants*, as the enforcers of local customs. Such tasks are progressively taken over by local representatives of central government (and subsequently by elected officials) who often are not themselves rich nor enjoy particular social prestige. The predominant arrangement for administration ceases to be patrimonialism and becomes *bureaucracy*.

From a certain point on, citizenship – an ensemble of rights and duties, of active and passive capacities of some political significance – connects to the state a growing multitude of mere individuals, ignoring in principle their socio-economic circumstances; it cuts across the class differences engendered by the distribution of property.

[...] But contend with one another

However! Once more according to Neumann (1986), the progressive institutional differentiation between the two powers did *not* entail that the respectively political and economic dimensions of social inequality and their effects on the individuals' total social position had become indifferent to one another. On the contrary, their relationship became a critical question, whose solution was historically contingent. A fundamental issue in the dynamics of modern society (signalled by such expressions as *politics vs markets*) (Lindblom 1977) is the extent to which each differentiated form of social power seeks – overtly or covertly – to constrain and control the exercise of the other. Each seeks to place the other at the service of its own interest; there is a rivalry between them concerning the extent to which each affects the structure and the dynamics of society as a whole.

The question, *which* power establishes its own superiority over *which*, and to what extent, is historically open-ended, and the answer to it is of great moment. For instance, contrasting answers played a major role in the central issue of the 'brief century' 1917–1991 – the contest over world hegemony between the West and the Soviet bloc.

One can roughly characterize the relationship between the two power forms in the West – to use the language of tennis umpires – as *advantage, economic power!*; in the Soviet system (and subsequently, for many decades, the Chinese system) as *advantage, political power!* But of course both contexts witnessed not insignificant variations between historical phases and between locales, suggesting again the intrinsic open-endedness of the answers to the question.

A critical difference between the two systems was the extent to which in each political and economic elites were differentiated and the way they related to one another. The Western pattern can be *very roughly* characterized by two American slogans – 'what's good for General Motors is good for the United States', and 'the business of America is business'. Both slogans on the one hand presuppose a relatively high degree of differentiation between economic and political power, on the other assert the legitimate priority of the former over the latter.

In the Soviet bloc (and signally, of course, in the USSR) the legitimacy of the differentiation itself was originally denied by the October Revolution's abolition of private property in the means of production, and subsequently (among other things) by the establishment of centralized planning. But there was some recognition of the advantage to be drawn from conceding a certain degree of autonomous control over the economic process to a relatively distinct elite operating at the level of direct productive activity. This happened first in the short-lived *New Economic Policy* of the twenties. Much later, from the fifties on, some Soviet policies allowed a relatively distinctive managerial elite to play a partly autonomous role in the implementation of centrally planned policies by particular industries and firms.

At this point, the Western and the Soviet economy represented contrasting institutional approaches to the pursuit of the same broad objective – the on-going development of an advanced industrial economy. Each preached to the world its own superiority over the other. But the competition between the two was very unequal; in the end, its ruinous outcome for the Soviet pattern was due to a large extent to the excessive leverage exercised upon the whole society by the political elite alone.

At the very top, the Politburo made the key planning decisions, but could not see many of them effectively implemented because it stubbornly denied sufficient autonomy to an economic elite. Thus there was no institutional *locus standi* in the system, for economic rationality, required among other things a proper price system generating and compellingly expressing the success or failure of individual production units. Thus many of the formidable human and material resources of the Soviet economy were condemned to remain undeveloped or – worse – to be ill-used and wasted.

The Western system was ultimately the winner in its contest with the Soviet one because it availed itself – among other resources – of very different institutional arrangements, established and tested in the previous two centuries. To characterize the early form of such an arrangement, let us quote from Sombart a saying (where 'powerful' designates only the holders of what we have been calling *political* power): 'One used to say "are you powerful? Then you shall be rich". Nowadays one says, "are you rich? Then you shall be powerful".'

The circuit: Economic → political power

The saying points up a significant change occurring in the course of Western modernization; but there were subsequently significant developments in the prevailing relationship between the two power forms in the West. The most significant development is one whereby from a certain point on the circuit (so to speak) *from economic to political* power the emphasis came to be flanked, moderated and to some extent displaced by a circuit *from political to economic* power.

The background to this phenomenon was the association between the industrialization of the economic system and the dominance of the capitalist mode of production, which led to a historically unprecedented increase in the production of material wealth by Western societies. One effect of this was to assign economic power a massive leverage over political power – as suggested by a sentence from *The Communist Manifesto*: 'The executive of the modern state is nothing but a committee for managing the common affairs of the whole bourgeoisie' (Marx 2000: 247).

Let us expand briefly on this pithy statement. To emerge and establish itself in the West as (very nearly) 'the only game in town', the capitalist-industrial economy required various conditions promoting more or less directly the interests of the bourgeoisie. Some such conditions could only be met by the parallel (though subordinate) development of a largely new, active and autonomous *political* system, which we can characterize as liberal. To this system the market economy centered on manufacture and industry, entrusted the development and management of new material and institutional arrangements, comprising among other things:

- the construction of more elaborate and secure road and transport systems;

- country-wide ways of measuring various resources;

- a unified monetary system and credit system;

- the loosening and successively the abolition of the rules and restraints imposed on production and consumption by local and corporate bodies;

- the production of a new body of private law, favoring the rapid formation and the reliable enforcement of diverse contractual arrangements between presumptively free, equal, and self-interested parties;

- arrangements allowing associations and partnerships between several individuals to be treated as single legal actors;

- the formation and diffusion (as far as possible) of a single, country-wide language, marginalizing and in the long run displacing vernacular, regional ones;

- frequently, policies regarding trade between countries which would either protect with high tariffs the nascent industrial sector of one national economy, or – on the contrary – establish *free trade* in capital and commodities between national economies at different stages of industrial development;

- politico-military initiatives establishing colonies in backwards parts of the world or otherwise inducing them to accept a subordinate position in the world economy.

In the Western countries, these and other policies could only be deliberated and carried out by political authorities widely recognized as legitimate, able to extract and deploy public resources to an extent previously unprecedented save for military purposes. Generally, the day-by-day implementation of such policies – at both the country and the local level – required an increasingly large and internally differentiated administrative system. Its units typically recruited, trained, funded, and controlled increasing numbers of personnel with professional qualifications and career prospects not common among previous administrators. (Think, as an important example, of an extensive, complex public education system.)

Other new political and administrative arrangements addressed not so much the *conditions* of the modernization of a country's economy, as its *consequences* – particularly those broad, diverse, disquieting consequences mostly referred to as *the social question*. Attending to some of them became the mission of various collective bodies within the civil society – old ones such as the churches or new ones such as diverse voluntary organizations. Other consequences, however, could only be dealt with (well or badly) by empowering new public organs, with activities funded from the public purse.

Urbanization, for instance, required the construction of new, city-wide systems of water supply and sewage disposal; new rules concerning bodily and vehicle traffic; some control over new forms of disease, pauperism and deviant behavior.

The 'great transformation' had another, massive set of consequences, overlapping with the social question, which induced the Western bourgeoisie to establish and activate various political authorities. As Marx phrased the matter – in a rather over-confident way! – the bourgeoisie's greatest historical feat was the production of its own 'grave-diggers': the modern working class. The bourgeoisie's pursuit of its own class interests generated unprecedented, threatening and virulent forms of organized social antagonism, dramatically transcending previous, locally-based forms.

In the latter, subaltern social groups mostly expressed (sometimes violently) their protest at violations of their own traditional, communal claims for protection and succor at the hands of their traditional betters. In the early phases of industrialization, however, the new subaltern groups were composed largely of individuals torn away from their local communities, thrown into the dark, satanic mills of the nascent factory system. Here they were compelled to labor under the most harrowing conditions for wages affording them at best the lowest level of survival. But they also discovered new opportunities for communication which allowed them to develop new collective identities and to seek to pursue shared interests.

We do not need to reconsider the steps (varying of course from time to time, from place to place) through which the new subaltern groups developed their own ways of articulating their protest, of contrasting and laying boundaries upon their own exploitation. Our point here is that mostly the holders of economic power confronted (more or less successfully) such development through numerous further uses of political power, such as:

- the out-and-out, bloody suppression of open workers' protest;

- the prohibition of early union activities, qualified and punished as criminal conspiracies;

- the promotion within the public, through the press, of ideologies which argued the moral superiority of shared, national identities over against class interests; extolled the liberating significance of the urban and industrial experience; pointed up the great debt the nation owed to the entrepreneurial, wealth-creating class, etc. (Many religious institutions played a similar, 'domesticating' role – the expression is Weber's.)

The dependency of economic on political power

Through these practices political power rendered essential services to economic power. But this does not hold straightforwardly for other practices which, at any rate on the face of it, protected instead significant interests of the subaltern groups themselves – interests to some extent in contrast with those of the bourgeoisie.

In Britain, for instance, the government mandated and empowered a body of civil servants to inspect the conditions under which factory workers (including women and children) were compelled to labor. Over time, their shocking findings, as Marx and Engels acknowledged, inspired statutes and administrative measures which progressively limited, and sometimes suppressed, managerial practices threatening the physical survival and integrity of employees (beginning with women and children).

Such political initiatives aroused concern and opposition in the ranks of the bourgeoisie, which saw them as encroachments on entrepreneurial prerogatives. By the same token, they evoked applause from some sections of the increasingly mobilized working class. Other sections articulated further demands of workers (or of the population at large) requiring governmental intervention. Others still did not so much advocate further interventions, as aim to promote revolutionary action on the part of the workers' own trade and political organizations.

Taken together, these phenomena amounted to something like a tug-of-war between contrasting visions of the legitimate scope and content of political (and ultimately coercion-centered) action. Over time, what had long constituted the prerogative of the bourgeoisie – the ability to activate and direct such action in order to foster its own exclusive interest – began to be contested by other sections of the public.

As a result (we would argue), those occupying significant governmental and administrative positions and controlling the use of public faculties and facilities, acquired a degree of autonomy with respect to both contenders. In the long run, by exercising and increasing such autonomy, political power began to loosen the lien laid upon it by economic power (including that recently acquired by actors other than the capitalist bourgeoisie, for instance by the professions and the unions). The resulting dialectic – let's call it, 'state *vs* markets' – became a dominant aspect of the continuing process of modernization.

The dialectic comprises two overlapping trends:

- the tendency for the state to absorb and deploy an increasing portion of the material resources of a society;

- the tendency for the administrative component of state institutions to become larger and larger and internally more and more complex.

Both trends are rooted not only in the requirements and demands of specific groups, but in characteristics of the society at large. *First*, the wealth produced and distributed by the industrial economy typically grew significantly, if not always from one year to the next, then from one decade to the other. Thus, the state could sometime increase, via the fiscal take, its own portion of the product yielded year by year by the country's economy, without reducing the absolute size of that product allocated by the market. It could then distribute that portion among sectors of the population placed at disadvantage by market allocation.

Second, the growth and the increasing internal complexity of the administrative apparatus largely reflected an increase in the society's own complexity, including that of its patrimony of increasingly differentiated forms of knowledge, most of them generated and managed by distinct bodies of professional personnel.

The state's growing involvement in societal management had also determinants of a distinctively political nature, such as a concern to strengthen the loyalty to the state also within the least favored sectors of the citizenry. The first major examples of this policy – and major milestones on the road to what was later to be called the *welfare state* – were three social legislation bills enacted by the German parliament on the initiative of Bismarck. They arranged respectively for compulsory health insurance (1883), accident insurance (1884), old age and disability insurance (1889) of workers. The second, in particular, was strongly opposed in parliament by the powerful National-liberal party, which saw it as a form of state socialism. But Bismarck insisted on it, arguably in the intent of loosening up the growing allegiance of workers to the German social-democratic party, which might at some point weaken in turn the disposition of youth to fight the country's war.

This is not the only manifestation of a paradoxical association between a nation being at war – or preparing for it – and its commitment to welfare policies. Twentieth century wars, in particular, have variously increased the leverage of political power and its administrative machinery upon the social process at large. Fighting wars required the state to lay boundaries on the automatism of the market and complement or replace it, however temporarily, with extensive planning arrangements sanctioned if necessary by the state's coercive faculties. For instance, countries at war established food rations, imposed on industries the standardization of certain products, fixed authoritatively their prices.

Though the most direct effect of these phenomena is a rapid increase in the size and complexity of the state's own administrative apparatus, the apparatus itself must call upon the cooperation of its counterparts in the industrial and financial system. This of course allows that system to make significant, self-interested inputs into the politico-administrative decisions; but its activities cannot challenge the priority of the national concern to win the war.

A war situation, furthermore, requires a country's politico-administrative system to pay close attention to at least the elementary needs of the masses – combatants and *non*-combatants, since modern warfare subjects also the latter to enormous stresses, deprivations, and sufferings. Also, the end itself of a war requires for some time the further involvement of political power in societal management at large. If the war was lost, that involvement was piloted by parties previously excluded from power, which now pursue significant reforms or seek regime change. But even after a victorious war, demobilization may entail considerable stresses, and activate unprecedented welfare measures. In Britain, for instance, after World War One policies characterized by the slogan 'homes fit for heroes' promoted a massive expansion of public housing. In the course of World War Two the Beveridge plan prospected the creation of the British public health system, and a commitment to full-employment. In the United States, after World War Two, the federal GI Bill allowed entire cohorts of former combatants to pursue higher education.

There is a further connection between the war experience and the growing intervention of the state in industrial affairs. Both World Wars, but especially the second, amply demonstrated the military significance of advanced scientific and technical knowledge. Such knowledge, however, is by nature a public good, optimally produced and distributed at the initiative not of profit-oriented economic units, but mainly of academic and research institutions funded from public moneys, whose operations do not prioritize the cost-and-benefit calculations orienting normal business operations. Paradoxically, after World War Two in particular, critical inputs of scientific and technical knowledge into the operations of industrial firms continued to be underwritten in large measure by public authority, both through the normal operations of academic units and through the governmental support of Research and Development activities within the industrial units themselves.

In any case, although at the end of a war the machinery expressly established by the state to manage the 'war effort' gets partly dismantled and loses many of its resources and prerogatives, generally this does not happen to the extent of re-establishing pre-war conditions. The dramatic wartime increase in public expenditure and in the size of the administrative apparatus is not entirely reversed. The state's active engagement in a country's social process has acquired a momentum of its own, which sometimes manifests itself also in countries which have not been involved in the conflict.

A very important role is played by the dynamics of liberal-democratic political systems, and in particular of adversarial policy formation by representative bodies. Increasingly, the content of a state's policies is the product of (more or less open) confrontations between the diverse and often conflicting interests of a more and more complex civil society. The formation of governments and oppositions depends on the returns of periodic electoral consultations; but those returns are the contingent outcome of an ongoing process of mobilization and organization of various sections of society, all competing to orient public opinion and to influence policy. Of course the economically powerful enjoy various advantages in this game; but there are other contenders, promoting initiatives those powerful oppose.

Finally, the bodies of personnel employed in the various units of the state's administrative machinery have a stake of their own in keeping those units in being, broadening as far as possible the scope of their operations, increasing the public funding available to them. The leading elements within each unit aim to exercise a decisive influence upon its activity, often at the expense of that of elected officials. To an extent, the units themselves compete with one another in promoting each its own interest, but their competition is bounded by a shared interest in securing the leverage of the administrative machine over the political system as a whole.

A countercircuit: Political → economic power

As a result of these diverse but convergent causal processes, in Western societies between the last part of the nineteenth and the first eight decades of the twentieth, what we have called the circuit from economic to political power was to an extent counterbalanced by one from political to economic power, sometimes characterized in the literature as *statism*. Its most visible and massive manifestation is, of course, the rise and development of the welfare state. To an extent and in forms variable from place to place and from time to time, the existential condition of a state's citizens comes to depend not only on the resources they autonomously bring to markets for capital, labor, or goods and services, but also on public provision for various individual needs – from education to housing to medical assistance.

Up to a point, as we have already seen, the welfare state itself renders critical services to economic power. It protects it from possible attacks on the private property of the means of production by revolutionary parties, or from the diffusion within the citizenry of attitudes threatening the social order. It moderates the effects of downturns in the economic cycle on the vitality of a country's industrial system, particularly on the disposition of capitalists to invest. Welfare provisions sustain the level of consumer demand the industrial system requires. The above-mentioned public funding of research and development activities by firms is just one indication that there is welfare state for the rich, not only for the poor.

In any case, through the welfare state or otherwise, while preserving the institutional differentiation between economic and political power, those holding the latter undertook to lay boundaries upon the exercise of the former, to contrast some of its outcomes, and to pursue interests of their own. Taking advantage of the unprecedented growth in the wealth produced and distributed by the industrial system, they increased the funds at the disposal of politico-administrative institutions by increasing the state's levy upon stocks and flows of private wealth, as well as upon the consumption expenditures by the public at large.

There emerged, in many national economies, a 'public sector' of the industrial system alongside its 'private sector'. The former, again, variously assisted the latter; in particular, it occasionally salvaged private firms threatened with bankruptcy; undertook large infrastructural projects which did not promise returns that were prompt, secure and large enough to attract private capital. By the same token, however, the public sector acquired considerable leverage on the operations of the economic system as a whole.

Such leverage lay sometimes in the hand of people who, although appointed and empowered by the state, had reached rewarding positions in the public sector by proving their usefulness for, and their loyalty to, political parties which had gained parliamentary majorities. After World War Two, the expression *razza padrona*, 'the boss race', was used in Italy to characterize individuals who in this fashion attained prominent positions in the public sector of the economy – and in some cases also in the private sector (Scalfari and Turani 1975).

In any case, the involvement of governments in the activities – sometimes also the day-to-day activities – of the main actors in a nation's economy, had become more and more massive, persistent, and demanding. In many countries it reached the point of replicating, during peacetime, arrangements previously associated with wartime conditions. For instance, ministers periodically convened the heads of both business associations and unions and officially negotiated their cooperation in the formation and enactment of public policies.

The high point of this trend was reached when governments expressly committed themselves, at least formally, to *programming* the main lines of the nation's economic policies. (The expression *planning* was mostly avoided, because of its association with collectivist economies.) Again, programming required the government itself to associate officially with official representatives of both business and labor. It was intended to prospect and to steer short- to medium-run developments both in main branches of the economy and in the economy as a whole. The understanding among all parties was that the promotion of advanced industrial development (including recent aspects of it which some observers labelled 'post-industrial') would benefit the whole society, but required some authoritative monitoring and express direction from the center and the top of each society. One can plausibly see events of this magnitude as signifying that both business and labor had at long last buried the hatchet. In our own imagery, the economic-to-political power circuit was now complemented and moderated by the institutionalization of a political-to-economic power circuit.

Whatever imagery one adopts, there was a more-or-less explicit premise to those events. All Western societies shared, more or less self-consciously, a view of their whole future focused on goals economic in nature: the pursuit of unprecedented, ongoing improvements in the material well-being of the population; the attainment of sustained and widely shared affluence; the triumph of the consumer society – and so on. The leverage governments currently exercised on the economic process was seen as legitimate to the extent that it contributed to the attainment of those goals.

The Italian political scientist Giorgio Galli synthesized this situation by arguing that in the first few decades after World War Two politics was essentially 'the organization of the economy' (personal communication). The German sociologist and anthropologist Arnold Gehlen has suggested (1988) that in the West the legitimacy itself of contemporary political authority was not (in Weber's terminology) traditional, charismatic or rational-legal in nature, but (for the first time in history) 'eudaimonistic'. That is: political authority was legitimate insofar as it promoted the *happiness* of the public. And what the public was increasingly interested in, was how satisfied its individual members were, primarily as private consumers, with their present and immediately foreseeable economic condition.

In sum, in the West political experience as a whole had become (so to speak) econo-centric. There is evidence of this not only in the internal politics of individual countries, but also in their external relations. Consider the development of the European Union. An early embodiment of it was the so-called European Community of Coal and Steel, whose very name unmistakably suggests the high priority of industrial concerns shared by the participant countries. This orientation to economic advance is echoed in the name itself of a successive phase, the formation of the European Common Market. Further evidence is provided by the central role performed in the whole European development by first-rate technocrats – Jean Monnet being the best example.

It is in the name of an urgent concern with economic matters that European states agreed to variously limit their own sovereignty and establish supernational institutions in Brussels.

Contemporary developments

But if, in the contemporary West, the leverage exercised by political power on the operations of economic power was closely tied to its role in promoting economic development, that leverage was bound to be compromised if economic development itself was halted or seriously slowed down. This began to be the case, by and large, in the middle seventies, for reasons too complex and controversial to be reviewed here; here, we shall just mention two of a very different nature:

- The so-called 'oil shocks' showed that many Western economies had become damagingly dependent on energy supplies originating from countries some of which had learned to use them aggressively as strategic resources in their own economic relations with the West.

- A diffuse sense that some of the institutional arrangements between political and economic power we have mentioned had intrinsic shortcomings and hindered the full display of the potentialities of unconstrained industrial and post-industrial development.

As we have seen, states had sought to re-distribute part of the economy's annual product and channel it toward certain sections of the public on grounds of solidarity, instead of compensating all sections solely for the market value of their contributions to that product. But some of these policies had become particularly controversial. For instance, apparently those promoting full employment and securing the earnings of employees had inflationary effects; the size of the state's fiscal take discouraged some entrepreneurial initiatives which could contribute to industrial development; above all, the bureaucratic machinery necessary for managing these and other public distributive undertakings was large, clumsy and costly. Even more alarmingly, such undertakings sometimes reduced the competitiveness of a particular national economy in the context of the international one and produced trade imbalances.

To understand a further, compelling reason for the increasing resonance of these and other criticisms of the accommodation between political and economic power, one needs a detour through considerations of a different nature. For a few decades the Western bourgeoisie (or at any rate its most significant components) had accepted and supported a growing role for the state in economic affairs. One reason for this was the intention to prevent significant subaltern sections of society from lending their support to particularly aggressive left-wing parties and factions.

For some of these, the continuing, massive presence of the Soviet system on the contemporary world stage seemed to represent an alternative, superior model for building and managing an advanced industrial economy and allocating its product. If such views were to mobilize politically ample sections of the working class, the social order in the Western countries would be seriously threatened. Such a concern had induced key exponents of the respective bourgeoisies to accept and support such policies as the nationalization of large sectors of industry, attempts at programming future developments of the economy, or the expansion of the welfare state.

However, over the decades after the end of World War Two, the prospect of massive subaltern groups lending their political support to forces inspired by the Soviet experience had been less and less plausible. There was growing public awareness of the discrepancy between the self-image of the Soviet system as a viable embodiment of the socialist idea, and what one could increasingly learn about the workings of (as it was sometimes phrased) 'actually existing socialism'. In 1989 the Fall of the Berlin Wall demonstrated that, socialist or not, the system which the Soviet Union had constructed and dominated in Eastern Europe, had failed miserably.

Such massive events relieved the holders of economic power of previous anxieties and induced them to, so to speak, *un-bury the hatchet* in their dealings not only with the working class, but also with the 'public sector' of the economy, and with other arrangements which for decades had given Western states a considerable hold on economic affairs.

Neo-liberalism takes command

In any case, in the last quarter of the twentieth century the *statist* trend was placed under heavy attack by holders of economic power who felt particularly damaged by that trend. They took for granted and emphasized the econocentric expectations of the Western publics formed in the previous decades. They argued that of late those expectations, previously frustrated largely by the advances of statism, had become both more legitimate and more plausible in the new horizon opened by the end of the Cold War – *globalization*. But now their realization depended on the scope and success of new policies inspired by the triumphant neo-liberal ideology.

Such ideology, constructed and communicated by a purpose-made, world-wide network of private institutions which influenced media of all kinds (including high-grade research institutes), justified a reactivation and reinforcement of the circuit from economic to political power. States could and should arrest and subvert the opposite circuit, which for too long had strengthened them at a heavy cost for society at large. In particular, regulation of private economic activities, public ownership of industrial assets and policies of re-distribution, had done enough damage. States were now advised to adopt a complex of self-denying measures of *de-regulation* and *privatization*, allowing the globalized market to place its own dynamic at the center of the whole social process.

The main import of this drastic policy change, both within the single national economies and in the global context, was of course to strengthen economic power. Large sections of national electorates advocated that change, and entrusted its realization either to parties which had reconsidered and recanted their previous support of the etatist trend, or to new parties and coalitions.

Public opinion increasingly exhibited:

- an increasing concern, within the electorate, over the growing burden which current fiscal policies imposed on firms and consumers;

- diffuse misgivings over the way the revenue so raised was allocated between the components of the administrative system;

- criticisms of the way some components managed (and often mis-managed) the expenditure of that revenue;

- indignation at various privileges political personnel enjoyed at public expense.

None of these criticisms were entirely unfounded; but neo-liberal discourse turned them into a wholesale condemnation of statism in all its aspects. In fact, that discourse was intrinsically biased because it unfairly counterposed to the empirically ascertained limitations and failures of *the state* the presumed merits of *the market*, conceived instead largely in ideal terms, with no sustained attention to how its past or present structures and performances matched its conceptual promise. To quote from Italian economist Federico Caffè:

> There are intrinsic limits to the functioning of the market economy, even in the heroic hypothesis that it operates in condition of perfect competition. All too frequently, within the current controversies, one notices a stubborn insistence on the advantages of the operations of the market system and objections to whatever hinders their 'spontaneity', with no concurrent warning on the defects inherent in the mechanism itself (Caffè 1978: 38).

The central tenet of neo-liberal ideology was memorably phrased in Ronald Reagan's Inaugural Address of 1981 as: 'government is not the solution to our problem; government is the problem'. What, then, was to be the solution? First, of course, the public had to withdraw the trust it had too long placed on *the state*, whose institutions were to be dis-empowered. Then, as we have seen, that trust had to be transferred to *the market*.

Contemplating with awe the joint effects of financialization, globalization, and de/regulation Alan Greenspan, then head of the Federal Reserve Bank expressed himself as follows in an interview with the TAGES-ANZEIGER on 9 September 2007, when a disastrous crisis was beginning:

> It is our good fortune that in the USA political decisions have been, thanks to globalization, to a large extent replaced by the world-wide market economy. Except for the theme of national security, it makes no significant difference, who will become President next. The world is governed by market forces (Greenspan 2007).

However, over the decades since World War Two the economic sphere had seen developments (including some supported and managed by public policies) which profoundly modified the market itself. The more significant protagonists of its actual workings had long been larger and larger, more and more powerful corporations, engaged at most in oligopolistic competition with one another and intent – for instance, via the promotion of brands and other marketing devices – on denying lesser aggregations of capital a more than marginal role in the market

Furthermore, alongside the developments taking place within the realm of the economy as traditionally understood, a new one of a somewhat different nature had lately imperiously asserted itself – *financialization*. Wikipedia characterizes it as a 'pattern of accumulation in which profit making occurs increasingly through financial channels rather than through trade and commodity production'.

Of course the formation and management of credit-debt relations between financial institutions (chiefly, banks) and productive units had always been a significant process in capitalist economies. But that significance had grown massively in the contemporary context, to the point of becoming 'the name of the game'. The game itself was played to a large extent by economic actors (mainly large corporations, beginning of course with banks) trafficking with one another in more and more sophisticated financial instruments (*derivatives* being one collective name for many of them).

Such traffics tended to direct huge resources away from productive investment, and toward speculative ventures. These, furthermore, were often piled on one another, to the extent that sometimes even people who constructed and traded in those instruments had little or no notion of the dimensions of the money values they referred to, though less and less directly and openly. (Descriptions of such processes may evoke in the reader's mind T. S. Eliot's 'All things become less real, man passes/From unreality to unreality.' *Murder in the Cathedral.*)

Because or in spite of this, the workings of financialization engaged a huge and growing portion of the world's total resources, exposing them to high and often incalculable risk. People constructing and managing the sophisticated instruments in question were most highly rewarded, and sometimes continued to be even after their ventures had come to a bad end, brutally impoverishing instead those who down the line had entrusted to them their own resources and very often their very livelihood. This phenomenon contributed significantly to the sharp increase in the inequalities of wealth and income over the last few decades.

The advent and the advance of financialization in its contemporary manifestations entailed, to use a commonplace phrasing, that the tail of the economic dog was vigorously and damagingly wagging the whole beast. Among the various determinants of this situation, let us mention two. First, globalization had hugely widened the geographical scope of traffics in capital; second, the systematic recourse to the Internet and related digital devices had spectacularly increased the velocity of those traffics. Huge financial resources could now be made to move across the planet with one touch at a computer keyboard; the spread of information about the operations of all stock markets had become instantaneous, and much more difficult and risky to interpret.

Both those determinants rendered the financialization a very opaque phenomenon, and one very hard to monitor and regulate. On this account, financial speculation could generate massive gains for those involved in it, either as producers and distributors of the new negotiable instruments, or as purchasers of those instruments. Risk was of course intrinsic to the whole process, but risk itself could be bought and sold in the form of ad hoc financial instruments.

Developments in the early 21st century

As was promptly demonstrated in the new century, financialization was liable to produce increasingly large, sudden, and disastrous boom-and-bust phenomena. These had rapid, massive and potentially disastrous effects which could only be moderated – for the sake of maintaining in operation the economy as a whole – by committing colossal inputs of state funds. This was paradoxical, for the most urgent demands for such inputs originated from firms which had previously benefitted greatly from inducing political authorities to cease monitoring, regulating and sanctioning the operations of financial actors – primarily the banks, but alongside them other significant components of the financial system, such as credit-rating agencies and the governing bodies of stock exchanges. In allocating their funds, states had to assign high priority to those actors, in view of the central position they had come to hold within the economy at large. Thus, many of them were protected from the consequences of their own ventures, and this at enormous expense for the public at large.

So much for some consequences (direct or otherwise) of the key neo-liberal policy – getting the state out of the way and allowing economic forces alone to control and steer the economic process. But that proposal constituted only the *negative* aspect of the revitalization of (to use our own terms) the economic-to-political-power circuit. There was also a *positive* aspect, which unsurprisingly was less self-consciously theorized in the neo-liberal ideology and less openly pursued in neo-liberal practice. It consisted in a set of operations intended to place personnel committed to neo-liberalism into leading positions within the state's own political and administrative apparatus, and to secure the widest possible echo for neo-liberal ideology within the media.

For example, Simon Johnson, a former chief economist of the International Monetary Fund and a close observer (and, subsequently, a sharp critic) of contemporary American practices, has spoken of a 'quiet coup'. Over the last few decades, an intense Southward traffic along what he calls 'the Wall Street-Washington corridor', introduced into the government of the US a large body of highly qualified personnel committed to neo-liberalism. They gained leading positions within the federal political and administrative apparatus and within the consulting and lobbying professions. Their performance in those positions continued to serve the interests of the sector of the economy they had come from and to which in many cases they intended to return. Through such practices, as Johnson emphatically puts, the finance industry in particularly 'effectively captured' the government of the US. His essay of 2009 in *The Atlantic* magazine states:

> Elite business interests – financiers, in the case of the U.S. – played a central role in creating the crisis, making ever-larger gambles, with the implicit backing of the government, until the inevitable collapse. More alarming, they are now using their influence to prevent precisely the sorts of reforms that are needed, and fast, to pull the economy out of its nosedive. The government seems helpless, or unwilling, to act against them (Johnson 2009).

Similar practices can be observed in other countries – among these, some of those one used to call 'underdeveloped'. To the extent that their conditions compelled them to apply for financial and other assistance from, in particular, the International Monetary Fund, such countries found themselves forced to adopt policies called 'economic re-structuring', based on the twin strategies of the neo-liberal project, de-regulation and privatization. Both were intended to encourage investments from foreign businesses, which often had such side-effects as overexploitation of natural resources and local labor, and an increase in socio-economic inequality.

There are two further, connected components, in the US, to what we called the positive aspect of the neo-liberal hegemony. First, the dominant economic interests, besides profiting from the traffic between Wall Street and Washington, managed to a large extent to inspire and orient public opinion. They did so via channels as diverse as, at one hand, foundations funding research in economics extolling the virtues of the market, at the other, the media system which broadcast to the public, on a day by day basis, news, entertainment and advertising loaded with neo-liberal content.

Second: huge aggregations of industrial and financial resources, often under the control of single individuals or families, undertook to play a more and more open and aggressive role in the political system itself. They supported, at all levels of the systems, particular parties, party factions, individual holders of or aspirants to public office, funding for them the services of well-connected lobbying and public relations firms. At election times their outlays underwrote chiefly the huge costs of TV advertising in support of certain parties and candidates.

The intent of such increasingly massive and visible intervention in the political process, is not just (and sometimes not at all) to promote de-regulation and privatization, but also the production of public policies which expressly favor the interests of the economically powerful. In the States, this is done for instance through:

- fiscal arrangements. Some years ago, Warren Buffett, a spectacularly successful financial tycoon, pointed out that he paid federal income tax at a rate lower that his own secretary;

- legislation on patents and copyright. The United States provides particularly strong and durable protection to such 'intellectual property', and via the World Trade Organization has induced many other states to adopt it. As a result, the original intent of the institution itself of intellectual property – to encourage industrial invention and innovation – has been perverted. It now largely constitutes a 'rent-seeking' device , and to an extent *discourages* those processes;

- large public subsidies for numerous agricultural products, mostly produced by a few large corporations which have rendered marginal the role of family and other small farming units.

We have spoken of these initiatives as *connected* with one another. Obviously, the connection lies chiefly in the increasingly decisive role which the ability to deploy large financial resources plays in all these processes. The significance of the whole phenomenon is suggested by the title of a recent American book – *Dollarocracy*. According to this work (Nichols and McChesney 2013), the phenomena we have reviewed, together with one deserving much greater attention than we have given it – the role of the media in shaping and biasing public opinion – render problematical the very nature of the whole political system, and that not only in the contemporary United States. An expression of much older lineage – 'plutocracy' – is being increasingly used to point up the problem.

In our own terms: in current times the circuit from economic to political power has not only successfully interrupted and displaced that from political to economic power, but is also subverting the institutional separation between the two power forms constitutive of Western modernity.

Conclusion

For quite some time, but more significantly in the last decades of the 20th century and in the first of the new millennium, fundamental aspects of public policy have ceased to emerge from open-ended confrontations between opposing political parties, all expressing contrasting demands and sentiments and recurrently ascertaining their respective standing in the national population via competitive elections. Policy is now largely a result of the persistent, more-or-less covert collusion between on the one hand the political class as a whole – which largely pursues interests entirely of its own, mostly shared across party lines – on the other the more commanding economic forces, ever more empowered by the central significance the society at large attributes to processes of production and distribution of wealth.

Such developments progressed, at the national level, without visibly encroaching on the prerogatives of constitutional organs and without openly displacing parties from their official position as mediators between society and the state. The political class has accommodated itself easily enough to the ever growing significance of the economic and financial elites. It has established with them arrangement of various kinds which assist political personnel (including its high-bureaucratic component) in the pursuit of their own dominant concern: maintaining their presence in the system of governance and the related privileges.

It seems fair to impute to such developments, among others, to the success of the neo-liberal drive, rendering it responsible, by the same token, for the disastrous crisis beginning in 2007. Paradoxically, however, the years immediately following did NOT see the settling of the accounts one could expect to follow from the awareness of that responsibility. Instead they saw a phenomenon best characterized by the title of a book by the English sociologist Colin Crouch: *The Strange Non-death of Neo-liberalism* (Crouch 2011).

That is: In spite of the large-scale and enduring crisis which by rights should lie at the door of neo-liberalism, this utterly refuses to lie down and die. Worse, it still provides the main mental framework within which a number of elite elements – within single countries, the EU, and numerous and powerful international agencies – continue to operate in both the political and the economic sphere. It's as if the arsonists were put in charge of fire-fighting and of arranging the repair of fire-damaged properties.

Neo-liberal ideology, with its persistent appeal to the virtues of the market, continues to hide a critical aspect of the situation, which has been hinted at above. To wit: huge aggregations of economic power, where multiple and diverse forms of capital are allowed to function as single actors by virtue of their corporate status, continue to play a decisive role in the contemporary social process. They do so within the economic sphere as well as in its relations with the political one. Their impact on the actual workings of the economic sphere could be labelled (rather inelegantly) a far-reaching (though not total) *de-marketization* of the creation and distribution of wealth. As far as the political sphere is concerned, that impact threatens the far-reaching *de-democratization* of the formation and implementation of public policy.

Chapter Nine

The Secularization of the State: Aspects of a Major Historical Development[*]

Approaching my topic from an expressly sociological perspective, I will consider the secularization of the modern state (an expression where the adjective 'modern' seems to me superfluous) as one manifestation among others of a much broader social and cultural social process of differentiation – the progressive separation and reciprocal autonomization between previously overlapping arrangements concerning multiple social and cultural phenomena.

That concept, in turn, constitutes the sociological refraction of an even broader concept of differentiation, comprising also biological phenomena, and lying at the core of the Darwinian theory of evolution, focused on two fundamental aspects of a transition between simple and complex biological phenomena. On the one hand, in the course of time the ensemble of vegetal and animal life forms becomes enriched by ever new forms, new species. On the other, the forms that come into being are in turn more complex, articulated, 'organized'.

Herbert Spencer transposes to the human-historical realm this understanding of Darwinian evolution, emphasizing such concepts as 'struggle for life' and 'survival of the fittest'. Ironically, however, Spencer's conception had an important precursor in pre-Darwinian theories dealing directly with cultural and social phenomena – in particular the theory of the division of labor advanced by the Scottish economists, who envisaged two components to that process: the social division of labor, whereby different economic subjects produce different goods and services (in the twentieth century, Colin Clark (1940) would point up the evolutionary succession between respectively the primary, the secondary, and the tertiary sector of the economy). And the technical division: the production and distribution of any particular good or service would require the organized cooperation between different economic subjects, each charged with a distinctive moment or aspect of those processes.

---

[*] In 2007, the Kessler Foundation at the University of Trento organized a multidisciplinary conference on the secularization of the state. In keeping with its statute, those taking part were Italian, Austrian, or German scholars. I was invited to contribute a paper which subsequently became a chapter in the proceedings of the conference (*Lo Stato secolarizzato nell'età post-secolare*, in G. E. Rusconi (ed.) Bologna: Il Mulino, 2008). It is translated below, with some revisions with respect to both previous editions.

The sociological concept of differentiation extends the division of labor to spheres of social experience different from the economy, while echoing more or less self-consciously the evolutionary hypothesis. It has been used to throw light on multiple, disparate processes of social change, as can be seen for example in a German book from the 1980's, *Soziale Differenzierung* (Hondrich 1982) which deals with the matter in a particularly elaborate and sophisticated manner. In his introduction, the editor, Karl Otto Hondrich defines social differentiation as the process whereby a given set of people – which previously satisfied a plurality of diffuse needs, often not easily distinguished from one another, articulates itself into two or more partial ensembles, each of which satisfies one relatively distinct need. One may note that this distinction echoes that between *Gemeinschaft* and *Gesellschaft*, advanced in the 19th century by Ferdinand Tönnies, and variously re-elaborated in the 20th by such authors as Talcott Parsons and Niklas Luhmann.

The latter, in particular, advances what one might call an ex post facto justification for both the division of labor and, more generally, social differentiation: internally differentiated social contexts are superior to non-differentiated ones as concerns the respective levels of rationality. This view presupposes Weber's understanding of rationality as a quality of action requiring a distinction between means and goals of action, and the deliberate selection, between diverse means of action, of those which maximize or optimize the attainment of a given goal. Contexts of individual or collective activity which are differentiated both externally, between one another, and internally, between their own components, enjoy the advantage of allowing each of their components to identify one specific goal, assuming it as the exclusive target of its own own activities. But if this holds for the several components, the rationality of the whole is enhanced.

The upshot of social and cultural differentiation thus understood, is a conception of modernity as an overall process of social and cultural rationalization. In the thinking of Weber and of other authors, such a process has its own costs for the individual – for instance such typical modern subjective liabilities as a sense of loss, an awareness of sharp and non-negotiable contrasts between different aspects of existence, a feeling of alienation and so forth.

The subtitle of the book edited by Hondrich – *Long-term analyses of changes in politics, work, and family* – points up a trio of institutional complexes, differing in the extent to which they lend themselves to rationalization, or represent diverse and potentially contrasting tendencies within its process. But one can also think of those components as having previously emerged in turn from a differentiation process within a previously undifferentiated whole.

Now, each component of the trio could claim a kind of priority, demand to be considered as a primordial matrix with respect to the other two. The Marxian tradition, with its emphasis on the priority of production and reproduction of the material existence of individuals and groups, would argue that for the 'work' component. Some anthropological traditions would instead emphasize the 'family' component, suggesting that the incest taboo constitutes the critical difference between the human species and the other animal species, or considering kinship affiliations as the primordial structure of human groups. One might, finally, claim the priority of 'politics', as in a Schmittian rendering of the primary political experience: each human collectivity derives its identity from its unavoidable (at least) potential enmity toward others, and can only become constituted and preserved if it is able to exercise collective violence in dealing with the threat those others represent.

One may observe that there is no place for religion in Hondrich's trio. This may seem highly problematical, at any rate for those who consider ritual and myth (arguably the primary components of religious experience) as the *ur-form*, respectively, of collective thought and collective action. It has been argued, in fact, that religion IS the primordial institution, from which all others – law, art, the economy, science, politics – originate through differentiation.

On what counts may one attribute such priority to religion? Consider the following:

- Originally, within the biologically open-ended realm of human activity, some forms and aspects become repetitive and stabilized ('stereotyped', to use a Weberian expression) to the extent that they are considered (and sanctioned) as 'sacred'. That is: some practices, persons, objects, places are seen as intrinsically privileged, as entitled to be considered and acted upon with a maximum of awe and respect on account of their symbolic, not – in principle – of their de facto significance. In this way sacralization lays boundaries upon the human tendency to make and unmake arrangements and objects, to consider existing ones as merely 'feasible' (*machbar*). Only in this way can some products of human activity acquire a capacity to abide, thus to structure and orient certain in principle arbitrary selections.

- Similarly, in view of the intrinsically open-ended realm of human thought, Tocqueville argues the necessity of a consensus, within a plurality of actors, around a distinctive, finite set of ways of construing and valuing reality. But that can only happen to the extent that those particular ways become 'dogmatic', that shared religious beliefs over against all possible ones, are conceived and justified as uniquely valid. They may differ enormously as between human populations, as long each of these subscribes to one set of such beliefs.

Many years ago, at Berkeley, I heard Kingsley Davis offer a characteristically irreverent justification of the peculiar advantages afforded a society by the moral views taught by religion. 'Salvation' religions, in particular, lead believers to carry out practices oriented to non-empirical goods and ends. These are viewed as NOT intrinsically scarce, thus can in principle be enjoyed by everyone; everyone can aspire to them without feeling envious or competitive toward anyone else, thus potentially in conflict with anyone. Two African-American 'spirituals' neatly convey this unique property of salvation: one announces that *the Gospel-train is a-coming round the curve* and instructs believers: *git on board little children, git on board, there's room for many a more!* The other promises *plenty good room, plenty good room, good room in my Father's kingdom – choose your seat and sit down.*

On the basis of this and similar arguments, many authors have seen in the relationship between religion and politics what one might call an 'asymmetric genetic affinity'; that is, historically, religious experience precedes and engenders political experience. (Note however that the opposite relation has been construed for Ancient Egypt (Assmann 2000).)

In any case some affinity between religion and politics can be evinced from the numerous historical situations in which they have established and maintained forms of alliance and cooperation. In particular, religious power often confers legitimacy on political power, domesticating its subjects (another Weberian expression). Consider a statement by Martin Luther: 'It's better when tyrants commit 100 injustices against the people, than when the people commit one single injustice against the tyrants.'

Furthermore, religious power makes itself useful to political power by rendering highly symbolically charged some of its manifestations, and turning it into the object of awe. Further: religious beliefs and practices can, as it were, distract the population from focusing critical attention on political authority by asserting the intrinsic priority of spiritual as against worldly interests and pursuits. Luther, again, comes to mind with his peremptory response to a female faithful who had asked him what she should do to be happy: ('*Leiden, Leiden, Kreuz, Kreuz ist der Christen Recht, das und kein anderes*').[1]

In turn, political power has often reciprocated the services rendered to it by religion by establishing and guaranteeing to a particular religious authority a monopoly of validity within a given population. It has put at its disposal its own 'secular arm' in order to punish and repress heresy; it has conferred on it immunity from fiscal burdens, authorized to establish and run an educational institution; prosecuted as crimes certain sins. And so forth.

How can one account for these and other forms of cooperation, which according to Weber (1922: 812) are historically more frequent than the 'primordial contrast' he posits between 'magic' and 'political charisma'? One possible response draws on the Machiavellian tradition, which – particularly

---

1. Translation: 'Suffering, suffering, the cross, the cross, that is the sole entitlement of Christians, this and nothing else'.

in the versions given of it in the last century – emphasizes the fundamental, unmodifiable difference between elite and mass. Such difference transcends the distinction between the two elites, political and religious: under certain circumstances they become aware of (and act upon) a compelling interest they share – to prevent the masses from challenging and subverting their own submission to the elites.

To this end, the masses must be made to cease and desist from struggling for an ideal situation where each collectivity manages its own affairs without a part of it becoming estranged from the whole and ruling over it. Both elites are chiefly interested in keeping the masses at bay, and to this end they accommodate each other, transcending or muting their 'primordial contrast'.

A significant example of this contingent convergence between the interests of the two powers – though one where the masses are not directly involved – can be seen in the joint opposition of Church and State to the modern phenomenon of 'libertinism'. The latter had two overlapping aspects: on the one hand a certain body of intellectuals sought to challenge their traditional subordination toward civil authority; on the other it attacked the moralistic prejudices typical of ecclesiastical authority. On both accounts, in various situations, libertines found themselves repressed and persecuted by political and religious authorities alike.

However, one aspect of the historical novelty embodied in the modern state is the extent to which this particular form of polity does not declare and cultivate its own affinity to and dependence on religious power. How can this be explained? One can see in the secularization of the state an express confirmation (though a gradual one, as is shown by the lengthy and tortuous itinerary at the end of which the State attains a more or less total separation from the Church) of the Weberian 'primordial contrast' between magical and political charisma. In effect, according to Weber, that particular contrast is one major instance of an even wider and very diverse phenomenon, which he emphasized in the so-called *Zwischenbetrachtung*, a component the 1920 edition of his collected essays on the sociology of religion.

That is: In principle, all human undertakings are inspired more or less directly and consistently by distinctive, subjectively entertained value preferences, each of which characterizes one of the institutional complexes characterized above as law, art, the economy, science, politics. However, such value preferences, *qua* existential commitments responsible for orienting and motivating individual action, are at bottom incompatible with one another: for instance, one cannot serve both God and Mammon (Matthew 6:24).

However, that between God and Mammon is only one of many contrasts of the same kind, which together allow Weber to speak (referring to a statement by J. S. Mill) of the inescapable 'polytheism' of socio-historical reality. Individuals cannot but experience a conflict between the diverse values in the name of which they can construe their existence as meaningful. On this account, a variety of institutional orders (bodies of personnel led by distinctive elites, generating and diffusing different understandings of reality, administering diverse cultural and material resources) contend for the privilege of generating and monitoring in individuals a prior commitment to one of those values, if not to the radical exclusion of others then by reducing their ability to inspire and orient their collective experience. Each institutional order seeks to impose the superiority of its own reasons at the expense of the reasons of other orders.

The complexity and the historical diversity of the relations between the institutional orders are suggested also by a dictum of the young Marx, which unfortunately I am unable to quote precisely, but sounds more or less as follows: Everything struggles to maintain the premises of its own existence; everything struggles to suppress those premises. Thus, even assuming that two institutional orders are bound to contend over the prior significance of each, their relations will over time shift back and forth between conflict and mutual accommodation.

Above, we have suggested a 'Machiavellian' reason for the fact that contrasting elites may at times work together to defeat the challenges represented by the claims for de-subordination of the respective masses. But materially those masses widely overlap: the subjects of the political elite tend to be also the faithful of the ecclesiastical elite. However, the forms of mass conduct conducive to their interests may differ from one elite to another. Or, to use a homely metaphor, the control over the mass as a whole tends to become a blanket too short to protect both elites from the cold. Each is induced to pull the blanket toward its own side, to loosen the hold upon it of the other.

Weber's *Zwischenbetrachtung* suggests a further, peculiar reason for tension and rivalry between political and religious power. The latter, by and large, grounds its privileges on its unique ability to impart meaning not only to various aspects of the lives of individuals but also to their death – an event which might otherwise be perceived as the voiding of the meaning of existence itself. Yet, says Weber, that uniqueness is challenged by one characteristic experience of the political sphere. The death of the warrior on the battlefield can be perceived (and celebrated) as an event loaded with intense, redeeming significance. To this extent political experience may appear as a rival to religious experience.

Finally, one may account for the historical exception represented by the modern secularization of the state by means of three variants of an 'economistic' argument. In the first variant, political power realizes that the costs of maintaining a close relationship with religious power exceed the gains it can derive from it. In the second, political power becomes convinced that it can do without the services traditionally rendered to it by religious power, it can become self-sufficient. In the third, political power turns to alternative suppliers of those needs. Let's consider briefly each variant.

a. The century-old collaboration between State and Church revealed very significant costs and risks for the former once the unity of Western Christianity was broken by the reformation. On this account the State undertakes the prolonged and difficult itinerary that goes from the Peace of Augsburg to the Treaty of Westphalia, to the praxis of tolerance, to more or less express and thoroughgoing secularization. Political power realizes that it cannot fulfill its own tasks of rule unless it reduces the extent to which the diverse religious affiliations of its own subjects/citizens require the state to relate differently to each sector of the population. It realizes, sooner or later, that it is not in its interest to remain (to some extent or other) in the business of sending souls to heaven; that it should no longer allow religious power to place a lien on its own distinctively, expressly mundane resource – the monopoly of legitimate violence.

b. The political order has attempted to render itself self-sufficient with respect to religious authority in three ways. First: it endows political experience with a halo of sacredness of its own by promoting and managing distinctive symbolic-ritual practices (political and military liturgies, monuments, holidays commemorating great political events, the naming of public places, national myths, the ideology of the 'ethical state'). Second: it attributes a universal value to its own worldly enterprises – see the parallel Tocqueville draws between the diffusion via conquest of Islam and the civilizing impact claimed for the French revolutionary wars. Finally, the State claims for itself an expressly modern and intrinsically secular form of legitimation, which Weber names legal-rational and contrasts with traditional and charismatic legitimation. (Let me mention in passing an interesting remark by the Norwegian sociologist Thomas Mathiesen (2000). The penal sanctions typical of archaic and early-modern political units on the one hand are spectacularly, cruelly corporeal and on the other hand are shot through with religious ritual. The penal practices of modern political units are less spectacular and cruel, and assign much more space and time to the distinctive rituals of law).

c. Finally, according to Gehlen (1988) contemporary states draw for their own legitimation on a realm which is neither expressly political nor religious – the economy. According to him, in the 20th century the legal-rational form of legitimation is largely replaced by a new form, which he calls eudaimonistic. Here the State grounds its own legitimacy more and more expressly on its capacity to assist and regulate the process of economic development, to promote and fund more advanced forms of industrialization which in turn raise the population's living standards. To the extent that it succeeds in these tasks the state can expect the citizenry to acknowledge the significance of its rule, and confer its consensus on political authority. Paraphrasing a well-known formula, one might say that the 20th century has witnessed an alliance between the throne and the market.

I cannot remember when Gehlen first spoke of the state's eudaimonistic legitimation, but presumably he did during the 'glorious thirty years' that followed the end of World War Two in the West. Already then, one could perceive some vagaries and limitations in the phenomenon evoked by Gehlen; even in places and at times when it more clearly manifested itself, what one witnessed (as Aron wrote (1964)) was *une satisfaction querelleuse*.

In any case, as we well know, the last phase of the 20th century saw the market turn its back on its own alliance with the State, opposing and to some extent disposing of some public policies which to an extent had re-distributed the national product to the benefit of strata deprived of market power. Furthermore, in the opening decade of the current century 'eudaimonistic legitimation' became less and less credible, as the autonomous dynamic of the economy was revealed to have drastically increased the inequalities within the populations since the mid 70s.

One may connect with Gehlen's thesis one final consideration. So far we have construed the secularization process as activated primarily on the initiative of political power, progressively reducing the public significance of religious beliefs and belongings. But perhaps there is another aspect to the story. At any rate in particular phases, modalities, and locales, the secularization process involved, next to political and religious power, also the evolving forms of economic power. Putting it otherwise, the process was not only à deux, but à trois. Consider, for instance, the interaction of Church, State, and market, in the story of the expropriation of monasteries in early-modern England.

Whether or not one accepts Weber's view that economic modernization itself had also religious determinants, it was clear to him that from a certain point on, modern capitalism had loosened its own initial dependence on expressly religious phenomena and begun to initiate and sustain a thoroughgoing process of cultural secularization.

In the circumstances of modernity, political power becomes aware that the 'health of souls' was less significant for it than the 'health of market', and views the promotion of the latter as more urgent and significant than that of the former. In this perspective, the secularization of the State appears as one component (however significant and complex) of a more comprehensive secularization phenomenon.

This is, of course, a rather obvious result of the discourse conducted so far. I will conclude it by referring it to an old statement by Franz Neumann on the relationship between political and economic power. During the whole course of pre-modern history various institutional arrangements had insured that, by and large, those two power forms coincided with one another. In a remark quoted by Sombart – in the past it was a rule that whoever was politically powerful would also be rich. It is again modernization that separates institutionally the economically from and the politically powerful. However, Neumann adds, that institutional separation itself renders intrinsically problematical (and contentious) the de facto relations between the two (Neumann 1986).

One may perhaps say the same of the relationship between political and religious power. Once modernization had differentiated them and led to their confrontating each other as distinctive and autonomous, there remained the problem of their reciprocal interferences, of their mutual claims and entitlements. The solutions of that problem may occasionally subvert or at any rate weaken their differentiation and make it plausible to speak of a process of de-differentiation. Something like that may be happening currently in many parts of the world, where indeed the relations between the two powers are a major theme of the social process at large. Some of its effects, however, may remind the observer of an ancient remark of Burckhardt's, according to which too close an alliance between Church and State may, in the long run, become damaging for both partners.

Chapter Ten

The Westphalian Design of the Modern States System[*]

The final signing (at Muenster on October 24 1648) of a series of treaties negotiated over several years in two Westphalian towns, Muenster and Osnabrueck, has long been seen as a turning point in European history, and particularly in the history of international affairs. In fact, 'until the days of the French Revolution, the Peace of Westphalia was considered to be the basis of the European state system' (Beller 1970: 358). The theme of this chapter is the broad design of that system, the institutional nature of its component parts and

---

[*] Over the years, much of my writing on political themes has focussed on the unique institutional embodiment of political power constituted by the modern state. This applies also to many of the texts in the present collection, whose focus however is not so much on the state in and of itself, as on its relations to other social and cultural phenomena – law, religion, the economy, the public sphere etc.

In pursuing this task, the writings making up this volume deal almost exclusively with what I would call the inside slope of the state. That is: their focus is on an understanding of the state which the French political scientist Badie characterized as follows while interviewed by Philippe Cabin:

> The state is in the first place a question of internal sociology: a public space which emerges over against civil society with a claim to establish a monopoly over public functions, to engender high-priority allegiances motivating civil obedience, to differentiate the political from the social by recruiting a personnel of its own and producing its own institutions (Badie B. 'Rencontre avec Bertrand Badie', *Sciences humaines*, February 1993).

This is indeed a tenable way of approaching the state as an object of sociological analysis; but one should not ignore the significance of a complementary approach, focussed instead on the outside slope of each state, on its nature as a component of a system of states, on the relations each state typically entertains with others.

The so far unpublished text that follows differs from the others by adopting such an approach, in however elementary a way. It was originally written as part of my own contribution to a book I was to write with a colleague – a project, however, which was subsequently abandoned.

That work as a whole was to deal with the dynamics of contemporary inter-state relations, and emphasize the novel aspects of those dynamics in comparison with those prevailing in previous phases of modern history. In order to do this, my prospective co-author and myself had decided that our joint work would deal in the first place, however schematically, with what could be called the classical conception of the modern states system. In keeping with established practice I focussed my presentation exclusively on the configuration originally imparted to that system by the Treaty of Westphalia (1648). (I often use the equivalent expression Peace of Westphalia.)

The text I produced and present here is on the one hand relatively diffuse and detailed; on the other, it aims at no more than an elementary and conventional discussion of its subject. On this account, it does not deal with two overlapping themes: the changes undergone by the Westphalian design of interstate relations in the subsequent centuries; the new understandings of the Westphalian system itself advanced by contemporary scholarship work – for instance the so-called postmodern interpretation of the nature itself of that system.

their relations.

The long-term import of the Peace

In its express terms the Peace of Westphalia dealt exclusively with German affairs, putting an end of the Thirty Years War, which had raged chiefly in German lands. But most of the larger European powers had been involved in the war, some of the multiple issues over which it had been fought were of continental scope, and the resolutions they received in the Peace had considerable long-term significance. In fact, the Peace of Westphalia structured the inter-actions of European states and shaped the nature of their involvement with one another in ways destined to be much more durable than the specific territorial and financial settlements the Peace embodied, and the power relations immediately resulting from it.

Not for the first time, but on some counts more expressly and self-consciously than had been done by other treaties, however significant, the Peace of Westphalia established that the larger affairs of the continent of Europe (affairs, however, which increasingly affected other parts of the world) were the sole concern of only one kind of political actor – the territorial, sovereign state – of which however there were several, all in principle equal to and independent of one another. 'The Peace of Westphalia [...] represented a new diplomatic arrangement – an order created by states, for states' (Holsti 1991: 35).

Sovereignty

Of the two adjectives we have attached above to the noun 'state' – 'territorial' and 'sovereign' – it is the second which warrants more explanation at this stage. Sovereignty is a qualification of 'political power'; it attaches (if to anything) to an entity involved in exercising political rule, that is, in issuing and if necessary enforcing commands, in carrying out its own interests even over the opposition of others. It is taken for granted in what would today be called 'the discourse of sovereignty' that the game of power is one which several numbers can play, mobilizing diverse resources, exercising distinct rights, pursuing different interests, affecting different aspects of the existence of different subjects, or for that matter of the same subjects. But, according to 'the discourse of sovereignty', this game can go on without threatening the possibility itself of civil existence ONLY IF within a given territory there is one power supreme and paramount, recognizing no peer and able to withstand any challenge to its own superiority. Such a power is sovereign insofar as it effectively reserves to itself the faculty of mobilizing the ultimate sanction, organized force, and uses it to back up generally and unconditionally binding commands, overriding if necessary those issued by all other power sources.

Only on this condition – only by being built around one sovereign power center – does a state exist as such; sovereignty is an intrinsic attribute of it. Where the contrast between opposing social interests routinely expresses itself through enmity – instead of being curbed and moderated by a sovereign power's monopoly of coercion, pursuing a shared, public interest in its own security and unity – the social body is condemned to internal dissolution; its several parts are liable to be overrun and conquered by other social bodies, capable of coherent action because within *them* a sovereign power has indeed become established.

The concept of sovereignty, so understood, stands in opposition to a situation where, within a territory, a number of power centers *compete*, none effectively able to prevent others from contrasting, weakening and neutralizing its own policies, directed to the preservation of the public order and the defence of the territory itself from outside encroachments. Sovereignty could not be said to be established within a land when, for instance, its magnates could with impunity make war on one another, perhaps with the declared intent of bestowing exclusive public standing on the religious confession to which each happened to subscribe. Its establishment requires that such pretentions to independence by several power centers be curbed by a single one, asserting its exclusive ability to lay down the law for the whole territory.

In other terms, the concept of sovereignty originally referred primarily to arrangements internal to a given settled society, and it is primarily in these terms that it was variously argued for and against and bloodily fought over in the European late Middle Ages and in the early modern era. That concept became an institutional reality, over most of Western Europe, insofar as royal dynasties imposed the superiority of their own power over that of barons and magnates, and sometimes over the pretensions of cities to statehood. In essence, it involved the principle that, when it came to forming and enforcing policies directly affecting a country's internal order and external security, the King would tolerate no power equal to his own.

Only in the later phases of the development of what one may label this *internal* aspect of sovereignty did its implications for a state's *external* position become clear. Curiously enough, however, those implications had already given notice of themselves in one of the early definitions of the concept, where a sovereign power was characterized as one *superiorem non recognoscens* – as a power which acknowledges no other as superior, rather than as equal to itself.

In fact the two aspects belong together. If the King is to have no peer within his realm it is necessary and sufficient that he should not be in turn subject to any power outwith that realm. Such a subjection would negate his own sovereignty over the realm and transfer it to the external power in question. In principle, on the other hand, a King's claim to sovereignty is compatible with the existence of equally sovereign powers in other realms, as long as these realms are juxtaposed to his own and similar in nature to it, that is intent upon (and capable of!) excluding any external subjection.

Thus, it was essential for the articulation of the external aspect of sovereignty that Kings should not acknowledge any overarching power capable of enforcing a lawful superiority over their juxtaposed realms, severally or jointly. However, for centuries Western Christendom recognized as many as two political entities insistently and self-confidently claiming such superiority – the Papacy and the Empire. Starting from the late Middle Ages, Kings were almost everywhere not just declaring but asserting in fact, within their own realms, the paramountcy of their own power over that of barons and of other jurisdictions aspiring to independence. It took longer for them to establish the principle *imperator in regno suo* – each king counts as emperor in his own realm – for this directly denied the empire's claim to universal jurisdiction. As to the Papacy, while its similar claim had long been contested in fact by rulers, an outright denial of it remained unthinkable (because blasphemous) through the late Middle Ages.

However, the very fact that both Empire and Papacy claimed (vaguely defined) faculties of rule transcending those exercised by territorial rulers, weakened the claims of both, if only because often it encouraged rulers to play one claimant against the other in order to assert their independence of both. Furthermore, the irreversible breach in the religious unity of Western Christendom caused by the Reformation had made the Papacy's claim ostensibly untenable. The Peace of Westphalia further sanctioned that breach by recognizing not only the Catholic and the Lutheran but also the Calvinist confession as entitled to a privileged political position wherever a ruler subscribed to the one or the other.

As to the Empire, by 1648 it had long renounced anything more than ceremonial supremacy over the Kingdoms of Western and Central Europe and had become a significant *regional* power, the overseer of several semi-independent German territories and cities. Its effective power rested largely on the fact that at any given time the Habsburg dynast who held the title of Emperor also exercised territorial rule over the eastern portion of the Empire, comprising the Kingdom of Bohemia and the Duchy of Austria. As we shall see, the Peace of Westphalia further 'declawed' the Empire by conferring on those German territories and cities independence in the conduct of their foreign affairs. But this provision only recognized what had long been clear for the rest of Europe: it was made up of a plurality of political units within each of which one power center had asserted its unchallengeable superiority over all others and did not acknowledge dependence on any outside power. Each unit, in other terms, possessed both internal and external sovereignty. It was the sole arbiter of its own interest, and in pursuing it depended only upon its own resources.

Territoriality

One can easily see what essential role territoriality played in this context: nothing less than establishing and by the same token delimiting the reach of each unit's power, thus acknowledging the legitimate existence of others. Each unit's territory marked the area over which rule was exercised in an orderly fashion, for its central power no longer had competitors in the business of determining general policy and enforcing the law. Further, the territory materially bounded that rule, establishing where it ended and where it came up against another territory and thus another self-standing area of internal order.

The relationship between sovereignty and territory, then, may appear obvious and straightforward. Yet, however conceptually transparent, by the time of the Peace of Westphalia that relationship had been for centuries, and was to remain for centuries to come, a very frequent and significant issue in the relations between states. It constituted the cause or issue of many of the bloody conflicts whereby the states themselves waxed or waned, flourished or perished. Some reasons for its permanent and bothersome contentiousness must be briefly reviewed.

The basic reason is that territory and sovereignty are realities of two very different kinds. At bottom, territory is a physical reality, no matter how significant a role memory and fantasy may play in its social construction, and no matter how profoundly the work of men and women may shape its natural features, enrich or deplete it. In fact, it has been suggested that the development of a plurality of sovereign, territorial states in Europe owes a great deal to the sheer geographical make-up of the area, which juxtaposes a number of physically and climatically highly distinctive habitats, often bounded by visible features such as mountain chains and bodies of water.

Sovereignty, on the other hand, is at bottom an institutional reality, a set of sanctioned arrangements, a property of a complex of inter-subjectively communicated understandings and claims, although (as we shall see) it lies under the burden of establishing itself initially, and proving itself from time to time, as factually valid.

Put otherwise – in the critical question, 'who rules here?' the 'here?' is intrinsically simpler to address than the 'who rules?' Perforce, then, the relationship between territory and sovereignty is an open-ended, highly contingent one, and the boundaries laid down to fix it at a given time between any two units share the ambiguity characteristic of the concept of 'horizon'. The horizon on the one hand limits one's sight, on the other hand necessarily hints at spaces beyond itself, and thus invites the surpassing of its own limits.

Whatever the conceptual reasons for the contentiousness of territory in the relations between sovereign entities, one can easily identify others of a purely historical nature. To begin with, throughout Europe the centers of rule acquired sovereignty, within each area, to a large extent by prevailing in battles over other power centers located within the same area, each seeking to maintain its own autonomy or indeed to compete, in turn, for sovereignty. For instance, over the course of generations the dynasty originally controlling the Ile de France had to make good its claim to kingship over a much wider territory by challenging, one after another, a large number of magnates, defeating their hosts, destroying their fortresses. Even when more peaceful processes were involved, such as – in the English case – the king sending his own judges to administer the common law over wider and wider circuits, the enterprise of asserting sovereignty had an intrinsic spatial momentum. It tended, over time, to push out from consolidated positions to exposed and contested peripheries, to stake out a wider and wider territory; and this momentum tended to carry over to the relations between a given sovereign unit, settled for some time within recognized boundaries, and other adjacent units.

A further root of this tendency lay in the cultural and economic physiognomy of the social groups which assisted the royal dynasties in their push for sovereignty. Most of those directly involved were aristocrats – greedy, quarrelsome people, keen to build up their fortunes from the proceeds of one military venture after another (Kautsky 1997). They inclined to cherish the opportunities for loot and acquisition represented by a military push beyond established boundaries. After all, such people were often the descendants of nomadic warriors and robbers, from whom they had inherited a rootlessness, an unwillingness to lock themselves within narrowly bounded locales. As the central ruler, in asserting his sovereignty, forbade the aristocrats to express these tendencies in feuds and private wars within the territory over which he ruled, the aristocrats developed a penchant for military adventure abroad. Besides, the cultural practices, the marriage policies of the European aristocracy often involved them in trans-local contacts and designs, and suggested to them dynastic aspirations favouring the spatial momentum of the sovereignty-building enterprise.

A further, related cause of the contentiousness of boundaries lies in an elementary military consideration. Seen from the center, the periphery of a territory has the vital import of distancing the center itself from direct attack, thus protecting it. Thus, outlying areas have a direct bearing on the problem of security. But the more the center's practices of rule extend uniformly over the territory, the more they solder the periphery to the center, making the former less and less distinguishable from the latter and more and more indispensable to it. To this extent, it made sense, in the light of the persistent problem of security, to add new outlying areas to those which had previously been incorporated within the whole. Once more, the spatial momentum tends to assert itself.

This last consideration, more explicitly than the previous ones, suggests an essential feature of the political environment consecrated by the Treaty of Westphalia – a plurality of sovereign, territorial states. Each of these is solely responsible for its own security, and is bound to consider it as potentially threatened by all the others' equal responsibility for their own security. Each state's denial of dependency upon and inferiority toward any other power necessarily throws it upon its own resources. In asserting interests threatened by other states (beginning with the interest in the integrity of its own territory – or in the acquisition of new territory) no sovereign state has the option of appealing to a superior political entity, producing and enforcing its own law. There is no place above the states, either physically or metaphorically, for such an entity; each must rely on 'self-help', on its factual ability to assert its own interests even when confronted by other states seeking to advance incompatible interests of their own.

The most fateful consequence of this circumstance has been spelled out long ago, with inimitable directness and authority, by Hobbes

> In all times, Kings, and Persons of Soveraigne authority, because of their Independency, are in continual jealousies, and in the state and posture of Gladiators; having their weapons pointing, and their eyes fixed on one another; that is, their Forts, Garrisons and Guns, upon the Frontiers of their Kingdomes; and continual Spyes upon their neighbours; which is a posture of warre (Hobbes 1953: 65).

In fact, 'warre' recurrently appears in the relations between European states as the ultimate way of settling conflicts of interest which cannot be settled otherwise. It does so by revealing, through a trial of force, which of the contending states is more mighty than the other. Thus it can compel the other to renounce its own designs and accept the realization of those of the winning party. Not all contrasts of interest are momentous enough to call for resolution through war, and many of them can be settled otherwise, or parties can learn to live with them. But which interests of a given state are momentous enough to justify pursuing them at all costs, which policies of other states threaten those interests directly enough to constitute enmity – such judgments must, by the nature of sovereignty, rest with each state. They constitute the most jealously guarded prerogative of whatever institution sees itself as the locus of sovereignty, be it the King, the King-in-Parliament, the supreme council of a republic, or (later) a national assembly.

In any case, while war itself is by nature an intermittent, contingent situation, a 'posture of warre' flows from the nature itself of sovereignty and is thus for all states, as they consider one another, a permanent condition, an inescapable burden. From this as from other aspects of the system derives, we have suggested, the particular significance of territoriality. Territoriality not only grounds and delimits the state, it also protects and projects the capacity for self-defence and if necessary for aggression on which the state's very existence as a sovereign entity ultimately depends. The gladiator's posture inexorably requires an *ubi consistam*, a firm location in space; but by the same token that location is the first thing to become an issue when two gladiators clash. Put otherwise, territory is what tends to make the relationship between any two contending states a zero-sum one.

Another way to construe territoriality relates instead to the internal aspect of sovereignty, and finds expression in the ascendance of *territorial* as against *personal* law. In asserting their own superiority over magnates and other power centers, Kings made much of the fact that those mostly claimed jurisdiction over relatively narrow locales, carved within the broader expanses of land making up the realms. These jurisdictions often crisscrossed one another, creating uncertainty over which body of law or custom would apply to which locales or to which relations within given locales. Furthermore, many of them originally owed their existence to private contracts between central rulers and local feudatories, who had subsequently usurped public powers and turned their backs on their patrons. Over against this situation (which tended to generate local, private wars) the King claimed to represent a distinctively public authority, reaching out into the political niches created by feudatories around their castles or their domains, encompassing even remote, forgotten corners of the realm, and claiming to produce and enforce the law of the land – a wide, more abstract space, comprising all manner of settlements, far and near, rural or urban, located on mountains, in valleys, or on plains.

The abstract nature of this space is suggested by the fact that German writers characterize the Westphalian kind of political unit as a *territorialer Flächenstaat*, a territorial state of the plains, although probably in Western Europe a state whose surface lies for more than 75 percent on a continuous plain is an exception. The French expression '*plat pays*', flat country, conveys the same emphasis on the continuity and homogeneity of the territory as against the variety of its physical features, which by itself would turn it instead into a set of strongly differentiated locales, possibly impervious to uniform central regulation.

The formation of regional estates in much of Western Europe in the late medieval period constituted a kind of way-station to a unitary conception of the state territory. On the one hand those estates established themselves (sometimes of their own initiative, sometimes at the ruler's behest) as public bodies transcending a variety of local jurisdictions, especially those based on feudal relations. They represented to the King the region as a whole, articulated its claims and committed its resources with regard to trans-regional policies. On the other hand, they tended to resist his preference for legal uniformity and for centralized decision-making, asserting the particularity of the region's customs and interests. In the long run, albeit to a different extent and with different vicissitudes from country to country, the ruler's centralizing drive won the day, projecting an ever more resolutely trans-local, territory-wide design of rule.

Simplified and over-generalized as it is, this account of the coming into being as territorial, sovereign units of most of the states involved in the Peace of Westphalia, suggests also their broad constitutional nature, as well as some aspects of the enduring logic of their operations. Essentially, we are dealing with monarchies, that is with polities where sovereign power is held by the current head of a royal dynasty. The monarch exercises that power within increasingly broad limits, ruling from his court but increasingly through an apparatus of councils, still largely manned, as we have already suggested, by aristocratic personnel.

The monarch is himself the first of the land's aristocrats, with whom he shares a dominant concern with the increase of his dynasty's patrimony and the enhancement of its glory. However, monarchs have the unique privilege of letting that concern inspire the land's public policies, beginning with those relating to other states. This is mostly an uncontested privilege, which means that dynastic interest is the acknowledged principle orienting a state's operations (with the exception of the few existent republics: Venice, the United Provinces, the Swiss Confederation. In the seventeenth century, for a while also England was a republic).

Two considerations suggest how powerful was the hold of that principle. In the first place, for quite some time the connection between the state and its territory was construed as a patrimonial one; that is, the monarch *owns* the land. Furthermore, the ownership in question resembles in nature that which had become the prevalent form of land-ownership, inspired by the Roman *dominium*, that is the owner's exclusive and unrestricted faculty of enjoying and disposing of his property in all its aspects, as against the earlier, feudal form, which allowed different aspects to be under the control of different subjects. Accordingly, a state's territory on occasion could be divided, and parts of it sold, or pawned.

Above all, in the second place, it was considered appropriate that possessions should accrue to the state's territories – thus, that the political map of Europe should change – not just according to the fortunes of war, but also by means of the royal dynasties' matrimonial alliances and the resultant dowries and hereditary entitlements. In a famous dictum addressed to Austria, war of conquest and judicious matrimonial alliances concerning the Habsburg children are considered as alternative strategies for territorial acquisition – *alii bella gerant, tu felix Austria nube*, let others wage wars, you happy Austria carry on marrying. In fact the two strategies intersect, as is indicated by the numerous and occasionally significant wars in the history of modern Europe fought over the very issue, *which* dynasty had a legitimate hereditary, marriage-grounded title to *which* land. Furthermore, the arrangement of matrimonial alliances was often a significant part of the settlement, through a peace treaty, of issues which the parties had just finished fighting over (Russell 1986: 86).

In any case, the rules of dynastic succession, including those pertaining to elected as against hereditary rulers, were for centuries widely agreed upon across Europe. They were clear and stable, and in the great majority of cases rendered the succession to a vacant throne unproblematical, allowing for remarkable genealogical continuity. In keeping with the dynastic principle, the rules also systematically allowed sovereigns to have among their subjects peoples of different languages and ethnic provenances.

What the Westphalian states share

The reader may begin to sense, at this point, some of the complexities concealed by 'the discourse of sovereignty', and lying behind the imagery of a plurality of mutually independent, sovereign, territorial states, permanently standing toward one another in 'the posture of Gladiators'. Such states, it turns out, all accept the dynastic principle (with the exception of the few republican states, which in fact acknowledge it for other states), and that principle underwrites the claims of all the crowned heads to unequalled authority and prestige, and induces them, among other things, to sponsor matrimonial unions between their respective lineages. It can be argued that around the dynastic principle there emerges considerable solidarity between European states, for the rulers of all major states share an interest: to have that principle persistently acknowledged as the foundation of the unity and continuity of each state.

What else, one may ask, do those mutually defiant Gladiators actually share? A great deal, it turns out. Chiefly, they hold in common a set of practices, many of them of fairly long standing, for dealing with one another, in peace or in war. Somewhat artificially, we may distinguish two components in those practices. The first is of an intellectual nature, a body of rules and principles, fairly widely agreed upon and understood to enjoy some legal validity, and originally referred to as *jus inter gentes*, literally 'law among peoples'. (The expression was first used in 1532 by one of the two greatest writers to expound those rules and principles, the Spanish monk Francisco de Vitoria; the other was the Dutch Protestant Hugo Grotius.) The second component is diplomacy: a complex of standing arrangements for the exchange of communications and informations between states, centered upon the activities of envoys (the most important of them called first 'orators', then 'ambassadors'). Diplomats on the one hand are committed to advancing the interests of the respective states, on the other increasingly see themselves as constituting together, across state lines as it were, a specialized, exclusive, highly skilled, prestigeful occupational body.

Furthermore, all European states share a sense that together they constitute, *vis-à-vis* the rest of the world, a privileged, peculiarly civilized community of political entities, profoundly marked by its century-old Christian heritage (however much the separate confessions may argue about the content of that heritage and about the related ecclesiastical structures). That community, furthermore, is also committed to some distinctive political values: for instance, the notion that proper rule should not be tyrannical and oppressive but embody justice, that is respect and enforce the land's customs and preserve the time-hallowed freedoms and advantages of (at least) the *meliores terrae*, the privileged element in the population; or the feeling that all political prerogatives, including the most exalted, are attributes of offices, of institutionally structured roles which do not only confer opportunities for glory and advantage but impose obligations on their holders. By virtue of their membership in such a community, all states recognize each other's existence as legitimate and treat each other, in principle, as equal parties.

Let us review this argument. Almost all European states subscribe to the dynastic principle as the ground of the legitimacy of rulers and they all consider it as a prime way of orienting, however broadly, their activities. In their mutual actions, even when these are hostile, those states respect some restraints originating from a diffuse body of quasi-legal rules and principles. Furthermore, their relations both hostile and non-hostile are to some extent patterned and tempered by a reliable, skilfully managed, flow of diplomatic communication. (Diplomacy does not terminate even during war, otherwise wars could not be terminated.) Finally, all states share a proud feeling (more and more self-consciously and complacently articulated in the two centuries after Westphalia) that they are part of a privileged community of civilized polities; together they constitute the political expression and articulation (in spite of confessional division) of the enduring reality of Christendom.

On all these accounts, Hobbes's 'Gladiators' are not just a set of actual or potential contestants engaged in, or keeping themselves in readiness for, a duel unto death; together, they also constitute, one might say, an Honorable Partnership of Gladiators. Protracted, large-scale war, when involving a majority of the greater states – and the Thirty Years War did involve them, a major exception being England – implies that the shared aspects of the partnership have somehow undergone an eclipse; but this, by its very nature, was meant to be temporary.

In the mid-seventeenth century resumption of inter-state business as usual was made difficult, among other things, by the fact that since the last decade of the previous century hostilities and animosities between Catholic states (or factions within states) and Protestant ones had been unusually bitter, to the extent of preventing the normal functioning of diplomatic activities (Magalhães 1988). On this account the Westphalian negotiations were particularly protracted, and had to be held in separate towns for Catholic and Protestant powers. However – and this is a further reason for considering Westphalia

1648 a landmark – they constituted the first major instance of what would be called today a multilateral negotiation, one involving more than two parties, and terminating therefore in a Peace Treaty of unusual scope and authority. The Treaty itself set a pattern for a number of subsequent attempts to impart some stability to the relations between European powers by convening to a 'congress' as many relevant participants as possible, in order to involve them all in underwriting and perhaps guaranteeing a settlement as wide-ranging and stable as possible.

We shall mention some of those attempts in due course. Meanwhile, let us point out that they constitute particularly infrequent, significant and solemn moments in an ongoing process of inter-state activity. The more frequent, diffuse, and routine aspect of that process is represented by two (sometimes more) states entering an agreement (frequently called a treaty) in order to regulate their interactions concerning a given matter – perhaps to control fishing in a body of water adjoining both states or to arrange common military activities in the face of what both states perceive as a potential or proximate threat to their security from a third state. This second kind of agreement – an alliance – is especially important because it imparts a structure to the apparently formless scatter of many discrete states standing toward each other in 'a posture of warre'. It generates potentially durable alignments between pairs of states (sometimes more) and prearranges their cooperative efforts in case of war against a common enemy.

Alliances

The alignments in question often register pre-existent commonalities among the states, based on their geographical proximity, similarities in their economic assets and in the resulting interests, genealogical relations between the respective ruling dynasties, cultural or linguistic or religious affinities between the peoples they rule, or whatever. But one should not overestimate how firmly and predictably these criteria sort out states as potential or actual enemies or allies, or neutral with respect to one another. Alliances provide an important scaffolding for inter-state relations, and colouring alike allied states on the map of Europe simplifies it significantly and gives a good sense of the prevailing policy orientations of existent states. However, each individual alliance is intrinsically a temporary arrangement, of uncertain duration. After all, as the Venetian ambassador to the Holy See reported Pope Leo X to have said, 'when a man has committed himself to one side, he must be careful to reinsure by negotiating with the other' (Wight 1973: 91).

There are reasons for the intrinsic tenuousness of the structuring principle represented by alliance policies. First, alliances are responses to two or more states' perceptions of threats from the same potential enemy or enemies; but such perceptions are very much a matter of judgment, and may vary more than the circumstances which they purportedly assess. Second, the circumstances themselves are likely to vary, particularly to the extent that, rather than being inexorably dictated by objective data, they consist in other states' dispositions to act in a friendly or hostile manner; and, in turn, those dispositions produce, or are evinced by, those other parties' alliances. Third, after an alliance is concluded a state excluded from it or indeed the very one against whom it has been negotiated can overtly or covertly, by means of threats or promises, induce one of the alliance partners to defect from the alliance, to enter a new alliance with itself, or at the very least to underperform its obligations toward the other partner(s). Fourth, as the previous point implies, an alliance is intrinsically a chancy undertaking, since it exposes each partner to two risks: that of being called upon to deliver military assistance to the other under conditions where its own interests are not actually threatened; on the other hand, that of seeing its partner fail to deliver the military assistance needed to fend off an actual threat. More broadly – fifth – like all cooperative endeavors, an alliance imposes burdens on each party in view of some advantages they may derive from cooperation; by the same token, however, it exposes each co-operator to the further risk of bearing a disproportionately high burden and deriving a disproportionately low advantage from the cooperation.

Of course these reasons for the fragility and unreliability of alliance arrangements apply also to many, more mundane kinds of undertakings, including the contracts we are often party to in our everyday private existence. In that context, however, those undertakings can be firmed up (to a greater or lesser extent) by legal mechanisms enforcing contracts, authoritatively monitoring their performance, exacting penalties for under- or non-performance, bindingly adjudicating disputes, and so forth. Thus, in the case of contracts for each party *quod antea erat voluntatis postea fit necessitatis* – what was originally a matter of voluntary choice has become a matter of constraint.

But this holds because the parties to the undertakings in question are not sovereign entities, and thus do not reserve to themselves the faculty of deciding autonomously with which of those undertakings or with which aspects to actually comply, in the light of their assessments of their own interests as they see them. But States *are* sovereign entities; explicitly or implicitly, they reserve the right to modify their own understanding of what they have committed themselves to when entering agreements with one another, including alliances, in the light of their unchallengeable judgment of where their interests lie in an ever-shifting constellation of circumstances. If their actions constitute violations of agreements, those violations, no matter how flagrant, can be redressed and those agreements enforced only through the 'self-help' of the other parties to those agreements. It is up to those parties to take the initiative for redress, and they must carry it out by committing their own might, at their own risk.

As we have insisted, there is no structure of authority arching over the individual states and in a position to 'lay down the law' to them, singly or collectively. The broad complex of rules and principles to which we have referred above, named successively *jus inter gentes*, *droit des gens*, international law, has, as a system of law, a rather peculiar nature since it possesses (as an ancient cynical saying has it) *ni loi, ni juge, ni gendarme* – 'neither statute, nor judge, nor policeman'. It claims *pacta sunt servanda*, 'agreements are to be kept' as its first principle; but it considers implicit to all inter-state agreements the clause *rebus sic stantibus*, 'as long as the situation remains the same'; which of course, miscreant states ever assert, it hardly ever does.

Of course there are constraints upon a state's potential preference for blithely disregarding agreed upon arrangements with another, be they alliances or of other nature; but they are mostly of a non-legal nature. Sovereign policy-makers are bound to consider that a state which in the past has earned a reputation as a frequent and blatant violator of agreements, betrayer of allies, can hardly expect to be sought as an ally and to enjoy the attendant benefits, whatever they are. It behoves a state, from this standpoint, to build up a record as a steadfast ally, or at least to be able to place a tenable construction upon its previous violations of agreed commitments.

To this last end, it also pays for states undertaking an alliance to insist on elaborately worded alliance agreements, specifying as closely as possible which circumstances – for instance, *which* kind of aggressive action on the part of which potential enemy would activate an engagement to offer military assistance to the ally, and which instead might justify a refusal to become so engaged. Above all, it is good policy to indicate precisely how long a given alliance is supposed to last, and when and how, before its termination, a state may give notice of its intention to withdraw from it. It may occasionally be useful to specify a 'third party' state whose good offices as a mediator two allies may seek in case of a dispute between them. It is in negotiating such clauses and subsequently finding for them the appropriate 'form of words' that diplomats specialize in. The resulting practices form to a large extent the substance of an evolving body of international law, still lacking 'statute, judge or policeman', but gaining some standing and some influence by the extent to which it codifies and systematizes such practices, and articulates a doctrinal justification for them.

We have insisted on the relatively tenuous nature of what we consider the chief structuring device of the system or inter-state relations – the alliance – for three reasons.

First, European states at the time of the Peace of Westphalia were little more (if anything) than machines for war-making, and to that extent the question of who might wage war alongside whom against whom – the question which alliances seek to address – goes to the heart of their policy concerns.

Second, by the same token the theme of the inherent impermanence and limited reliability of alliances points up a key characteristic of the European states system: its highly contingent nature, the rapidity with which it is liable to structure and de-structure itself by means of shifting alignments; hence the pressure of danger and fear of surprise borne by rulers and other decision-makers involved in its affairs. (Only a direct consideration of the 'fortunes of war' would reveal that characteristic even more sharply than the theme of alliance does.)

Third: at the same time, paradoxically, the phenomenon of shifting alliances betrays, at a higher level of abstraction, a stable ordering principle of the European states system, a way of making sense of its tendency intermittently to generate new alignments, often of short duration. This principle is the so-called balance of power.

The balance of power

In European history, this principle shows itself in operation for the first time in Renaissance Italy, where it is also originally theorized, for instance in the image of the Florentine ruler Lorenzo de Medici's as *l'ago della bilancia*, 'the needle of the scale'. It refers to what had been emerging as the dominant preoccupation of the several small states of the peninsula (many of them city-states): to prevent at all costs the rise in their midst of one state powerful enough to subjugate all others or otherwise to suppress their autonomous existence.

From this concern flowed one key rule of what might be called the operational code of those states: wherever one of them appeared to constitute a credible candidate for supremacy, it had to be challenged and contained, and if necessary eliminated, by a coalition of the others. The dominant partner in such a coalition, however, could always be expected in turn to seek to use its advantage to promote its own general supremacy once the other state's attempt had been defeated. Thus, each coalition on the one hand was intrinsically provisional, having no reason to be persisted once it had done its job; on the other hand, it was likely to be soon replaced by a new alignment.

This game was in principle never-ending, since at bottom each of the players nourished its own aspirations to supremacy; each of them saw in the current candidate to supremacy *son semblable, son frère*, and merely sought to keep it from accomplishing what, left to itself, it would also seek to accomplish. The ever-changing, ever-renewed outcome of the game was thus a dynamic equilibrium ('balance'), resulting from the pushes and counter-pushes of a succession of supremacy-seeking states and of coalitions intent on teaching each of them a lesson.

Attentive readers will note that such a view of the dynamics of a system suits particularly well one composed of sovereign, territorial states, each committed in the first place to keeping itself in being as a self-standing player, and having to do so chiefly by means of 'self-help', by mobilizing and deploying its own power. On this account, after the balance-of-power game had been played out in Italy (the local states played it so successfully against one another that they could not withstand, either singly or jointly, the overpowering hand played by foreign invaders) its logic was rediscovered and applied on the larger, European checkerboard in the seventeenth century, and theorized in the successive one.

Within the second decade of the eighteenth century, the Treaty of Utrecht (1713) expressly stated as its own purpose 'that the peace and tranquillity of the Christian world may be ordered and stabilized in a just balance of power, which is the best and most solid foundation of mutual friendship and a lasting general concord' (Wight 1973: 98). In the middle of the same century Eméric de Vattel, in his famous *Droit des gens* (1758) argued that the balance-of-power principle was the fulcrum of the 'political system' which in his view the European nations jointly constituted:

> Europe forms a political system in which the Nations inhabiting this part of the world are bound together by their relations and various interests into a single body. It is no longer, as in former times, a confused heap of detached parts, each of which had little concern for the lot of others, and rarely troubled itself over what did not immediately affect it. The constant attention of sovereigns to all that goes on, the custom of resident ministers, the continual negotiations that take place, make modern Europe a sort of republic, whose members – each independent, but all bound together by a common interest – unite for the maintenance of order and the preservation of liberty. This is what has given rise to the well-known principle of the balance of power, by which is meant an arrangement of affairs so that no State shall be in a position to have absolute mastery and dominate over the others (Vattel 1916: 251).

We follow Martin Wight's exposition (Wight 1973) in giving a brief account of the balance of power principle. Its first feature is the one we have repeatedly mentioned: the resolute disposition to prevent any single state from becoming strong enough to dominate all the rest. The key means to this end, the distribution of power among the states, does not have to confer the same amount of power to each – an intrinsically implausible condition, among other reasons because it could easily be subverted through the formation of alliances – but should be such as to confer upon each state some freedom of action.

The maintenance of this condition, furthermore, is seen as preserving a broader, collective value, often referred to as 'the liberties of Europe'. Indeed, a generally dominant power could be expected to behave tyrannically and in disregard of the principles of justice European states see themselves as deriving from the continent's Roman legacy and from the Christian tradition.

Also to be preserved through the balance of power is, as far as possible, a condition of stability and order among the states, from which also the civil society might benefit.

These values are of such significance that, in order to preserve them, the balance of power principle may occasionally override even dynastic right, although (as we have seen) the commitment to this right is common to almost all states. In particular, marriage alliances between ruling dynasties should not be allowed to produce all their legal effects when doing so would lead to the formation of an overwhelmingly powerful state. As Fénelon, a domestic critic of Louis XIV's hegemonic ambitions, put it, 'a particular right of succession or of donation must yield to the natural law which guarantees the security of so many nations' (Wight 1973: 102). Thus one key import of the Peace of Utrecht (1713) was to regulate the succession to the French and Spanish thrones in such a way that no individual could become the ruler of both.

Peace settlements constituted the standard device by which threats to the balance of power would be terminated. Each of them, of course, gave the balance a particular shape, generating a status quo which a war, and a successive peace, could legitimately modify. The balance, in other terms, was by nature a changeable, dynamic equilibrium, subject to the thrusts of each state's policies. In particular, Wight states (1973:128),

> To maintain the balance of power required flexibility of alliances. Every member of the states-system should be prepared to co-operate with any other member [...] as circumstances demanded, towards this great political end. There should be no political alignments or exclusion that overrode it.

And in fact, from the Peace of Westphalia through to our own times, '[e]very one of the grand alliances which have successively restored the balance of power has cut across doctrinal divisions, uniting Catholics and Protestants, constitutionalist states and despots, capitalist states and communist' (Wight 1973: 128).

In the intervals between the great peaces which reasserted it and reshaped it, the balance of power could only be maintained by the constant attention of each power to the immediate or potential threat which innumerable developments internal to individual states, or undertakings shared between a few of them, could pose to it. It was in monitoring and interpreting such shifting events, and in proposing and when necessary negotiating responses to them, that diplomacy had to prove its worth. But, in the nature of the case, those responses occasionally had to encompass the recourse to coercion, by individual states or by coalitions, against states whose policies threatened the balance. More broadly, to quote Wight again, in the presence of such a threat from a given state other states 'had a right, collectively and severally, of intervention, that is of interference in the domestic affairs of that state'; for, as the British Foreign Minister Castlereagh stated in a memorandum of 1818, 'no State has a right to endanger its neighbours by its internal Proceedings, and [...] if it does, provided they exercise a sound discretion, Their right of Interference is clear'(Wight 1973: 95).

That a balance of power system existed in post-Westphalia Europe does not mean either that no state enjoyed a degree of power superiority over the others, or that such a state would not attempt to convert such superiority into a position of visible, legitimate dominance. In fact, the whole period 1648–1815, following upon a century and a half of Spanish dominance, saw a de facto preponderance of France. (We adopt the periodization suggested by a German historian of international law, Wilhelm Grewe (Grewe 2000).) During the first century of that period the French monarch Louis XIV threatened to upset the balance of power by seeking to construct a Europe-wide imperial system, a kind of universal monarchy; during its last century Napoleon took up the same undertaking on a very different basis. However, in each case the balance of power withstood the challenge.

Chapter Eleven

The Genesis of Weber's Talks on the Vocations of Science and of Politics[*]

This paper discusses two texts originating from the last phase of Max Weber's life, known to English readers respectively as 'Science as a vocation' and 'Politics as a vocation' (Weber 1992). However, it deals not so much with their content as with their genesis, with reference both to what one may call its external context, that is the public circumstances under which each talk was given, and their internal context. By this we mean the place the themes of both talks held in Weber's mind, the value and significance he personally attributed to the distinctive activities respectively of the scientist (or scholar) and of the politician.

The sources

In treating this topic, but especially in dealing with what we have called the external context of the genesis of both texts, I shall avail myself of some secondary treatments of that topic, most especially the introductory and other editorial material contained in a volume of the *Max Weber Gesamtausgabe* (Weber's *Collected Works*) published in 1992, and containing both 'Wissenschaft' and 'Politik als Beruf' (Weber 1992). My discussion is hugely indebted to the extensive work of biographical and historical interpretation, textual reconstruction, or conceptual analysis, undertaken for that volume by

---

[*]   As I indicated in my Preface to this volume, much of my teaching and most of my writing have dealt with two broad thematic areas: 'classical' social theory (in lectures, essays or books on Tocqueville, Marx, Durkheim, Max Weber or Simmel) or the sociology of political institutions, signally the modern state. There has been some overlap between my contributions to these areas, especially those dealing with Max Weber, given the significance, in particular, of his theories regarding political processes and institutions.

   One text in particular, 'Politics as a vocation', always evoked and rewarded my attention, provoked to some extent by the disconcerting views Weber advanced in its last section on the phenomenon of political leadership in the context of democratic regimes.

   At some point, I decided to devote a book to a relatively extensive discussion, in two separate chapters, both of that text and of an earlier, companion one, 'Science as a vocation'. However, I subsequently abandoned that project, probably because I did not feel up to the challenge represented by the necessity, in dealing with science, of confronting philosophical and methodological issues with which I have always been ill-at-ease.

   Before abandoning the project of such a book, however, I had drafted an introductory chapter, dealing not so much with the substance as with the genesis of the texts in question. In later years, I expounded the contents of that chapter to a few audiences, mainly colleagues and advanced students. In this essay, the content of those presentations appears for the first time in print.

the two editors, Wolfgang J. Mommsen and Wolfgang Schluchter, and their collaborator Birgitt Morgenbrod.

Let it just be mentioned that the volume is approximately 300 pp. long, but less than half of these contain the texts themselves. The rest of the book (printed, *nota bene*, in considerably smaller type) contains commentaries specially written for this edition, to which should be added a largish number of footnotes added to the texts themselves. In this manner the editors, (and chiefly Schluchter, in his extensive and most penetrating Introduction to the volume as a whole) have clarified all the questions one might have asked about what we have labelled the genesis of the texts, and made our understanding of them much easier.

Previous to their joint appearance in the *Gesamtausgabe*, the original German texts had been published separately. 'Wissenschaft' had been incorporated by successive editors into a volume containing Weber's essays on methodology and related matters, 'Politik' into a volume containing his political writings. Interestingly, that separation had not been observed in at least three *foreign* editions of Weber's writings. In 1946 Hans Gerth and C. W. Mills had placed both 'Science as a vocation' and 'Politics as a vocation' at the beginning of their most successful collection *From Max Weber: Essays in sociology* (1946) destined to be reprinted innumerable times. In 1948 the Italian version of the two essays had constituted the content of *Il lavoro intellettuale come professione* (1948). 1959 had seen their publication in French in *Le savant et le politique* (1959). During all this time, as we said, the texts could be read in German only in two different volumes.

The circumstances of the original presentations of the texts

Both the texts we are dealing with were first presented by Max Weber, on two separate occasions, as public talks, the content of which he subsequently edited for publication (to what extent we do not know for sure). Both talks were given in Munich; the dates of them, definitively established not long ago, were respectively 7 November 1917 for the 'Wissenschaft' talk, 28 January 1919 for the 'Politik' talk. Later that year they were published as two distinct pamphlets of the same format.

What was going on at the time each talk was delivered, in Germany and in Weber's own life? By November 1917 the German empire had entered the fourth winter of what was to be called The Great War. Early in the war, in association with the forces of the Habsburg Empire, the army of the German Reich had broken the back of Germany's main opponent on the eastern front, Tsarist Russia, by routing its army.

After that it had easily dominated that front, first against the remnants of that army, then against whatever forces the Republic born of the Russian revolution of February 1917 had been able to field.

However, at the very time the 'Wissenschaft' talk was delivered, the October Revolution was taking place (it takes its name from the Russian calendar of the time, which lagged behind the Western one). An early outcome of the Bolshevik power take-over in those days was to be a hasty Russian surrender and then an armistice at Brest-Litowsk – an enormous though not long-lasting success for Germany.

Things, however, were NOT going well for the German Empire (and its main ally, the Habsburg Empire) on the Western front. Here the German army had begun to feel the adverse, and in the end decisive, impact of the entry of the United States into the war. Nor were they going well on what might be called the internal front. In fact, in Germany itself, though it remained territorially intact, the population was suffering deeply both from the huge human losses inflicted on the German armed forces by the Allied armies, and from the deprivations imposed on the country by continually worsening conditions as concerned supplies of food and other resources. Furthermore, the political climate had become very tense. The German High Command was imposing tight restrictions on public debate over the course and the purposes of the war, allegedly for the sake of maintaining morale, but with the effect of creating something of a military dictatorship over the domestic population.

As to Max Weber himself, the war had had a complex impact on his personal and professional circumstances. Early on, he had joined the army as a reserve officer – he had qualified as such while conscripted during his University studies – and had been assigned to administrative duties in a military hospital in his home town, Heidelberg. By the autumn of 1915, however, he had had to accept the fact that his age (he was 50 at the time the war started) and his physical and mental conditions, which had previously compelled him to retire from his teaching post at Heidelberg University and to assume there the position of a research professor, no longer allowed him to play an active military role.

From that point on, Weber had focussed his energies on two massive scholarly projects, his own comparative/historical study of the economic ethic of the world religions, and the editing of a large, collective work on the modern economic system. At the same time, however, he had entered the public arena by publishing essays and occasionally giving talks on major political affairs – not day-to-day ones, rather such themes as the changes in the German constitution which he expected to become mandatory after the end of the war, whatever its outcome, or broad issues of foreign policy and strategy.

In 1917, finally, both the March and the October revolutions in Russia had re-activated in Weber a long-standing interest in Russian affairs, which again was to find expression in two substantial essays, the last of which – commenting on the outcome of the Bolshevik takeover – were written and published after Weber had given the 'Wissenschaft' talk. One of the major themes of the latter, the notion of 'value-freedom' (to use the conventional rendering of the German expression *Wertfreiheit*) had already been explored by Weber in a major essay a few months before.

By the time of the 'Politik' talk – late January 1919 – both the public situation and Weber's personal circumstances had changed: dramatically the former, substantially the latter. Germany had lost the war. A Republic had been proclaimed and was being governed chiefly by representatives of parties previously excluded from the experience of rule.

Some parts of the country were in turmoil. In particular, in the capital of Bavaria, Munich, where both talks were given, a motley crowd of alienated intellectuals, previously persecuted politicians, and bohemians, had established a so-called 'republic of the councils' (where the term 'council' was expressly a translation of the Russian 'Soviet') which had tried ineffectually to proclaim the city's independence of Berlin AND to rule over the rest of Bavaria.

The mood of the allies toward their defeated enemies was distinctly punitive, and was about to find expression in the harsh terms of the Versailles *diktat*, such as the termination of German rule over sizeable territories both east and west, the dismantling of the German army, and the imposition of unbearably heavy financial 'reparations'.

Somehow this situation, while it constituted a personal, deeply felt tragedy for a keen German nationalist such as Max Weber, also energized him. Aware as he had been of the fact that the Hohenzollern dynasty had grievously failed the German nation, he had regretted the sudden proclamation of a Republic. However, not long after that, he had publicly accepted that event as *a fait accompli*. The Republic was now the political framework within which one was forced to operate in order to confront and remedy the country's disastrous situation.

In that framework, at the time still ill-defined and contested, Weber chose to perform a more openly public and expressly political role than before. (Previously his keen interest in political matters had found public expression mainly in articles commenting on current matters.) He became a prominent member of the German Democratic Party – a middle-class party committed to the new republican order – gave a number of acclaimed talks on its behalf, and was urged to present himself a candidate on its ballot. He considered the possibility and decided against it, but indicated that he would keep himself ready for such a commitment in the near future.

Meanwhile, Weber was for a time a member of the German delegation to the Versailles peace conference. He also made a significant input into the drafting of the new German constitution (the so-called Weimar constitution). He even took it upon himself to try (in vain, as it happened) to persuade General Ludendorff – who as the chief of the German General Staff had become something of a dictator in the last phase of the war – to deliver himself to the Allies and be put on trial for war crimes. Alongside these activities Weber continued to operate as a publicist and took part in debates on a number of the dramatic issues raised by defeat, the subsequent social and political disorder, and constitutional change.

This outburst of activity (mostly undertaken with great determination though in a pessimistic spirit) was not limited to Weber's political involvements. Not only did he continue to pursue energetically the two big research-and-writing commitments we mentioned earlier. Not long before giving the 'Wissenschaft' talk he had also decided to try and return to the other academic task – lecturing on a regular basis – which he had abandoned over ten years earlier, feeling psychologically incapable of performing it properly.

This decision, as soon as it was known, brought Weber various offers. He chose at first to accept an invitation from the University of Vienna, where in the summer semester of 1918 he gave a most successful course. It was while holding this post that he returned to the Bavarian capital to give his talk on 'Science as a vocation'. In the subsequent months, after the bloody end of the tragic-comical episode of the Munich 'council republic', and after turning down the offer of a chair in Vienna, he accepted instead a call from Munich University, and undertook there a full schedule of teaching. It was while he held this post that Max Weber fell ill with pneumonia and died in the early summer of 1920, several months after the simultaneous publication of the edited and extended texts of the two 'Beruf' talks.

Student life in Weber's Germany

We continue this account of the circumstances both public and personal under which the two texts came into being by considering what occasioned the two talks where they first took form. This question has been extensively addressed by the editors of the relevant volume of the *Max Weber Gesamtausgabe*, and it is wholly on the results of their inquiries that the following account rests. Following their lead, we come to answer the question, *on whose behest were the talks given?*, by way of a digression into Weber's relation to the associational aspect of student life in the Germany of his time.

As a University student at Heidelberg Max Weber had joined *Alemannia*, one of several student corporations (*Burschenschaften*) active at the time (some still are!) at various German Universities. The nature of the *Burschenschaften* is not easily characterized. They were of course voluntary associations of young men attending University, but differed on some counts from the student organizations of our own time, although the American fraternities vaguely remind one of some aspects of them, beginning with the fact that normally the members resided on the local premises of their association.

Most *Burschenschaften* had their origins in the rather distant past, and cultivated a keen sense of continuity with it. Each inherited from its traditions various symbols of collective identity – not just its name but a flag, an anthem, insignia, a ceremonial garb to be held at recurrent occasions. They all cultivated a code of conduct and a set of practices reminiscent of the earliest student corporations – distinctive collective rituals, festive occasions focussed on choral singing and boisterous drinking. They typically produced within their members a keen and potentially lasting sense of affiliation to their own *Burschenschaft*, thus of brotherhood with one another. Most *Burschenschaften* established chapters within several universities, and to those went the primary loyalty of members. But there were also bonds between the chapters, broader identifications of their members with the entire *Burschenschaft*, across the academic map of Germany.

To these traditional features, the nineteenth-century German student corporations had added a peculiar emphasis on a quasi-military sense of honour – dramatised by the practice of ritual (but not bloodless) duelling – and a tendency to assume or to cultivate in their members an outspoken, aggressive patriotism and nationalism. On these and other accounts, the *Burschenschaften* were socially exclusive. Even within the relatively small constituency of German university students, the mechanism of co-optation of new members by the existent ones favoured students from wealthier, more established backgrounds, with a more conservative orientation on social and political matters. Among those excluded (not necessarily in formal terms) were not just students from less privileged social groups, unable to fund the perquisites of membership (such as fencing lessons and equipment, and regular attendance at drinking parties), but also women, Jews and anybody with unconventional political and ideological propensities.

Membership in a *Burschenschaft* was supposed to be held for life, though naturally in a more attenuated fashion after the members had left university, and to commit those holding it to trust and support one another whenever they interacted. Though as we have seen each corporation had traditions and requirements of its own, and the primary obligation of loyalty and mutual recognition applied within each, all *Burschenschaften* shared a broad code, and a keen sense of constituting, within each University's student body, and thus within German youth at large, a social elite, destined to hold more exalted and exalting positions in adult life.

In his salad days at University (first Heidelberg then Berlin), Max Weber practiced and valued his own membership in *Alemannia*, but later became more critical of the *Burschenschaften* in general. They embodied and fostered among the scions of the bourgeoisie Germany a tendency he had come to consider a major problem of Wilhelmine Germany: to a large extent the members of its bourgeoisie (the class which Weber expressly called his own) accepted and indeed endorsed the general superiority of the *Junker* stratum and its entitlement to rule the country. They sought to hang on to such views, and to the correlated nationalistic and militaristic feelings, even in the face of the national disaster the Great War was coming to represent. On that account, in Weber's judgment the political preferences typical of the members of the

German bourgeoisie had become more and more anachronistic. Indeed, they represented an obstacle to the changes imposed on the German social and political order by the country's defeat, the demise of the Hohenzollern ruling dynasty, and the advent of the Republic.

Weber had publicly prospected some significant changes in the constitution of the Reich even when it still seemed that the war could be won and the Empire maintained. After those expectations had been brutally negated by the course of events in 1918, one of the ways in which he expressed his willingness to accept the end of the old order was his decision to resign from *Alemannia* (November 1918). That association and the others of the same kind seemed incapable of accepting, let alone actively participating in, the process of democratization which in Weber's opinion would have been inevitable even under a reformed constitutional monarchy, and which the proclamation of the Republic rendered even more urgently necessary.

But the *Burschenschaften* were not the only associations of University students in imperial Germany. In more or less explicit opposition to them, others had been founded in the second half of the nineteenth century or successively, sometimes with the claim or the intent to represent the student body as a whole as against the relatively narrow constituencies of the *Burschenschaften*. Accordingly, these associations had more modern, less exclusive organizational structures. (One may get a sense of this contrast by recalling how in the mid-twentieth century US some groupings of students, mostly housed in dormitories and cooperative houses, felt about and opposed the fraternities and sororities, all of them with their own residences, each marked by a different trio of characters from the Greek alphabet – hence the designation of their residents as 'the Greeks'.)

But there was variety also among these associations, and there were contrasting orientations, to some extent sharpened by the confrontation with the dreadful events of the war and their dramatics outcomes. Students and former students had died in their thousands, and others had remained physically or mentally maimed and impaired. Both before and during the war, Weber took an intense interest not so much in the organizational life of such associations as in the cultural, moral, and political views they espoused and in the issues their activities raised. More generally, he kept himself attuned to the youth movements of his own time, though he was often critical of them. (He was also attentive to, and well-disposed toward, what today we would call *feminist* initiatives and organizations.)

The initiative leading to the two talks

In 1917 an association called *Freistudentischer Bund* (literally, 'League of free students') – or, more precisely, its Bavarian chapter, based at the University of Munich – took the initiative to sponsor a series of public talks by prominent personalities on the general theme of *Geistige Arbeit als Beruf* – 'Intellectual work as a vocation'. We might characterize the general tendency of the association in question as left-of-center. Its constituency comprised a relatively high number of Jews, young women, and individuals whose views on political, social, and cultural matters were more progressive than those entertained by the majority within the student body, and definitely at variance from those the *Burschenschaften* inculcated into their own membership.

Immanuel Birnbaum, a member and local leader of the League who had taken the responsibility of organizing the series, many years later gave a detailed account of the circumstances. He relates among other things that some other members would have preferred to have the theme of 'Politics as a vocation' addressed not by Weber, who had already been asked by talk on 'Science as a vocation', but by a prominent Jewish intellectual, Kurt Eisner, at the time President of the short-lived Munich republic. (Eisner was to be assassinated shortly after Weber's second talk by a right-wing fanatic, Count Arco. In due course, Weber would oppose, as a matter of principle, the decision to spare Arco the death penalty.)

A third personality, the Protestant pastor and publicist Friedrich Naumann (who was on good terms with Weber) had also been considered as a speaker. In any case, some left-wing students disappointed by the choice of Weber as a speaker on politics tried to disrupt his performance. Of Weber's two talks the first, 'Wissenschaft' had by far the most favorable public reception, although a number of people witnessed later to the powerful impression made upon them by both presentations.

The fact itself that the Munich chapter of the *Freistudentischer Bund* had chosen *Geistige Arbeit als Beruf* as the theme of a series of talks addressed in the first place to the local students, had a somewhat polemical import, suggesting again that the League held a left-of-center position on the spectrum of concerns and perspectives prevalent among German students at the time.

'Beruf' is a complex notion, to the extent that the expression itself raises problems for translators. In English, one might translate it as 'calling, 'vocation', 'profession' or 'occupation'. In fact, an English translation of 'Politik' from the 1990's, has at its title 'The *profession AND vocation* of politics' (Weber 1994). In any case, however you translate it, the title itself of the series of talks implied that intellectual pursuits of the kind cultivated by Universities could legitimately serve to prepare individuals for their occupational future, and was intended to prospect some professional positions worth aspiring to.

Now, this view, obvious as we may consider it today, was somewhat controversial in the particular context in which the *Freistudentischer Bund* sponsored the series of talks. It opposed the view that the University experience was chiefly intended, instead, to endow individuals with *Bildung* – another complex, hard-to-translate expression, akin to the French 'formation' or the Italian 'formazione'. On this view, you went to University in order to become an educated individual, a cultivated person. This entails exploring and familiarising oneself with the noblest intellectual and artistic products of the past, enriching one's own soul and intellect. The point of the University experience was NOT, instead, to train, and to qualify, for a professional position in the society's occupational structure.

The title of the series sponsored at Munich by the *Freistudentischer Bund*, and more broadly the ideology of the league and of other student associations of the same nature, did not deny some validity to *Bildung* as *one* goal of the University experience, but definitely denied it *exclusive* validity. Whatever else a University education was for, it was appropriate to focus it also on the professional positions for which it qualified students.

The *Gesamtausgabe* edition of the two 'Beruf' texts relates that in 1917 an influential young intellectual, Alexander Schwab, had aggressively articulated a contrary view, – extolling *Bildung* and disparaging *Beruf* – which had a long and glorious past in German academic culture, and on that account a somewhat archaic tone to it. Rehearsing several motifs within the German tradition of critique of modernity and of the West, Schwab had focussed on 'Beruf' as a central aspect of both those targets. According to him, to focus one's education on training for an occupational position posed a real danger for a young individual's moral, cultural and intellectual development. The very idea of it was something monstrous, a 'modern perversity', typically associated with American practices. In fact, according to Schwab, in the proper view of things, inspired by the Greek notion of *paideia*, an individual's occupational achievement itself would constitute, 'no honor, but at best a form of success […] and sometimes indeed a shame'.

The resonance and approval accorded to this view of Schwab's by his readers, according to the *Gesamtausgabe*, provided the stimulus for the *Freistudentischer Bund*'s talk series on 'intellectual work as a profession' at Munich. We translate with 'intellectual' the expression *geistig* (following the lead of the Italian translation of the two 'Berufe'). But that expression is an adjective deriving from *Geist*, meaning 'spirit'; another expression with the same root, *Geistliche*, refers to a minister of religion. This suggests, again, that the title itself of the series had a somewhat polemical intent and import, for it paired something generally understood as noble and lofty (*Geist*) with something which, at any rate in Schwab's well-publicised views, was common if not tawdry – *Beruf*.

In his two talks Weber did not waste much time in attacking Schwab's views, and those of other authors who abhorred *Beruf*, but argued explicitly and compellingly that in the modern world it was necessary, not to mention appropriate, to focus one's life on an occupation, indeed to make the preparation for it and the practice of it the center of one's moral life.

The two talks by Weber were, so far as one can find, the only ones actually offered in the series. Others, concerning respectively 'education', 'art' and 'religion' were planned, but there is no evidence that they were ever given, and at any rate were not subsequently published as Weber's did. Those two, as we have already indicated, had been originally presented *as talks*, not read, and according to all indications from contemporary witnesses the actual delivery of them was, we would say today, quite a performance.

In the case of 'Politik' we happen to have two separate but overlapping sets of scribbled notes where Weber constructed a fairly detailed outline of his presentation, though probably one set was intended for another, lesser public discussion of a related topic, offered by Weber more or less at the same time, but never intended for publication. The *Gesamtausgabe* text of 'Politik' comprises both a photographic version of those notes in Weber's own hand (they were apparently jotted down on the backs of envelopes, but the physical originals were not preserved after being photographed) and a printed version of their content. Furthermore, the *Gesamtausgabe* reproduces that content as a set of headings alongside the text, allowing readers to use them as signposts to their own reading.

The contents of the talks were taken down by professional short-hand specialists as they were being delivered, and the transcriptions of those shorthand notes were delivered to the author, who corrected them and added to them to an extent we cannot precisely determine. Thus edited, the texts were printed sometime in 1919, as two separate brochures. It is the content of these that is reproduced in the *Gesamtausgabe*, accompanied, as we indicated, by a wealth of introductory and editorial materials. This arrangement, one might suggest, amply compensates for the fact that previously, as suggested above, the original texts had appeared in two separate volumes.

The internal context

So much, then, for what we have called the external context of the genesis of the two texts discussed in this volume, including the occasions of their being first presented as talks, and subsequently published. The balance of this paper discusses some aspects of what we called the internal context of that genesis. That is: what did it *mean*, for Weber, to find himself discussing the nature of both science and politics, each seen as a potential professional pursuit? What personal resonances did each theme evoke in him? What place did both science and politics occupy in his biography, as well as in his aspirations, in his understanding of what might make his life meaningful?

Max Weber himself did not expressly address these questions in the talks themselves. His remarks on the nature respectively of 'science' and of 'politics' do not have a retrospective, much less an autobiographical slant. Of course much of what Weber said in the two talks did draw upon his personal experiences, which were often at variance with those of his contemporaries. For instance, his repeated and relatively elaborate remarks on how both science and politics were practiced in the United States, are grounded on the impressions he had formed during a fairly long stay he had made in that country in 1905. Subsequently, he had continued to take a keen interest in what went on in America – an interest which, we surmise, very few people in his academic milieu shared with him. Also, when he argues that often journalists are much more honorable men than they are generally supposed to be, he assures his audience that this remark reflects his personal experiences with journalists.

Finally, his pointed assertion that in no other professional career mere chance plays as great a role as in the academic profession may have been inspired to an extent by his own career. Having qualified himself for a faculty position in *law* and/or in *classical history*, he had found himself called by the University of Freiburg to its chair in *economics*. This, it seems, on account of the active and productive role he had found himself performing in *non*-academic inquiries into the contemporary situation of the rural population in the Eastern part of Germany. What had been for him an *a*-vocational undertaking had the unexpected result of his becoming professionally associated, for the rest of his life, with a discipline – economics itself – with which he had very little previous familiarity and within which he never felt wholly at ease. Although such past experiences informed to an extent the content of Weber's *Beruf* talks, he definitely did not treat his speaking assignments at Munich, in 1917 and 1919, as an opportunity to muse and discourse at length on the personal significance of lessons taught him by his own involvement in either of science or politics. As he says expressly at the beginning of 'Politik', he wants to go straight to 'the matter at hand'; furthermore, he deals with it from the perspective not of the past but of the immediate future, icy and dark as it may be.

His arguments in both talks were clearly intended in the first place for young men, particularly of course for those currently at Universities. Weber, especially in the later phase of his life, was aware of and variously encouraged and assisted the slow-moving progress of women into positions from which they had been previously utterly excluded, beginning with higher education. But the individuals he seems to envisage as constituting the audience of his talks *are* chiefly young men. It is in the first place to them that Weber indicates, to put it simply, *what it takes* for young adults to commit themselves to the professions respectively of science and of politics, in view of the requirements these pursuits impose on individuals in the contemporary world, and the opportunities they represent.

Weber's constant emphasis lies on the objective nature of those pursuits, on the moral and intellectual challenges they pose, on the renunciations they require, on the structure of the institutions within which they are normally practiced. There is not as much express concern with *what it feels like* to practice them, except perhaps to condemn some potentially dangerous emotions, for instance vanity in the case of 'politics as a vocation'.

Much less, as we already suggested, is there anything like a confessional unburdening of the speaker, an express revelation of what science/politics meant *to Max Weber himself*. Interestingly, when presenting his second theme, he made no overt reference to the first, addressed to the same constituency some months before. Also, neither talk refers to his famous earlier essay of 1904–05, *The Protestant Ethic and the Spirit of Capitalism*, where he had for the first time discussed at length the notion of *Beruf*. In fact, one may well surmise that one reason why the name of Max Weber had occurred to the organizers of the Munich talk series was that he was still identified, years later, chiefly as the author of *The Protestant Ethic*, and thus as the proponent of a distinctive, elevated view of the potential moral significance of the practice of a profession.

In spite of this, I do not deem it inappropriate to raise the question of what science and politics did mean to Max Weber; indeed, this is what I mean by the 'internal context' of the genesis of the two texts. I do not approach this topic, however, by narrating how Weber came to practice science, by recounting his own (tormented) career as a scholar, or by detailing the various aspects of his prolonged (though discontinuous) engagement with the politics of his own time. There are excellent books that do that, drawing among other things on Weber's correspondence, on the views he expressed, privately or in public, on political or scholarly issues, on what his contemporaries thought about those views, and so on. What we consider below, is the personal resonance those pursuits found in him, his answers to the question 'what of it?' which, one surmises, must have been raised by the demands of his professional experience as a scholar, and his assiduous observation of, and occasional involvement in, contemporary political affairs.

The uneasy relation between science and politics

Bearing in mind, then, that Weber was in the first instance a scholar, but one passionately involved in politics (above, I mentioned some aspects of this involvement in the last few years of his life), I suggest that the relationship between these two dimensions of his personal experience was loaded with tensions, and engendered something like a sense of tragedy. I develop this argument in three steps.

(1) Weber was acutely aware that science and politics were two sharply opposed realms of human experience. An agent could deal competently with the demands and opportunities of each realm only by fostering and mobilising within her/himself subjective qualities and capacities strongly contrasting with those appropriate to the other realm.

This view, it should be noted, does not hold only for those two realms of experience. In a number of texts, including both 'Wissenschaft' and 'Politik', Weber put forward what he called a 'polytheistic' view of life. Drawing on a suggestion from J. S. Mill, he argued that the world, and human existence, are essentially disorderly, for they possess no intrinsically valid meaning and no objectively given center. They can only be ordered subjectively, by the agent's committing her/himself to the prior significance of one of life's multiple, contrasting aspects over against all others – by her/his worship of one god to the neglect of all others asking for allegiance.

One reason why Weber was fascinated by the historical experience of the Jewish people was probably that the covenant between the children of Israel and Jahweh exemplifies and dramatizes an essential human paradox. Sometimes, in the Bible, it is as if Jahweh tells the Jews, 'Do you see all those other Gods? *They* are not there, only *I* am.' The children of Israel ground their identity, as we would say today, and depend for their collective survival and success, on deliberately ignoring all alternative allegiances, on their passionate commitment to one God *as if* it were the only one.

Similarly, at bottom each individual can make sense of her/his life, orient her/himself in the world, only by centering her/his existence on the demands and opportunities of one central pursuit, and ignoring or sharply downgrading others, although in principle these might offer the individuals equally valid understandings of reality and directives for action.

Furthermore, the Gods worshipped respectively by the men of science and by the men of politics are in strong opposition to one another. The former, if they embrace *their* God firmly enough to center on it their own existence, are committed chiefly to objectivity, impartiality, abstention from the passing of value judgment and from the interference of practical preferences into professional activity. This, if competently conducted, should eventuate in findings and arguments compelling the assent of whoever is interested in premising her/his action on objectively givens, even while remaining oriented to different value premises and goals.

Men of politics, on the other hand, are necessarily committed to one goal: promoting the fortunes and enhancing the power of one singular collectivity – be it (in the modern world) a nation or a party. Accordingly, their activity must be appraised and sanctioned according to whether and to what extent it accomplishes this goal. They operate necessarily in a situation of latent or open conflict, and are expected to make a difference to the outcome of conflict by seeking exclusively to advance the interests of that collectivity, and damn all others. They are NOT expected to be impartial but to be partisan. When the situation requires it, they must be able to say, 'right or wrong – my country!/ my party!'.

(2) Weber was a man of science through and through, and his public persona was chiefly that of a scientist. HOWEVER, he often proclaimed that political values were more significant for him as a person than those pertaining to the practice of his own profession. There was nothing in which he was personally more interested than the might and power of the German nation. His keen awareness that the political institutions of Imperial Germany prevented the emergence of gifted and effective leaders and condemned the Empire's policy to being incompetently and irresponsibly conducted, caused him keen anguish and, during the war, a sense of despair.

Interestingly, this existential commitment to what one might call 'the primacy of politics' reflected itself, more or less directly, also in Weber's scholarly work. Let us take three examples.

(a) In 1895, in his inaugural lecture at Freiburg, the young professor of economics proclaimed that his own discipline made sense only as a *political* discipline, to be explored, taught, practiced with a keen sense that the interests of the German nation trumped, so to speak, any narrowly conceived economic interest. While declaring his affiliation with the German bourgeois class, Weber refused to celebrate the remarkable economic successes of that class because it had not stepped forward to claim its political birth-right, to acknowledge its responsibility for, and assert its entitlement to, guiding the nation in its pursuit of power. He blamed the Junker stratum for managing their estates with an eye chiefly to economic advantage, and allowing a process of 'polonization': that is, an increasingly dense settlement on their estate by Polish peasants, that potentially compromised the security of Germany's eastern border.

(b) A letter of Weber's reveals to his correspondent (a famous German theologian) that there was, so to speak, a political sub-text to his most famous essay, *The Protestant Ethic*, which ostensibly considers only the relation between the religious and the economic spheres. Apparently Weber was motivated to write it also by his ambivalent feelings toward his Lutheran background. For all its merits from other viewpoints, he felt, the persistent Lutheran imprint on contemporary German culture had negative political consequences. The prevalent, excessively submissive attitude toward authority, generated the German public's unwillingness to take charge of its own political affairs. On account of the Lutheran legacy, unlike the English and the French, the Germans had never committed the ultimate act of political self-affirmation – the beheading of a King!

(c) According to Reinhard Bendix's authoritative view of Weber's scholarly work, a significant trend in that work during the last years of Weber's life had been the progressive emphasis on political institution, and something of a turn away from sociology toward political science. In spite of its title, *Economy and Society*, his unfinished masterpiece, was to affirm this development by devoting much attention to matters of law and politics, culminating in what Weber himself called a *Staatssoziologie*.

Putting the matter plainly, then, Max Weber was stuck in a professional role in the sphere of science while expressly proclaiming the priority of politics among his personal concerns. Respected as he was as a commentator on affairs of policy (especially foreign and constitutional policy) he yearned in vain to prove himself in a more active and responsible role. In the years during which he presented his 'Wissenschaft' and his 'Politik als Beruf', however, Weber, was becoming progressively convinced that he had to abide by his proven vocation as a scholar rather than reaching out for a chance to prove himself in the practice of politics, and to assist and perhaps lead his country in confronting its dire circumstances.

(3) Finally, Weber had reasons to feel that in *both* the sphere of science and in that of politics he had been something of a failure. As far as politics is concerned, we have indicated that his aspiration to play a significant, perhaps a leading role in public life remained unfulfilled. Even as a commentator, especially as concerns a number of foreign policy issues, one might have said of him that he suffered the plight of the mythical prophetess Cassandra – always to foresee correctly the future and announce it, BUT never to be believed.

As far as science is concerned, it is difficult to understand what grounds Weber might have had for not considering himself a success – unless one knows something of his biography. In 1904 he had powerfully signalled his return to the world of active scholarship, having overcome at last the painful depressive condition which had started in 1897 and nearly paralysed him for the next 5–6 years. Subsequently, in spite of occasional relapses into that condition, he had – we might say today – maintained a high profile through his publications and other scholarly activities. But, as we have already indicated, he had *not* been able to resume teaching – and he perceived this as a critical disability, which he had only unsuccessfully tried to overcome. So far as he was concerned, that disability markedly diminished him as a man of science, and gave him a galling sense of professional impotence. As long as he could not regularly confront an audience of University students, he felt that he was not personally living up to the specific honor of the academic scholar. Even after accepting a trial appointment at Vienna and experiencing a great success in his teaching there, he felt that the practice of teaching took too much out of him. All indications are that he performed even better in his subsequent appointment at Munich: but it is doubtful that to him such success (again, achieved through great effort) made up for the failure sustained during the previous twenty years.

I have thus tried to give the reader an idea of the complex and to an extent painful resonances that the themes of 'Wissenschaft' and of 'Politik' – both singly and jointly, one might say – had for Weber as a person.

Bibliography

Anderson, B. (1983) *Imagined Communities: Reflections on the Origin and Spread of Nationalism*, London: Verso.

Anter, A. (1996) *Max Weber's Theorie des modernen Staates*, Berlin: Duncker & Humblot.

Assmann, J. (2000) *Herrschaft und Heil: Politische Theologie in Altägypten, Israel und Europa*, Munich: Hanser.

Beller, E. A. (1970) 'The thirty years war' in *New Cambridge Modern History*, vol 4, Cambridge: Cambridge University Press.

Bobbio, N. *et al.* (eds) (1983) *Dizionario di Politica*, Torino: UTET.

Brunner, O. (1956) *Neue Wege der Sozialgeschichte*, Göttingen: Vandenhoeck & Ruprecht.

Caffè, F. (1978) *Lezioni di politica economica*, Torino: Bollati Boringhieri.

Calvez, J. (1995), *Politique: Une Introduction*, Paris: Aubier.

Cloward, R. A. and Piven, F. (1975), *The Politics of Turmoil*, New York: Vintage Books.

Cohen, J. and Arato, A. (1992) *Civil Society and Political Theory*, Cambridge, Mass: MIT Press.

Coleman, J. S. (1974) *Power and the Structure of Society*, New York: Norton.

Collins, R. (1975) *Conflict Sociology: Toward an Explanatory Science*, New York: Academic Press.

Crouch, C. (2011) *The Strange Non-death of Neo-liberalism*, Cambridge: Polity Press.

De Jasay, A. (1998) *The State*, Indianapolis: Liberty Fund.

Di Palma, G. (2013) *The Modern State Subverted: Risk and the Deconstruction of Solidarity*, Colchester: ECPR Press.

Easton, D. (1965) *Systems analysis of political life*, New York: Wiley.

Eisenstadt, S. N. (1993, 2nd ed) *The Political Systems of Empires*, New Brunswick: Transactions Publishers.

Ertman, T. (1997) *Birth of the Leviathan: Building States and Regimes in Medieval and Early Modern Europe*, Cambridge: Cambridge University Press.

Etzioni, A. (1975) *A Comparative Analysis of Complex Organizations*, New York: Free Press.

Field, G. L. and Higley J. (1980) *Elitism*, London: Routledge.

Finer, S. (1976) *Man on Horseback: The Role of the Military in Politics*, Harmondsworth: Penguin.

Gehlen, A. (1988) *Man: His Nature and Place in the World*, New York, Columbia University Press.

Gellner, E. (1969) *Plough, Sword and Book: The Structure of Human Society*, Chicago: University of Chicago Press.

— (1994) *Conditions of Liberty: Civil Society and its Enemies*, New York: Viking.

Greenspan, A. (2007) quoted in http://deutschlandradiokultur.de/die-krise-der-demokratie.1270.de.html?dram:article id=249382

Grewe, W. G. (2000) *The Epochs of International Law*, Berlin-New York: De Gruyter.

Habermas, J. (1991) *The Structural Transformation of the Public Sphere*, Cambridge, Mass: MIT Press.

Hayek, F. (1960) *The Constitution of Liberty*, Chicago: Chicago University Press.

Hinsley, F. H. (1966) *Sovereignty*, New York: Basic Books.

Hirschman, A. O. (1997) *The Passions and the Interests: Political Arguments for Capitalism Before its Triumph*, Princeton: Princeton University Press.

Hobbes, T. (1953) *Leviathan,* New York: Dutton.

Holsti, K. J. (1991) *Peace and War: Armed Conflicts and International Order*, Cambridge: Cambridge University Press.

Hondrich, K. O. (1982) (ed.) *Soziale Differenzierung: Langzeitanalysen zum Wandel von Politik, Arbeit und Familie*, Frankfurt: Campus Verlag.

Johnson, S. (2009) 'The quiet coup', *The Atlantic*, May 2009.

Jouanna, A. (1989) *Le devoir de révolte:la noblesse française et la gestation de l'Etat moderne, 1559–1661*. Paris: Fayard.

Jouvenel , de B. (1962) *On Power:Its Nature and the History of its Growth*, Boston: Beacon Press.

Karlson, N. (1993) *The State of State*, Uppsala: Almvist & Wiksell.

Kautsky, J. H. (1997) *The Politics of Aristocratic Empires*, New Brunswick, N. J.: Transaction Books.

Lindblom, C. E. (1977) *Politics and Markets: The World's Political Economic Systems*, New York: Basic Books.

Luhmann, N. (1975) *Soziologische Aufklärung 2*, Wiesbaden: VS Verlag für Sozialwissenschaften.

Lukes, S. (1994) *Power: A Radical View*, Basingstoke: Palgrave.

Magalhaes, de J. C. (1988) *The Pure Concept of Diplomacy*, New York: Greenwood Press

Mann, M. (1986) *The Sources of Social Power: Volume 1, A History of Power from the Beginning to AD 1760*, Cambridge University Press.

— (1993) *The Sources of Social Power: Volume 2, The Rise of Classes and Nation States 1760–1914*, Cambridge University Press.

— (2012) *The Sources of Social Power: Volume 3, Global Empires and Revolution, 1890–1945*, Cambridge University Press.

— (2013) *The Sources of Social Power: Volume 4, Globalizations 1945–2011,* Cambridge University Press.

Marshall, T. H. (1950) *Citizenship and Social Class and Other Essays*, Cambridge: Cambridge University Press.

Marx, K. (1976) *Capital*, London: Penguin Books.

— (2000) *Selected Writings*, Oxford: Oxford University Press.

Miller, L. (2010) '"The master switch": is the Internet due for a takeover?', *Salon*, December 2010.

Milner, M. J. (1994) *Status and Sacredness*, Oxford: Oxford University Press.

Neumann, F. L. (1986) *Demokratischer und Autoritärer Staat: Beitrage zur Soziologie der Politik*, Frankfurt: Europäischer Verlagsanstalt.

Nichols, J. and McChesney, R. W. (2013) *Dollarocracy: How the Money and Media Election Complex is Destroying America*, New York: Nation Books.

North, D. C.and Thomas, R. P. (1972) *The Rise of the Western World: A New Economic History*, Cambridge: Cambridge University Press.

Piven, F. F. and Cloward, R. (1971) *Regulating the Poor: The Functions of Public Welfare*, New York: Pantheon Books.

Poggi, G. (1978), 'Economy and polity: a chastened reflection on past hopes' in *Contemporary Sociology*, VII(4): 397–399.

— (2001) *Forms of Power*, Cambridge: Polity Press.

— (1998) *Il gioco dei poteri*, Bologna: Mulino.

Popitz, H. (1992) *Phänomene der Macht*, Tuebingen: Mohr-Siebeck.

Proudhon, H. (1998) *La teoria della proprietà*, Roma: SEAM

Renan, E. (1997 [1882]) *Qu'est-ce qu'une Nation?*, Paris: Mille et Une Nuits.

Rokkan, S. ([1970] 2009), 'Nation-Building, Cleavage Formation and the Structuring of Mass Politics', in *Citizens Elections Parties: Approaches to the Comparative Study of the Processes of Development*, reprint Colchester: ECPR Press.

Rousseau, J. J. (1993) *The Social Contract and Discourses*. London: Dent.

Runciman, G. W. (1983–88) *A Treatise in Social Theory*, 2 Vols., Cambridge: Cambridge University Press.

Rusconi, G. E. (2008) (ed.) *Lo stato secolarizzato nella società post-secolare*, Bologna: Il Mulino.

Russell, J. G (1986) *Peacemaking in the Renaissance*, Philadelphia: University of Pennsylvania Press.

Scalfari, E. and Turani, G. (1975) *Razza padrona: Storia della borghesia di stato*, Milano: Feltrinelli.

Schmitt, C. (1996) *The Concept of the Political*, Cambridge: Cambridge University Press.

Somers, M. (2008) *Genealogies of Citizenship*, Cambridge: Cambridge University Press.

Stein, L. von (1921) *Geschichte der sozialen Bewegung in Frankreich von 1789 bis auf unsere Tage*, Munich: Drei Masken Verlag.

Tarello, G. (1976) *Storia della cultura giuridica. Assolutismo e codificazione del diritto*, Bologna: Il Mulino.

— (1988) *Cultura giuridica e politica del diritto*, Bologna: Il Mulino.

Tilly, C. (1975) (ed.) *The Formation of National States in Western Europe*, Princeton: Princeton University Press.

Titmuss, R. M. (1971) *The Gift Relationship: From Human Blood to Social Policy*, New York: Pantheon Books.

Tocqueville, A. de (1985) *L'Ancien régime et la révolution*, Paris: Gallimard.

Vattel, de E. (1916) *Le droit des gens ou Principes de la loi naturelle etc*, Washington: Carnegie Institution of Washington.

Weber, M. (1922) *Wirtschaft u Gesellschaft*, Tuebingen: Mohr.

— (1978) *Economy and Society*, Berkeley: University of California Press.

— (1992) *Wissenschaft als Beruf – Politik als Beruf*, Tuebingen: Mohr(Siebeck)

— (1994) 'The profession and vocation of politics', in P. Lassman and R. Speirs (eds) *Weber: Political Writings*, Cambridge: Cambridge University Press.

Wight, M. (1973) 'The Balance of Power and International Order' in A. James (ed.) *The Bases of International Order*, Oxford: Oxford University Press, pp. 85–115.

Williamson, O. (1975) *Markets and Hierarchies, Analysis and Antitrust Implications*, New York: Free Press.

Wrong, D. (1980) *Power, its Forms, Bases, and Uses*, New York: Harper and Row.

Appendix: The Concept of Power
(*Heinrich Popitz*)[*]

Translation of Chapter One, Heinrich Popitz,
Phänomene der Macht, Tübingen:
J.C.B. Mohr, 2nd edn, 1992.

The aim of the following reflections is to construct a general frame of reference for the analysis of power phenomena.

In the first place, I seek to identify the historical premises of the problematization of power. On what presuppositions is our understanding of power, both currently and for the foreseeable future, grounded?

As we shall see, one can assume that power constitutes a universal element of the human condition, fundamentally affecting the very essence of human sociability. On the basis of this assumption, we may also ask: on what grounds does human power rest? On what capacities for action, what conditions of existence? These questions lead us to distinguish between four fundamental anthropological forms of power. Together with some additional comments, these forms may in turn serve as analytical signposts of the discourse that follows.

---

[*] As I stated at the end of my Preface, and as a glance at this volume's Index will confim, much of my own thinking about power and related themes is hugely indebted to a close reading of, and frequent reference to what I consider an insufficiently known masterpiece within the huge and diverse literature about those subjects – the second edition of Heinrich Popitz, *Phänomene der Macht* (Tubingen: Mohr-Siebeck, 1992). To further acknowledge my own debt to the author, I present here my own translation of the introductory chapter of that book. I hope that, besides further enlightening my book's readers as to the significance of Popitz-on-power, this sample from his masterpiece will encourage a publisher to produce a full English edition of it.

The references provided in the footnotes to the text reproduced Popitz's original. Most of the footnotes are made out entirely of bibliographical references, except for some short text, which is translated because its content complements or qualifies that of the main text. The quotations from Sophocles' *Antigone* are taken from the translation by Marianne Macdonald available online at: http://www.24grammata.com/wp-content/uploads/2012/09/antigone-mcdonald-24grammata. com_.pdf)

I am grateful to my friend and colleague Joerg Friedrichs, of Oxford University, for suggesting a number of corrections to the original text of my translation. [G.P.]

Historical premises of the problematization of power

Why do we problematize power? Which aspects of it do we take for granted, and which do we question? Duly addressing historically these questions (to the extent that they lend themselves to historical treatment) would require a comprehensive history of both the problem and the concept. Here, however, we can simply identify some premises almost universally agreed to, which are particularly consequential for the way in which we perceive power phenomena.

The feasibility of power

The fundamental premise is the belief in the *feasibility* [*Machbarkeit*] *of power-based orders*. These are not divinely ordained, predetermined by myths, imposed by nature, or derived from sacrosanct tradition; rather, they are the product of human activity. Inasmuch as they have been brought into being, they can also be re-fashioned.

This idea that social orders are the products of human agency is one of the incredibly abrupt and radical discoveries of the Greek *polis*. If anything deserves to be called the 'idea of the political', this does. It renders the over-arching political ordering of collective human existence something open to shaping and modifying. In this manner, the status quo is experienced from the distance resulting from the fact that it can be imagined differently. It can now be viewed as a result of human capacity.

The status quo cannot be imagined differently but for the fact that it is possible to imagine something better. The idea of the political entails the belief in the possibility of designing a good order, 'in order to share a dignified existence', according to Aristotle.[1] And, should it not be possible 'to attain the best possible constitution, then the legislator and genuine statesman must approximate [...] what is best within the given circumstances'.[2]

In a quest for the best constitution, whether the absolutely best or the best possible one, were formulated postulates which have ever since accompanied the idea of the political, whenever it was encountered in the course of history: justice, rule of law, equality before the law (since 'a law became lord and king over men instead of men exercising tyranny over laws'),[3] as well as the understanding of the *polis* as 'a community of free men'[4] or an aggregation of citizens who 'see happiness in freedom'.[5]

---

1.   Aristotle, *Politics*, 1252b (Book One, Ch. 2).
2.   *Ibid.* 1288b (Book Four, Ch. 1).
3.   Plato, 8. Letter, 354.
4.   Aristotle, *Politics*, 1279a (Book Three, Ch. 6).
5.   Thucydides, *History of the Peloponnesian War*, Book Two, §43.

The presence in close proximity to one another of the diverse political orders of Greek city states – all experiencing in various ways the precariousness of any constitution, as well as war and civil war, tyranny and revolt – must have inspired the making of comparisons. A critical turn of mind led to the awareness that political orders can be expressly designed and improved, for 'all that exists is destined to decay'.[6] Thus the first comprehensive theories of political power systems came into being as *comparative theories of constitutional forms* such as those of Plato and Aristotle, the intellectual intensity of which remained unmatched until Montesquieu.

The second great phase of the belief in the purposive making of power relations begins with the bourgeois revolutions of the modern era. Here too, as previously during the phase of the culture of the *polis*, that belief is one aspect of a broader assumption that one can produce changes and improvements through methodical action – an aspect of an overriding 'consciousness of feasibility'.[7] Notably, in the modern era this creative consciousness expressed itself in the same domains of action as in antiquity: not only in the ordering of political affairs but also in the knowledge of nature, metaphysics, navigation, architecture, military strategy, and education. Here, again, the prospecting of political-institutional changes eventuates in democratic constitutional designs.

An example may suffice to characterize the idea of the political that was emerging from new conditions. In the first article of *The Federalist Papers* (1787), which recommended to the electors of New York the adoption of a draft constitution for an American federal state, Alexander Hamilton writes:

> It has been frequently remarked that it seems to have been reserved to the people of this country, by their conduct and example, to decide the important question, whether societies of men are really capable or not of establishing good government from reflection and choice, or whether they are forever destined to depend for their political constitutions on accident and force (Alexander Hamilton, *Federalist Papers*, n. 1).

Not making the right decision would 'deserve to be considered as the general misfortune of mankind'.[8]

Now is the time to make that decision and that for *everyone*.

As happens also in France at about the same time, an expression can be found of here an acute sense for the moment's epochal significance for humanity, transcending national boundaries. The belief in the power of reason

---

6. Plato, *Republic*, 546a (Book Eight).

7. Christian Meier, 'Ein antikes Äquivalent des Fortschrittsgedankens: Das "Könnens"'-Bewußtsein des 5.Jahrhunderts v.Chr., in *Ibid.*, *Die Entstehung des Politischen bei den Griechen*, Frankfurt 1980, pp. 468ff.

8. Alexander Hamilton, James Madison, John Jay, *Der Föderalist*, Vienna 1958, p. 33.

which inspires this sense of significance is not naïve – various risks are considered and debated – but at the end of the day it remains unshaken. Chance and violence can be overcome if we find the right concept. A constitution for free citizens is a matter of design, and that design can be put into being: we can do it.

Today, we may share neither the confidence nor the enthusiasm of the American founding fathers. We may disagree about the scope for variation and the degree of urgency of new institutions. None of this affects the certainty that one *can* do things differently, and do them better. One of the taken-for-granted premises of our understanding of power is once more the conviction that power is 'made' and can be re-made otherwise, than is now the case.

The ubiquity of power

Another premise of our historical understanding of power is the assumption that power is *ubiquitous*.

The awareness of this, too, emerges with the bourgeois revolutions. One no longer senses, as under absolutism, that all power phenomena converge toward the institutions of the modern state, that power is intrinsically a property of the state itself. On the contrary, power is now perceived as a property of society itself.[9] New classes develop power potentials of their own. The educated bourgeoisie seizes upon the power of public opinion, asserts the power of reason, the power of ideas.[10] The property-owning bourgeoisie establishes the 'power of mobile property', the power of money, 'the supremacy of the bankers', the 'force of property' (Marx).[11] Within the proletariat emerges as a counter-power 'the elemental force of the popular masses' (Engels).[12] These new powers oppose the old ones: nobility, land-owners, the Catholic Church.

The bourgeois configuration of societal powers does not dis-empower the state. Externally, the nation-state takes charge of new interests in territorial expansion, internally of new aspects of societal management. But power as such is no longer concentrated within political institutions. Tensions arising from power conflicts pervade the whole society.

The two essential human relationships, that between man and woman and that between parents and children, are also increasingly understood as power relationships. Behind every contrast between the genders and between the generations one detects a question of power, and wrong answers to that question

9. Otto Bruner, Werner Conze, Reinhard Koselleck (eds), *Geschichtliche Grundbegriffe*, Stuttgart 1972 ff., Vol. 3, 'Macht, Gewalt' §I (Karl Georg Faber) p. 818. Cf. Helmuth Plessner, 'Die Emanzipation der Macht', in *Ibid. Diesseits der Utopie, Ausgewählte Beiträge zur Kultursoziologie*, Düsseldorf, Köln 1966.

10. *Ibid.*, 'Macht, Gewalt', §V2 (Karl Georg Faber) p. 900.

11. *Ibid.*, pp. 922f.

12. *Ibid.*, p. 923.

may occasion the breakdown of the relationship. It is simply presumed that the power at stake here is of the same kind as any other kind of power, for example that of making political or economic decisions.

In a competitive society, power conflicts become a constant experience for the individual. Under conditions whereby the individual's life course revolves around the opportunity for status gain or the risk of status loss, around success or failure in the competition with others, the individual's own biography comes to be perceived as a sequence of voluntary or involuntary power conflicts leading to victory or defeat. The more society appears open to processes of vertical mobility, the more strongly power experiences become individualized and the more individual experiences are interpreted in terms of power.

When the critique of power reaches the private sphere, it concludes a process that can be called the *generalization of the suspicion of power*. Every relation, every personal bond is now exposed to the suspicion of either maintaining conventional power inequalities or promoting new ones. Power lurks behind everything – all one needs to do is, to see it. It does not matter whether this view is advanced as a theoretical claim or only finds expression in a generalized suspicion of power: power is assumed to be a component of all social processes. It is ubiquitous. A search for a power-free space or for a domination-free discourse appears as merely a subject for academic speculation. There ought to be a power-free space, somewhere – but where? It should be possible for communication to be free of domination – but how?

Let us remember Max Weber's definition: '*Power* means any chance, within a social relationship, of giving effect to one's own will even against opposition, whatever such chance rests on', within any relationship, for whatever reason. Weber's own gloss on his definition underlines the point: 'All thinkable qualities of an individual and all thinkable situations may place anyone in a position to give effect to one's will under existing conditions'.[13] The assumption of the ubiquity of power is not expressly articulated here, but the independence of power from context is strongly emphasized. Power is not necessarily connected with relations having any particular content, it can associate itself with relations of whatever sort, and it intervenes everywhere. This definition is not, as it may seem, out of touch with the real world. It reflects a historical process which has eventuated in the generalization of the power suspicion.

The need to justify power

The third premise of the understanding of power results from the contrast between power and freedom. *All exercise of power is a limitation of freedom.* On this account, all power needs *justification*.

---

13. Max Weber, *Economy and Society*, Ch. 1, §16, Studienausgabe, Tübingen 1980, pp. 28f.

Wherever a new, more acute consciousness of freedom makes itself felt, power relations are called into question. The times when consciousness of freedom became more acute and intense were also the times of the great theories of power. Once again, the most significant examples are offered by the Greek *polis* and by the modern, bourgeois revolutions.

In writing about 'The constitution of Germany' (1802), the young Hegel remarks:

> Given that over the last ten years Europe as a whole has become aware of an awful struggle of a people for freedom, and Europe as a whole has been put in motion, unavoidably concepts regarding freedom have undergone a change and have attained clarity beyond their previous emptiness and indetermination.[14]

What did the new content and the new determination consist in? To begin with, they express a will to liberate oneself. The initial impulse to this new striving for liberty comes from the emancipation of consciousness. In Germany, Kant has famously formulated this as 'the exit of man from the self-imposed status of a minor'.[15] Marx goes one step further: 'We must emancipate ourselves before we can emancipate others'.[16]

So this is the first half of the equation: the recovery of the concept of freedom from its 'previous emptiness and indetermination' means a demand for self-emancipation, a call to come of age. The freedom movements inspired by the Enlightenment are movements toward 'awakening'.

The other half of the equation is that this process of liberation is expressly characterized as a power struggle intended to subvert the existing power relations. Hegel: 'This thought has to do with reality and has become a force opposing the present condition, and this force entails revolution in general'.[17]

Power conflicts *qua* liberation conflicts have marked the history of the last two centuries: the overthrow of the feudal order, the national liberation struggles in North America and Europe, the liberation of peoples outside Europe from colonial oppression, innumerable movements for the self-determination of minorities, the beginnings of the emancipation of women and, above all, class conflicts (which overlapped with many of those conflicts). Here, in the struggle for the emancipation of the proletariat, finally emerges the

---

14. G.W.F. Hegel, *Politische Schriften*, edited by Jürgen Habermas, Frankfurt 1966, p. 129. Cf. *Geschichtliche Grundbegriffe*, Vol. 2, 'Freiheit' §V (Horst Günther), p. 469.

15. Immanuel Kant, 'Beantwortung der Frage: Was ist Aufklärung?', *Ausgewählte kleine Schriften*, Hamburg 1969, p. 1.

16. Karl Marx, *Zur Judenfrage* (Deutsch-Französische Jahrbücher 1844). Marx-Engels-Studien-ausgabe I, Frankfurt (Fischer) 1966, p. 32.

17. G.W.F. Hegel, edited by Georg Lasson, *Vorlesungen über die Philosophie der Weltgeschichte*, Leipzig 1920, Vol. 4, p. 924.

most radical speculative venture of the new liberation movement: the struggle of the proletariat, in its specifically German alliance between proletariat and philosophy, leads to the emancipation of the human being, which in turn means the abolition of *any* kind of servitude, the suppression of all relations 'in which man is a humiliated being, a being enslaved, abandoned, despicable'.[18]

Insofar as the modern European-American liberation movement in its call for the self-emancipation of the individual expresses the search for an awakening, the power conflict it unleashes entails also a search for redemption.

Very different consequences can be drawn from this confrontation between power and freedom. However, it has become impossible not to put into question every exercise of power as an interference with self-determination. This does not mean a wholesale condemnation of all power, for one can view power as inevitable: consider, for instance, the impossibility of dispensing with protective and educational power over children, the need for organized power within larger collectivities, the necessity of concentrated power for securing law and peace.[19] Yet, in modern society all power, all imposition of limits on freedom needs to be accounted for. There no longer is any power – neither in the state nor in the family – whose legitimacy is so unquestionable as to exempt it from justification. Every determination by others must come to terms with a claim to self-determination, and every claim to power arouses as a response the consciousness of freedom. Power, in all contexts, in all forms, is indissolubly connected with the question, 'why?'. Never again will it be possible to answer that question once and for all.

The argument so far

[1] Power is a product of action; power orderings can be modified; a good ordering can be designed; one can *do* all this. [2] Power is ubiquitous; it permeates social relations of whatever content; it presents itself everywhere. [3] Power lays limitations on freedom; it interferes with the self-determination of others; therefore it requires justification; all power is questionable.

The first of these premises, namely that power relations are a matter for human design, is part and parcel of the modern awareness that the world in which we live is something *made*. No power ordering is either divinely ordained or imposed by nature. Reflection on power means reflection on something in principle amenable to deliberate, planned human intervention.

---

18. Karl Marx, *Zur Kritik der Hegeischen Rechtsphilosophie*, Marx-Engels-Studienausgabe I, aaO., p. 30 u. 44.

19. Incidentally, even Jakob Burckhardt did not mean that all is evil ('power in itself is evil'), but rather, as the context makes clear, all *arbitrary* power. Jakob Burckhardt, *Weltgeschichtliche Betrachtungen*, Munich 1978 (dtv), p. 25.

This is the basic constellation on which the second and third premises rest: the diffusion of the suspicion of power and the activation of a more acute claim for self-determination. Together, they render the problematic of power both wider and more intense.

These premises themselves are the outcome of a historical process, but are not limited to a particular historical constellation. They inherently claim universal validity. Power has come to be understood as a universal component in the genesis and operation of human societies. It is universally the case that power is a product; its effects are also universal, not connected with any specific social context; the danger it poses to self-determination is equally universal.

If one accepts these premises – and I fail to see how one can escape their intellectual and moral cogency – they lead to an obvious theoretical consequence. One must identify theoretically the implicit anthropological grounds of the power concept, and argue why power is universal. On what rests the power of human beings over their fellow human beings? Of what capacity for action, what ability to prevail over others can we avail ourselves? Why is it possible to construct power relations and modify their design? What accounts for the suspicion that the power bacillus is present in all human relations? While reflecting on these questions, one must also locate the roots of un-freedom. What generates the particular susceptibility of the human being to power, its exposure to suffering from power? Power as ability and power as suffering – only if we pose questions of such general nature can we hope to attain understandings whose scope matches the premises of our historical consciousness of power.

Basic anthropological forms of power

'Power', in a general anthropological sense, refers to something the human being *can* do – it entails the ability to assert oneself against external forces.

The history of concepts reveals numerous expressions which, often vaguely and fleetingly, point to this or that aspect of the power phenomenon. However, within all this variety, over and over again there has emerged a conception that the human species possesses a potency, an ability to assert oneself. *Kratos* means a general superiority, a capacity to subjugate, a force that can overcome extraneous forces.[20] In the same way, *potentia* remains both in Rome and in the Latin Middle ages an undifferentiated concept pointing to a superior force of any kind.[21] Linked with *potentia* are *power* and *pouvoir*, as well as *Macht*

---

20. *Geschichtliche Grundbegriffe*, Vol. 3, 'Macht, Gewalt' §II (Christian Meier), p. 821.

21. *Ibid.*, pp. 830, 833.

in its medieval and modern German usage[22] (Kant: 'Power is a capacity which can overcome great obstacles').[23]

The concept circumscribed by *kratos*, *potentia* and *Macht* appears to possess generality or indeed universality. It can encompass the whole position of the human being in the world, as well as its social constitution in both a static and a dynamic sense. This tendency can be reconstructed also in conceptual terms. The most general category underlying the power concept is the ability to *modify* (a capacity constitutive of all human action), i.e. a disposition to alter the world through our action. Ever since humans began to settle, and thus committed themselves to secure their own provisions,[24] they have modified nature in increasingly efficient ways; and in so doing they have also modified the mode of their own social existence. Human action has increasingly become the capacity to define anew one's own situation. In the light of this broad capacity to produce change, the history of human power is the history of human action.

Our analysis however does not require such a stretching (or overstretching) of the power concept. If we limit ourselves to the question of why, on the basis of what faculties, men can exercise power, and to the complementary question of why they must suffer from power, we can differentiate the generic human ability to assert oneself against external forces. That ability appears be connected with a variety of determinate faculties of action and a variety of equally determinate vital dependencies. In my attempt to identify more precisely these faculties and these dependencies, I have encountered four anthropologically irreducible conditions. Accordingly, I distinguish four fundamental forms of power.

To clarify these distinctions, I shall resort to a chorus from Sophocles's *Antigone* – at the same time the most solemn paean to human power and one of the most precise descriptions of that power we know of: *Manifold is power, yet nothing is more powerful than man*.[25] What are the grounds of human powerfulness?

---

22. *Ibid.*, 'Macht, Gewalt' §III (Karl Georg Faber), pp. 836f.

23. Immanuel Kant, *Kritik der Urteilskraft*, Hamburg 1948, p. 105.

24. *Lebensmittel* quite simply denotes food, apart from the literal meaning of means for existence, and the best term in English I could find for this is 'provisions'. Popitz alludes to the theory that at some point hunters and gatherers were forced by the circumstances to become agriculturalists. [G.P.]

25. [In the text, Popitz uses the German translation by Georg Peter Landmann (Neue Zürcher Zeitung 23./24. 8. 1986): 'Mächtiges gibt es vielerlei – nichts ist mächtiger als der Mensch'. The translation here used is Marianne Macdonald's, from http://www.24grammata.com/wp-content/uploads/2012/09/antigone-mcdonald-24grammata.com_.pdf, (G.P.)]

(1) Active Power

Sophocles describes the power of the hunter who captures and kills the animals of the wilderness and the sea:

Skillful man of clever thought
Traps in the woven coils of his nets
The birds, with thoughts as light as wings,
And tribes of wild animals,
And the creatures of the deep.
With his devices he overpowers
The wild beast that roams the mountain.

The hunter asserts himself against external forces with both cleverness and violence. He shows the superiority of his own power. The weaker party must suffer what the hunter does to it.

A capacity to inflict damage on others, an active damaging power: this is what man possesses with respect to all organisms, including other men. As the hunter does to animals, so men can capture and kill other men. But as a rule this power is unequally distributed. Its inequality results from inborn endowments, muscular strength, dexterity, swiftness, cleverness; it also accrues from exercise and, above all, from unequal control over contrived devices that enhance the efficiency of the damaging action – the material facilities and the organizational arrangements for combat. Since there is apparently no limit to this artificial enhancement of efficiency, the potential dangerousness of man for other men is also unlimited.

At the same time, man is exposed to being damaged in multiple and subtle ways. Anything alive can be deprived of its life, and indeed the vulnerability of the human body to damage is particularly striking. Deprived of fur and carapace, standing erect, his vital organs are open to external attack. (The particular vulnerability is matched by a particular disposition of human fantasy toward ways of inflicting damage. Just listing the various ways to inflict the death penalty would require pages.) To the humans' physical vulnerability is added economic vulnerability, the multiple ways of depriving others of their means of subsistence, such as robbery, devastation of resources, denial of access to them, and to cultivable land in particular. Finally, there is the vulnerability related to limitations on social participation imposed by some on others. Sophocles:

[Man] is lofty in the city; but exiled, and homeless
Is the man who consorts with evil
For the sake of greed and ambition.
He has my curse upon him.

The loss of social affiliations entails an unending series of exclusions and humiliations, which can jeopardize an individual's very existence.

This, then, is the first root of power: Men can exercise power over other men because they can do damage to them. In historical terms this appears as the beginning of various forms of subjugation. Damaging acts do not presuppose any continuous methodic control, nor do they necessary lead to organized exploitation, but some can literally be performed by simple gestures of the hand.

(2) Instrumental Power

Often the power to damage expresses itself in a single act. It can sometimes be routinized, as happens in the seizing of booty by hunters, but *qua* single act it remains limited to a given trial of strength which is undertaken ever anew and asserts itself in each case. This differentiates the active damaging power of the hunter from another form of power, which Sophocles introduces in the same passage. Man is also capable of taming and domesticating both *the rough-maned horse and the untiring mountain bull* into submitting to *a yoke over their necks*. Here power becomes durable, it can continually direct the conduct of those subjugated. The wild beast has been captured and been taught to obey. Again, active damaging power comes into play: the beast obeys because it fears the blows. Or it may do so because it also hopes for rewards (as in the common-place coupling and contrasting of the stick and the carrot). Power is rendered durable to the extent that certain acts – punishments or rewards – can be turned respectively into threats and promises, extending across time and space the effect of the mere power to damage. What may happen at any time can control conduct at any time. A credible danger and a credible opportunity can be put to use in securing permanent submission.

The basis of this *instrumental power* is the ability to give and take, to have at one's disposal rewards and punishments, or more precisely to be able to make dispositions over punishments and rewards that appear credible to those concerned. The exercise of instrumental power requires that this credibility be generated and maintained.

In the case of instrumental power, the exercise of power entails the formulation of an alternative – this, or that. Who poses the alternative assigns the conduct of those affected to one of two categories: submission or insubordination. He dichotomizes anything the affected party can do into yes-actions and no-actions. Whatever the affected party will do unavoidably constitutes an answer to a question posed by somebody else. The affected party cannot avoid answering. The definition of the situation is imposed. In the case of threat the alternative can be characterized as blackmail; in the case of promise as an act of corruption. The motives generating compliance are respectively fear and hope.

Such alternatives can only work because our social action is oriented to the expected conduct of others, and social interaction itself is guided by expectations relating to the future. What functions to control conduct is what we believe we can foresee (or what we unconsciously anticipate). Hence, one who can credibly formulate power alternatives, as a rule can also avail himself of the fact that no future state can be precisely predicted and that all orientation to the future is uncertain; hence the anticipated future is intrinsically volatile. It is possible to manipulate hopes even over the long term. It is possible to upgrade threats into a power to frighten others, to cast a shadow over their calculations.

In the case of active damaging power, men cannot successfully defend themselves from something which others do to them. By means of instrumental controlling power men are durably induced to act as the tools on an alien will. One should note that social power – as distinct from power over animals, as with the horse and the bull – is exercised over subjects who in principle are capable of action just as are those exercising power: they, too, are speaking, thinking subjects. The distinctive human capacity for action also of those subjected to power renders them also exploitable in a specific fashion. They can be induced to place their diligent and planned action at the service of systems exercising power. As helpers and helpers of helpers they can serve not only as tools but as intelligent power multipliers.

The instrumental power to threaten and to promise is the typical power of everyday life, the standard way of asserting one's will against external forces. By the same token it is a necessary component of all durable exercise of power. Every long-lasting power relationship rests *also* on instrumental power.

(3) Authoritative Power

Among power phenomena one can contrast those involving such 'external power' that manifests itself in threats and promises, with 'internal power'. The latter does not need to operate by means of extrinsic advantages and disadvantages: it produces a willing, compliant disposition to obey.

The effectiveness of such power is suggested by its inducing compliance also where one's actions are not subject to another's control. It works beyond the limits of what it can control. You carry it with yourself as internalized self-control. It works even in a dark hole. Such power is effective not only in guiding actual behavior, it also guides the attitudes, perspectives and criteria of those affected by it, the manner in which they perceive and judge something.

What are the grounds of power of this nature? Its broadest anthropological foundation is the fact that, in order to act, man needs standards and norms by which to orient himself. His 'as yet unsettled' nature must itself engender the constraints that guide his action. This happens via the great objectifications of normative orders. In the words of Sophocles:

He follows the laws of the land
and swears to keep the justice of the gods.

Such norm-setting power accrues to the great mediators of those orders: priests, kings, patriarchs. As we know, this power to impose standards of action can lose its transcendental legitimacy, but its ultimate ground, the need for standards, can survive such loss. Today, standard-setting power is present everywhere in secularized, banal forms.

To understand the effectiveness of 'internal power' there is something else to consider. The need for standards entails also that if we are to esteem ourselves we need to assert our conformity with standards. Those who need standards hankers after assurance, after signs of approval which various kinds of success can evoke. Since certain individuals and groups function as standard-setters, recognition on their part constitutes a decisive sign of approval.

This kind of dependency brings forth what we may call authority in the strict sense. The authority relation rests on a twofold process of recognition: recognizing the superiority of others as standard setters, and striving to be ourselves recognized, to receive from those standard-setters signs to the effect that one has proven himself. What is at stake in this submission to authority is nothing less than the reassurance about one's social orientation and about one's self-esteem.

Here we find again the dichotomous structure already seen as structuring instrumental power relations. In this case it appears as the alternative between hoped-for recognition and dreaded withdrawal of it. Whoever can and does intentionally establish such alternatives in order to guide the conduct and attitude of others, exercises *authoritative power*.

(4) The power of imposed circumstances

We have started from the power of man over the animals which he hunts and tames. But power over nature does not limit itself to our relations to such life forms. Man can assert himself also against alien forces of *inanimate* nature, and even here establish his superiority over whatever comes in his way: the tree is felled, the ore is smelt, the clay is baked, the stone is quarried. Sophocles mentions the key activity on which depends man's systematic overwhelming of nature.

He harrasses the almighty immortal unwearying Earth,
Turning his plow back and forth year after year,
Turning up the soil with the help of mules.

Clearly, to Sophocles it was obvious that this furrowing and harrowing of the earth, this putting nature to human use constitutes one of the fundamental manifestations of human power. This has become particularly evident in the light of the current awareness that the destruction of nature has come to constitute a danger to humanity. We have become conscious that we find ourselves in conflict with foreign forces operating on their own behalf.

When we modify for our own benefit what is naturally given, we exercise power over nature – but besides that also power over other men. As a rule, the artifacts we produce do not only act back on the producer by serving him more or less well. They also act upon other men: the road restricts and the wall obstructs passage to many, farmed land offers food to many, the overexploited earth condemns many to starvation. Those who plan and design a new settlement determine the conditions of existence, the degrees of freedom or the constraints encountered by many other men. They build worlds for others.

Not all technical action has such wide-ranging consequences. However, every new artifact adds to the previous state of the world a new given, a new circumstance. Those responsible for imposing new circumstances upon others exercise a peculiar power over them, bound to affect them.

The *power of imposed circumstances* is a power mediated by objects. It is brought to bear on others in material fashion. On this account it is by no means a power of things over men – although it suggests the ideological imagery of 'reified' power – but the power of the producing and of the producer, built by the latter into things, which often remains long latent, but can manifest itself any time. We can dig such power mines into the ground for tens of thousands of years, affecting generations to come. Thus, there is good reason to reflect on the twin ways by which technological action has the imprint of power: on the one hand it is the power over the forces of nature, on the other it is an indirect power to determine the life conditions of other men. Man as *homo faber* asserts himself against recalcitrant forces of nature that obey laws of their own, turns nature into artifacts and thereby also modifies the life conditions of all those who must insert themselves into the world of artifacts.

Retrospect

Men have power over other men because one can damage the other by prevailing upon his resistance. He can *do something* to him: interfere with his bodily integrity, his economic livelihood, his social participation. Every individual, every group is susceptible to and endangered by damage. ('Active power'.)

Men have power over men because they can take something from others or give others something, and this enables them to formulate threats and promises that guide the others' conduct. The basis of such power is something in one's possession, the (at least presumed) capacity to dispose of punishments and rewards. But this possession produces power only when it affects the orientation to the future constitutive of human action, availing itself of men's concern over the future. It is part of such concern that men are fearful of other men and hope to receive something from them; their action is thus influenced by fear and hope. ('Instrumental power'.)

The other form of power guiding conduct is authoritative. It rests on men's need for standards and their quest for recognition from those individuals and groups whom they recognize as sources of standards. Our self-esteem depends on such confirmation. Men can exercise authoritative power over other men because the need for standards and recognition engenders psychical dependencies. ('Authoritative power'.)

Men have power over other men by virtue of their capacity for technical action, their creative intelligence. We are affected by power via technical action because we are bound to an artificially modified world of objects, which surrounds us because it has been entirely or partially produced by others. Man as the 'tool-making animal' cannot but produce the conditions of his own existence, and equally he cannot but embody power decisions into things. ('Power of imposed circumstances'.)[26]

The roots of social power lie in the correspondence between faculties of action constitutive of the human being and the dependencies of their existence. The latter are: man's liability to suffer damage, his concern for the future, his need for standards and recognition, his dependency on artifacts. The respective action faculties are: the capacity to act so as to inflict damage, the capacity to engender fears and hopes, the capacity to set standards, the capacity for technical action.

Power relations arise because relations between humans are determined by their ability to inflict damage and their openness to such damage; by fears and hopes which can be manipulated; by the inescapable necessity to orient to standards; and by the compulsion and the ability to modify the objective world. Or, in a nutshell: human beings can directly *do something* to other human beings; furthermore they can engender expectations, standards and artifacts with exercise effects upon others.

We live a damageable existence, we depend on artifacts, our action is future-oriented, and needs orientation. Therefore we must suffer power. It is possible (it seems to me) to derive from these four roots most of the concepts of power that have been suggested in the literature.[27]

---

26. Power, with its institutionalization, whereby emerges 'domination' (*Herrschaft*), and power becomes connected with position, acquires stability and societal continuity. But this does not entail a new, self-standing way to exercise power, beyond those discussed here.

27. This does not mean there is consensus on how to conceive these phenomena. The boundless extension of the power concept to 'influences' of all kinds should be discussed separately. Such extensions, which in the end seek to encompass every effect a person may have upon another, show how even apparently plausible formulations can lose sight of the problem. But also the distinctions put forward may differ significantly. For instance one can divide up instrumental power of threat and promise into 'coercive power' and 'reward power'. (J. R. P. French jr., B. H. Raven, 'The Basis of Social Power', in: D. Cartwright (ed.) *Studies in Social Power*, Michigan 1959, pp. 150–167.) One can qualify as 'inner power' various manifestations of what is here conceived as authoritative power (for instance, 'referend power' *Ibid.*) or, as one frequently does, reduce all authority phenomena to the recognition of prestige. Also, institutionalised power (domination) can occasionally be treated as a distinctive power form, whereas it is here understood as the

Relations between power forms

Instrumental power and authoritative power have something in common: they guide the conduct of those affected by them. They both work on the basis of alternatives: in the case of instrumental power the alternative between 'external' advantages and disadvantages; in the case of authoritative power the alternative between attainment of recognition and withdrawal of recognition. Instrumental power guides only conduct, whereas authoritative power guides both conduct and attitude.

Active power and the power of imposed circumstances have one thing in common: they modify the situation of those affected, and thereby the degrees of freedom of their conduct. Active power affects the person directly. Imposed circumstances operate by shaping and modifying the settings of other people's existence.

Clearly these forms of power can at any time affect social processes of any kind. This holds also if (as we consider appropriate to do) we have recourse to the power concept only in situations where power is exercised *intentionally*, to fulfil an intent to do damage, to guide the conduct and attitudes of others, or to modify their life circumstances. It equally holds if we limit ourselves to cases where the exercise of power is particularly evident.

If someone does something that affects others, then as a rule he is also in a position to do serious damage to them. Whoever influences the action of others by posing the alternative of yes-or-no reactions, can make use of multiple opportunities to corrupt or blackmail. In the most varied contexts, what we do and what we don't do is determined by the need for standards and for recognition, and thus by psychical dependencies which can be exploited. In the end, all social dramas in which we perform a role can be manipulated by shifting about the stage props.

The *opportunity* to exercise power is part and parcel of all day-to-day social interactions. It can be put to use, intentionally and in evident ways, in innumerable constellations.

Such opportunity is always used, and must always be used, in the process of socialization. Every child learns how to deal with power. It suffers from its own vulnerability to damage even when something is taken away from it in order to protect it; it learns that its actions can have good and bad consequences, and that these may be brought about by others (the masters of

---

consolidation and stabilization of one power form or of more than one power form combined (*see* note 26). Also, I do not consider the legitimation of power as a distinctive power form; rather, for me legitimation itself amounts to an additional stabilizing quality which can be attained by any of the power forms I distinguish, singly or in combination. The conceptualization of a self-standing 'power of imposed circumstances' is here proposed for the first time. The remarkable variety of conceptual proposals to a large extent overstates superficial differences, which can instead be disregarded if one refers to the four basic conditions described here.

its own fear and hope); it comes to depend on the attention and recognition it receives from adults, accommodates itself to a world fabricated by somebody else. The awareness of their own inferiority is a component of children's social awareness, no matter how well or how badly the culture understands this experience. Wherever human beings take care of and educate children, they exercise power intentionally and with a marked sense of superiority: as active power, instrumental power, authoritative power, and as the power of imposed circumstances.

The distinction between power forms can be put to three analytical usages.

(1) Each of the four forms of power can establish power relations in and of itself: as sheer violence, outright blackmail, unquestioned sense of worth, or sheer effectiveness of technical action. We can comprehend each of these cases to the extent that we learn to see in them the effects of a distinctive form of power.

(2) Many constellations, however, are more difficult to grasp because several forms of power are present in them and operate. How can they be combined? Examples are easy to come by: active power can manifest itself in the conquest of foreign lands; the new possessions can becomes the sites of the instrumental power of exploitation; enduring oppression can be transfigured into authoritative power; and all these processes can find physical expression in walls and fortifications. Alternatively: by allowing himself to be blackmailed by threats somebody can allow a quantum of active power to accumulate in the hands of its counterpart, and this can subsequently be put to use in further threats.

There are frequent connections between instrumental and authoritative power. The latter can be turned into the former. The guru can convince his devoted followers to hand over to him their possessions and thus acquire complete control over them. Or, instrumental power can become authoritative. Even the most cruel potentate can acquire a kind of hieratic charisma. The result of such connections amounts to a twofold power situation. 'External' and 'internal' alternatives become fused into combinations that are often difficult to analyze; but it remains worthwhile to detect the bipolarity behind such combination.

The structure of every form of power has aspects that lend themselves to the acquisition of other forms of power. Accordingly, it is possible to distinguish between two ways by which power is accumulated: *either* one particular form of power grows upon itself (active power leads to even more active power, authoritative power becomes more deeply rooted); *or*, the opportunities afforded by any form of power are put to use in adding further forms to the existing one. One may indeed speak of a 'tendency of power forms toward reciprocal attraction'.

Power accumulations via the acquisition of additional forms of power are assisted by the fact that power experiences tend to become generalized. Demonstrations of superiority and experiences of inferiority become generalized. If one has shown superiority or experienced inferiority in *that* situation, the same will happen in *this* situation. Similarly: who is superior in *this* respect will be also superior in *that* respect.[28]

(3) Apart from the combinations between power forms, the specific modalities of their interplay are equally interesting. Such interplay can operate as a coalition between associated forces, with the different forms of power complementing and enhancing each other to such extent that all the exits potentially open to those subjected to them are closed off at the same time.

To conclude and somewhat extend this argument, let us consider a childhood's memory from Peter Weiss:

> At the fence of our neighbor's garden at the time of our arrival, stood Friederle, with his arms close to his chest, and in a superior tone he asked for my name. Are you going to live here, he asked, and I nodded yes while looking at the men who were carrying our furniture into the house. The house belongs to my father, said Friederle, he just rents it out. My father is the mayor, he said, what does your father do. I did not know. What, you don't even know what your father does, he said. I searched for an answer that might impress him or one that would gain me his favor, but found neither. Again he asked, what is there on your cap. I took it off, it was a sailor's cap, with golden letters on its headband. What does it say, he asked once more. I did not know. Can't you even read what's on your own cap, he said; it says: I am stupid. And with that he grabbed the cap from my hand and threw it on a tree, the cap got stuck on a branch, its long blue ribbons fluttered in the wind. My mother stepped on the balcony of the house and saw us together. Have you already found a new friend, she called out, enjoy playing with him. And I shouted back, yes we are enjoying ourselves a lot.[29]

Here, a child is thrown into a new environment: a residential area with bourgeois houses, a garden, few neighbors, and hardly any children. It doesn't matter, least of all to the child, whether the parents have themselves shaped the environment or are merely transmitting its effects upon the child's future action. Friederle, the neighbor's son, starts off in a boastful tone (the house belongs to my father, my father is mayor) and then quickly raises the level of

---

28. The generalization assumption corresponds with the so-called 'force-conditioning model', as formulated by James G. Marsh, 'The power of power', in D. Easton (ed.) *Varieties of Political Theory*, Englewood Cliffs 1966, pp. 39–70.

29. Peter Weiss, *Abschied von den Eltern*, Frankfurt 1966, p. 27f.

aggression (it says: I am stupid). Finally, he grabs the stupid child's cap and – here the power of action – throws it away.

The child under attack, just barely arrived and younger of age, is scared. Friederle has successfully threatened him, and the best he can do is 'gain his favor'. Thus the ground has been laid for the consolidation of instrumental power.

However the child could run away, complain to his mother, try to make a new start. It is only the apparition of the mother with her authoritative power that blocks off all exits. 'Have you already found a new friend, enjoy playing with him'.

This is a breath-taking concentration of clichéd expectations. The cliché of friendship: when small boys meet, they quickly make friends; that's how children are. The cliché of adaptation: children adapt quickly to new situations. And the cliché of play: when children are together, they play.

The child's answer to his mother is easily understood. He will not 'disappoint' her (the key term for all authority relations); he will be the way his mother sees him, he needs the mother's approval and on that account he accepts her definition of the situation.

It is only the authoritative bond with the mother that exposes the child to the power of the neighbor's child. It is truly over the child's head that the interplay of power forms begins. The child, bound to the approval of his mother and thus to her wishful thinking, becomes entrapped in helplessness. 'Yes, we are enjoying ourselves a lot'.

Index